WHAT THE EXPERTS ARE SAYING ABOUT THIS BOOK

"This is the **FIRST** guide about living in Costa Rica and has been often imitated but never equalled by a slew of copycat books. It is by far the most **REALISTIC** and **INFORMATIVE** work on the subject by an author who actually lives in the country."

- Jay Trettien, *Central America Weekly*

"It's **FULL** of **VALUABLE** information, paints a **CLEAR** picture of what life is like for foreigners living there and is very **DOWN-TO-EARTH**."

- USA TODAY

"Another splendid comprehensive guide to making the break. The **BEST** of several books geared to would-be residents. It leaves **NO** stone unturned.

- Christopher Baker, *Costa Rica Handbook*.

"If your life is meaningless, let me **TURN YOU ON** to this **GREAT** book."

- D. Lopez, *La Prensa*, **San Diego**

"Mr. Howard makes it **EASY** for anyone to leave the 'rat race.' This is by far the BEST guidebook on the subject."

- Los Angeles Times

"This book is **PACKED** with **PRACTICAL** information for both retirees and tourists."

-Chicago Tribune

"Potential residents of Costa Rica, shouldn't leave home **WITHOUT** this guide."

-Dallas Morning News

"The Golden Door to Retirement and Living in Costa Rica offers **LOADS** of **USEFUL** information for the permanent resident."

-Jack Reber, *The San Diego-Tribune*

" This book offers **HELPFUL** advice to any would-be resident of Costa Rica."

-Mary Ellen Botter, Travel Editor, *Denver Post*

HEAR WHAT OUR READERS HAVE
SAID ABOUT THE BOOK

"**FANTASTIC BOOK!** Great, useful information for first-time visitors. A real VALUE at any price." - **Cory Brey, Siesta Key Florida**

"Your book is the most **COMPREHENSIVE** informative help I could find, you have done a fine job." - Niki Lesko

I just read your book and hope to run into you someday so you can sign it! Don't get me wrong, I'm not a typical Autograph Hunter, you may remember that I'm in Corporate Aviation? Thanks to the owner of the airplane and his circle of friends, we fly the likes of Don Henley, Ann Richards, etc. around. **NEVER** have I asked them to sign anything, you're the first, my man! - **Hank Guichelaar**

"I picked up your book about a year ago. I have found it very useful. Thanks for providing a good **INSIGHT** into Costa Rica." **William Baio**

I received a copy of the "12th Edition" from the library and was so impressed that I have been telling everyone I know that they **MUST** own this book!!. - **William F. Wessely**

"I have read your excellent book -the **BEST** I´ve read yet on the subject. I am returning to CR after a 25-year absence and consider your book an invaluable reference tool." - **Thomas Marino**

"**NEVER** before have I been so thoroughly prepared for moving to a new location as I was after reading "The New Golden Door to Retirement and Living In Costa Rica". In fact, after arriving here, I was utterly and continuously amazed at how much **VALUABLE** knowledge I had previously obtained through reading this book. Furthermore, I find it **INDISPENSABLE** as a constant reference source for day-to-day operations. Subsequently I had purchased two similar, popular guide books and after several attempts at trying to read them, I find that they are incapable of holding my attention." - **Steve, San Jose, Costa Rica**

"I just picked up your book (The New Golden Door to Retirement and Living in Costa Rica) and I **LOVE** it. My wife and I have had a long time dream to someday retire (young) in paradise. It sounds like we have a found our future destination. Your book has been very **HELPFUL.**" Dan Graham

THE NEW GOLDEN DOOR TO RETIREMENT AND LIVING IN COSTA RICA

A guide to inexpensive living, making money and finding love in a peaceful tropical paradise

Written by
CHRISTOPHER HOWARD

THE NEW GOLDEN DOOR TO RETIREMENT AND LIVING IN COSTA RICA

By Christopher Howard

Fourteenth Edition

First Edition, published in Costa Rica
Second through Fourteenth Editions
Published in the United States

© 2005-2006 Editora de Turismo Nacional, S.A.

ISBN 1-881233-58-8

Costa Rica Books
Suite 1 SJO 981
P.O. Box 025216
Miami, FL 33102-5216
www.costaricabooks.com
www.liveincostarica.com
www.amazon.com

"If there be any splendor in peace, let it rest in a country like this. . ."

Lambert James

"Costa Rica is a proud example of a free people practicing the principals of democracy. And you have done so in good times and in bad, when it was easier and when it required great courage."

Ronald Reagan 1982

ACKNOWLDGEMENTS

This edition would not have become a reality without the invaluable help of many people.

I would first like to thank my graphic designer, William "El Mago" Morales, for his hard work and patience.

I am also very grateful to Mary De Waal at Blue JewelTravel.

A special thanks to the following local writers and Costa Rican residents for their contributions to this edition: Jay Trettien, Rob Hodel, Roger Petersen, Martha Bennett, Todd Staley, Michael Pierpont, Ryan Piercy, William Lytle, Carlos Morton, Les Nuñez and Landy Blank.

I am indebted to all the critics whose many favorable reviews made my previous editions a success.

I would like to acknowledge all of the help I have received from the Publishers Marketing Association's andAmazon.com's programs for independent publishers. Thanks to them, this book is now available in the U.S., Canada and rest of the world. A special thanks to my Costa Rican distributor, 7th Street Books, for a job well done.

Finally, I would like to express my eternal gratitude to members of my family, especially my late mother and wife, for their constant support when I needed it the most.

Christopher Howard
San José, Costa Rica

MORE ABOUT THE AUTHOR

Christopher Howard has resided in Costa Rica for over fifteen years and is a Costa Rican citizen.

During this time he has had the opportunity to gather a plethora of information about living , investing and retiring in Costa Rica. It is not surprising that he has first-hand knowledge and insight into all aspects of Costa Rica's culture and its people. Because of his expertise he is a frequent lecturer at numerous investment seminars.

Mr. Howard has an extensive foreign language background, having earned a B.A. in Latin American studies and a Master's degree in Spanish from the University of California. He also has credentials to teach Spanish at all levels from California State University, San Francisco.

Howard was the recipient of scholarships for graduate study at the University of the Americas in Puebla, Mexico and the Jesuit University of Guadalajara, Mexico in conjunction with the University of San Diego, California. He has written three foreign language books including the best-selling *Costa Rican Spanish Survival Course* and, in 1985, founded a successful language institute in San José, Costa Rica.

The author in front of his new home in Lagunilla de Heredia.

At present, Chris Howard has been busy leading monthly relocation tours for people thinking of moving to Costa Rica; working as a paid consultant for *National Geographic Magazine*; putting the finishing touches on a book about Costa Rican idioms; publishing articles for various newsletter about living abroad and working on a feature action movie script to be filmed in Central America.

Mr. Howard has also served as an officer on the Board of Directors of the Association of Residents Costa Rica.

In 1998 he published the visionary guidebook, *Living and Investing in the New Cuba*. His most recent guidebooks are *Living and Investing in the New Nicaragua* (2000) and *Living and Investing in Panama* (2004).

Due to a multitude of requests from the readers of this guidebook, Chris Howard began to offer relocation and retirement tours to Costa Rica starting in 1997. Since then he has personally introduced 1000's of people to Costa Rica through his one-of-a-kind monthly tours, seminars and private consultation services.

- The Publisher

CONTENTS

CHAPTER IV

CHAPTER V

CHAPTER VI

CHAPTER VII

CHAPTER VIII

CHAPTER IX

CHAPTER X

WHY LIVE IN COSTA RICA?

Recently I led a group of prospective residents on a trip around Costa Rica. After a week of traveling and attending a series of informative seminars, the majority had decided they would like to live here for at least part of the year. It comes as little surprise that they felt this way. Costa Rica has more Americans per capita than any other country outside the United States. Why do so many people want to live here?

The most obvious reason is the climate. People are tired of freezing winters, scorching summers and the high utility bills that go with them. In Costa Rica they can enjoy one of the best year-round climates in the world (72 degrees average in the Central Valley.) We have only two seasons here, dry and rainy, both with an abundance of sunshine. We rarely need air conditioning and never need heat. Costa Rica has more winter sunshine than Hawaii or Florida and fewer people.

Costa Rica is called by many "the Switzerland of the Americas" due to its neutral political status and spectacular mountains. From the huge, curling waves of the Pacific coast, to the sight of molten rock tumbling down the sides of a volcano, Costa Rica's natural beauty has something for everyone. This unique little country offers a real paradise for the nature lover, the fishing enthusiast and water sports fanatic as well as the retiree.

Many come here for the lifestyle. Costa Rica fits the bill for anyone sick of the hustle and bustle, seeking a more laid-back way of life. One of the tour participants remarked, "Costa Rica reminds me of the U.S. about 40 years ago when everything was unspoiled, unhurried and less crowded." It will also appeal to people of all ages seeking to move to a new and exotic land outside of the States and Canada and the energetic entrepreneur, the burned-out baby boomer, those

sick of long rush-hour commutes and anyone seeking an alternative way of life.

This beautiful country is so appealing because it has the warmth and flavor of Mexico, without anti-Americanism and fear of government expropriations; the physical beauty of Guatemala without a large military presence; and the sophistication of Brazil without the abject poverty and far less crime.

But Isn't It Expensive?

Although much has been written about the high cost of living here, what you spend depends on your lifestyle. If you must have a luxurious home, drive a late model car and buy imported goods, you will spend as much or more than you would in North America. But if you live more like the locals and watch your spending, you will spend considerably less.

Many Americans living below the poverty line in the United States can live in moderate luxury on a modest retirement or investment income in Costa Rica.

The favorable exchange rate and low rate of inflation let you stretch your dollars here. The cost of food, utilities and entertainment are all substantially lower than in the United States.

Costa Rica's affordable medical care is among the best anywhere. The quality of health care is comparable to North America but the prices are one half or less! Considered by many to be the healthiest country south of Canada, Costa Rica has a higher life-expectancy rate than the United States (76.3 for men, 79.8 for women), rumored to be the third longest in the world.

Housing costs are a fraction of what you are accustomed to paying in the U.S. My wife and I just purchased a new three-bedroom home in Lagunilla de Heredia, about five miles from downtown San José, for $62,000. It has a cathedral ceiling, sits on a 250 square meter lot and is very comfortable for three people and a dog. We have a 15-year mortgage and pay $452 monthly including insurance, with a 9% loan from a Costa Rican state bank.

Besides our home we have a car and a full-time maid. Household help makes life easier. (You can hire a full-time maid for as little as $200 per month or $1 per hour.) My son goes to one of the best private schools in the country. We eat out a few times a week and enjoy various types of entertainment. We spend a week at the beach during Easter and go to the United States every Christmas. Our monthly expenses are about $2500.

The country's inexpensive medical care, affordable housing, excellent transportation and communication networks, an abundance of activities to stay busy and happy, contribute to Costa Rica's appeal and place it at the top of the list of retirement and expatriate havens.

According to a survey of potential foreign retirement areas in the Robb Report, due to the high quality of life Costa Rica surpasses all countries including Mexico, Puerto Rico, Spain, Portugal, Australia, the Caribbean Islands and Greece.

What Sets Costa Rica Apart from Its Neighbors?

Countries such as Nicaragua, Belize, Honduras and Guatemala have lower living costs, but you get what you pay for. The quality of life and lack of infrastructure in those countries leave a lot to be desired. Safety is a concern, especially where paramilitary police have power or where police are corrupt, as in Mexico. Costa Rica is politically stable and is unique in having no army. Although theft occurs, violent crime is minimal.

A Place to Invest

Costa Rica has a myriad of business opportunities awaiting creative, hard-working individuals. You can run a global business from here by using Internet access, fax machines and cell phones. It is also relatively easy to start a small business on a shoestring. Tax incentives and a government that encourages investments and affords investors the same rights as citizens contribute to a propitious business climate. Many countries either do not permit noncitizens to own property or place restrictions on foreign-owned real estate, but this is not the case in Costa Rica. Anyone may buy real estate with all the legal rights of citizens. Actually, an investment in Costa Rica today is much better than an investment in California real estate was 30 years ago.

What gets people excited about Costa Rica, however, is that it offers some of the best real estate on the planet at affordable prices. The price will eventually go up as the rest of the world catches on. There's only so much beautiful beachfront and prime real estate left in the world. When you think that almost every bit of the coastline in the U.S. is becoming overcrowded and overpriced, Costa Rica seems like a bargain.

Passive investors will find CD's, second mortgages or other investments that pay 25% to 30% in dollars annually. These numbers are fantastic when you consider that a million dollars invested in the U.S. at a standard 4 to 5 percent annual rate, will generate only $45,000 to $50,000 a year.

A burgeoning global economy and the Internet communications revolution have created unlimited possibilities for doing business in Central and South America. Furthermore, trade pacts between Costa Rica, U.S., Mexico and South America will soon become a reality. These free trade treaties promise to link all of the nations in the hemisphere in to one trading block.

Costa Rica's current prosperity is being fueled by the emigration of affluent baby boomers from around the world seeking their own piece of paradise and the same engine that fueled the growth in California for the last 30 years, technology. When Intel decided it needed more capacity, they looked all over the western hemisphere and chose Costa Rica for the very same reasons you will.

Word is getting out about Costa Rica. And that's why now is such a good time to invest.

The Adventure of Starting Over

Some move here to start over and seek adventure in an exotic land. They are tired of dead-end jobs or the rat race and want new challenges, a chance to pursue their dreams and achieve greater personal growth. As an foreigner, you have the challenge of immersing yourself in a new culture and, if you choose, the rewards of learning a foreign language.

Newcomers can make friends easily because foreigners gravitate towards one another. One Florida transplant told us he had lived in Florida for 20 years and hardly ever had contact with his neighbors. He claims not to be the most sociable person in the world, nevertheless he has made over a hundred friends in Costa Rica. He proudly says, "Everywhere I go I bump into people I know."

Adjusting and Keeping Busy

Adjustment to a new way of life can take many months. However, an open mind, a positive attitude and a willingness to seek out new experiences can make the transition relatively painless.

Costa Rica has come a long way in the last decade. Satellite and Direct TV, private mail service and the Internet make it easier to stay in touch with family and friends in the United States and keep up with what is going on all over the world. If you don't own a computer, you can go to an Internet café.

Costa Rica's modern technology has made life easy for foreign residents. In most areas of the country you can get cash at a local ATM, manage your investments online and read almost any major newspaper in the world the day it comes out.

A friend of ours, a 20-year resident of Costa Rica, said, " My days are so filled with exciting activities and interesting experiences that each day seems like a whole lifetime. I really feel that I have discovered the fountain of youth."

Single men are attracted to the country since it has the reputation of having the most beautiful, flirtatious and accessible women in Latin America. It comes as no surprise that Costa Rican women are highly sought as companions by foreign men of all ages. Single men will have no problem finding love, romance and a second chance in life with a devoted Costa Rican woman.

You will never be bored here unless you choose to be. Costa Rica has something for everyone. In the Tico Times, the weekly English-language newspaper, you can find hundreds of interesting activities: movies in English, support groups, computer and bridge clubs. You name it, Costa Rica has it.

Living in Costa Rica can open the door to a new and exciting life. Who knows? You may never want to return home.

One Expatriate's Experience

Michael Pierpont, the founder of Sunburst Coffee, fell in love with Costa Rica a few years ago and knew right away that this was where he wanted to live. You too may find that you want to spend more than just a few weeks every year in this delightful country.

"People ask me all the time why I chose Costa Rica," says Michael. "I like this country for several reasons. First, it is a spectacularly beautiful place. Along the Pacific coast you will find rocky outcrops and pounding surf. The beaches look just like those in California, which is where I am from. But you can buy here for one-tenth the cost of California. Inland you'll find a lush jungle...Lake Arenal...the Irazú volcano, and coffee plantations...and the most beautiful rain forests in the world. In the northwest you will find white-sand beaches, many declared turtle reserves, one of the numerous areas in this country set aside for wildlife research and preservation.

"Second, and important to me is the cost of living. I can live well in this country on as little as $1,500 per month. You can rent a comfortable house in San José, where I chose to settle, for $500 per month. You can employ a full-time maid for $185 monthly. You will spend $300 per month on groceries, $65 per month on electricity. You can see a movie for $3 and have a nice dinner with drinks for $15.

'Third, I was smitten by the people. Costa Ricans are good-natured and kind, trusting and friendly and extremely beautiful. I knew I'd be happy living and making friends here."

"A few more notes on why I came to Costa Rica: The weather is great, the Spanish colonial history and architecture is delightful, the small expatriate community is welcoming and an extremely interesting bunch. Everyone's got a story. And best of all the taxes are low and easy to deal with."

INTRODUCTION

WELCOME TO BEAUTIFUL COSTA RICA

Costa Rica's friendly three million people, or Ticos as they affectionately call themselves, invite you to come and experience their tranquil country, with its long and beautiful coastlines, alluring waters of the Caribbean and the Pacific, pristine beaches and some of the most picturesque surroundings you have ever laid your eyes on.

Many visitors say Costa Rica is even more beautiful than Hawaii, and best of all, still unspoiled. In Fact, Costa Rica took over Hawaii's place as best adventure destination last year, as revealed by the publication Pacific Business News, of Honolulu. Costa Rica has Hawaii's weather, spectacular green mountains, and beaches without the high prices. The country offers more beauty and adventure per acre than any other place in the world.

In the heart of the Central Valley, surrounded by beautiful rolling mountains and volcanoes, sits San José, today's capital and largest city in the country. Viewed from above, this area looks like some parts of Switzerland.

Downtown San José is always bustling with activity.

San José is the center of the country's politics and cultural events. It has a mixture of modern and colonial architecture, yet remains charmingly quaint and retains a small-town feel despite being a fairly large city with a slightly international flavor. It feels more like a town that has grown in all directions, rather than a metropolis. Even though San José and adjacent suburbs have a population of around one million people, you always get a small-town feeling due to the layout of the city. San José along with Panama City are considered to be the most cosmopolitan cities in Central America.

In a 2004 survey by Mercer Human Resource Consulting, San José ranked 130 out of 140 cities world wide with respect to cost of living. Tokio and London were at the head of the list.

San José or *Chepe*, as the locals call it, is also the cultural and business center of the country and a mecca for North Americans. There is something for everyone. The city boasts the three largest shopping malls in Central America, with all of the stores to which you have become accustomed back home. The city also offers a variety of night life, a wide range of hotels, restaurants serving international cuisine, casinos, quaint cafés, lovely parks, an old national theater with a wonderful orchestra and lots of outside attractions on a regular basis. Other things of interest are a zoo, art galleries, theatres, museums, parks, two English newspapers, places for people watching and much more. Virtually everything in a large U.S. city can be found here. Americans have no trouble feeling at home. It is very easy to find something to do to entertain yourself. At an altitude of just over 3,750 feet above sea level, San José offers year-round spring-like temperatures which add to its appeal.

The city is laid out on a grid plan. *Calles* (streets) run north and south and *avenidas* (avenues). Avenues to the north of *Avenida Central* have odd numbers and those to the south even numbers. Streets to the east of *Calle Central* have odd numbers and those to the west even.

San José's convenient central location, make any part of the country accessible in a matter of hours by automobile. We recommend you use San José as a gateway, starting point or home base while you explore Costa Rica and look for a permanent place to reside. Due to the county's size it is possible to spend the morning at the beach, visit a volcano by noon and dine at a mountain resort overlooking the Central Valley for dinner.

COSTA RICA
A country that lives up to its name.
by Julie Campbell

"In my capacity as Fashion and Travel Editor of *Sports Illustrated magazine*, I've produced every one of the magazine's swimsuit issues from 1965 to 1996, thirty-two in all. My annual search for beautiful and unspoiled locations has led me to every continent except Antarctica, and I've walked literally hundreds of miles of beaches, mountain trails, deserts, and even glaciers in order to take our readers to some of the most exotic, and often overlooked, corners of our planet. Sometimes my choice was a resort so new that it could only be envisioned from an architect's blueprint; in other years I've settled on an island or a country or even an entire continent— Australia.

So what brought me to Dominical, Costa Rica? Looking at the map I was struck for the first time by how near a neighbor Central America was, and at the same time how little I knew about it. I had to know more, and when i discovered Costa Rica, the jewel of the Central American chain, and traveled its length and breadth, I knew I had found something very special—a country that truly lives up to its name.

Costa Rica means Coast of Abundance or richness of nature. Its rainforests comprise a virtual cornucopia of flowers, lush vegetation, birds and wildlife—all still unspoiled. Rising from the coastline at Dominical are the majestic green mountains with rushing clear streams leading to crystal waterfalls and swimable fresh-water pools.

Coming down from mountains that were often tucked behind mist and clouds I found myself in a beautiful and varied stretch of coast. One side of the country faces the Pacific and the other the Caribbean. For our shoot I chose the Pacific at a place called Dominical, where one beach is more lovely and dramatic than the next. The diversity was breathtaking. And on these immaculate beaches there is no one to step over you while sunning, and only the sound of tropical birds and rolling surf.

I came to Dominical to take gorgeous pictures of gorgeous models in a gorgeous setting, and indeed I was able to do that. But the real discovery was a small piece of God's Country that I'll want to revisit again and again—and on my own time!

*Courtesy of Sports Illustrated

THINGS TO THINK ABOUT BEFORE MOVING TO A NEW COUNTRY OR MAKING FOREIGN INVESTMENTS

❑ What is required to become a legal resident? Can I meet these requirements? What is the cost? How often does residency have to be renewed, what are the conditions of renewal and what is the cost?

❑ What is required to visit, or stay while I'm waiting for residency?

❑ What is the political situation? How stable is the country?

❑ Weather (Will I like the weather year-round?)

❑ Income taxes (Will I be taxed on income brought into the country?) (Am I allowed to earn income in the country?) If yes, (How is it taxed?)

❑ Other taxes? (Sales tax, import duties, exit taxes, vehicle taxes, etc.)

❑ How much will it cost in fees, duties, import taxes to bring my personal possessions into the country? (Cars, boats, appliances, electronic equipment, etc.)

❑ Rental property - How much? Availability?

❑ Purchase property - Property taxes, restrictions on foreign ownership of property, expropriation laws, building regulations, squatters rights, etc. Is there a capital gains tax?

❑ Communications - Are there reliable phone and fax lines, cellular phones, beepers, connections to Internet and other computer communication service? Is there good mail service between the country and the rest of the world? Are there private express mail services like DHL, UPS and FEDEX? Are there local newspapers, radio and TV in a language I will understand? Is there cable or satellite TV available?

❑ Transportation - How are the roads? Are flights available to places I will want to go? How are the buses and taxis ? How costly is it to travel to and from other international destinations?

❑ Is it difficult for friends and family to visit?

❑ Shopping - Are replacement parts available for the items you have brought from home? If so, what are the costs? If not, how much will it cost to import what I need?

❑ Are the types of food I am accustomed to readily available in both markets and restaurants?

❑ If I have hobbies, are clubs, supplies and assistance available?

❑ What cultural activities are available? (Art, music, theatre, museums, etc.)

- ❏ What entertainment is available? (Sports, movies, nightclubs, dancing, etc.)
- ❏ What recreational facilities are available? (Golf courses, tennis, health clubs, recreational centers, parks, etc.)
- ❏ If I like the beach, are good beaches available? Can they be reached easily? What is the year round temperature of the water?
- ❏ What is the violent crime rate? Minor crime (theft, car and house break-ins)? What support can be expected from the police department? Are the police helpful to foreign residents?
- ❏ How do local residents treat foreign visitors and residents?
- ❏ What are the local investment opportunities? Is there any consumer or protective legislation for investors? What return can I expect from my investments?
- ❏ Is the banking system safe and reliable? Can they transfer funds and convert foreign currency, checks, drafts, and transfers? Are checking, savings and other accounts available to foreigners? Is there banking confidentiality? Is there a favorable rate of exchange with the U.S. dollar?
- ❏ Are good lawyers, accountants, investment advisors and other professionals available?
- ❏ How difficult is it to start a business? What kinds of opportunities are there?
- ❏ How is the health care system? Is it affordable? Do they honor U.S. and Canadian health insurance? Are there any diseases which are dangerous to foreigners, and if so does the local health care system address the problem? What is the quality of hospitals, clinics, doctors and dentists? What is the availability of good specialists?
- ❏ How is the sanitation? Can I drink the water? Do the restaurants have good sanitation standards? Are pasteurized milk and other dairy products available? Do meat, fish, and vegetable markets have satisfactory sanitary standards?
- ❏ If I am interested in domestic staff, what is the cost of cooks, housekeepers and gardeners, etc.? Is the local help reliable? What regulations are involved in hiring employees? What are the employers' responsibilities to the workers?
- ❏ What legislation is there to protect foreign residents? What rights do foreign residents have in comparison to citizens?
- ❏ What natural disasters are there? (Hurricanes, tornadoes, typhoons, earthquakes, droughts, floods.)
- ❏ Can pets be brought into the country?
- ❏ Is there religious freedom?

*Courtesy of the Costa Rican Residents Association

COSTA RICA'S LAND, HISTORY AND PEOPLE

The Lay of the Land

Costa Rica occupies a territory of around 20,000 square miles in the southern part of Central America, and includes several small islands mostly on the Pacific side. It is much like the state of Florida with two long coastlines. The country is only about 200 miles long and 70 miles wide at the narrowest part.

Costa Rica is often compared to Switzerland and Hawaii because of its mountains and forests. Costa Rica's three mountain ranges create five geographically diverse areas. The Northern Central Plains, the Northwest Peninsula, the Tropical Lowlands on the Pacific and Caribbean coasts and the Central Valley where 70 percent of the population reside. They make up the seven provinces of Alajuela, Cartago, Guanacaste, Heredia, Puntarenas, Limón and San José.

Unlike many areas of Mexico, Central and South America, Costa Rica remains beautiful and warm year-round. This is partly because it borders the Pacific Ocean on the west, the Atlantic Ocean on the east, and has a string of towering volcanoes on the Central Plateau. Combine all this and you have a unique tropical paradise with 11 climatic zones.

COSTA RICA GENERAL INFORMATION

Capital	San José
Population	4,000,000
Size	19,730 square miles
Quality of Life	Excellent,(good weather, friendly people, affordable)
Official Language	Spanish (English is widely spoken)
Political System	Democracy
Currency	Colón
Investment Climate	Good-many opportunities
Per capita income	$3,700
Official Religion	Catholicism
Foreign Population (U.S., Canadian and European)	Over 50,000
Longevity	77.49 is almost as high the U.S.
Literacy	95%
Time	Central Standard (U.S.)

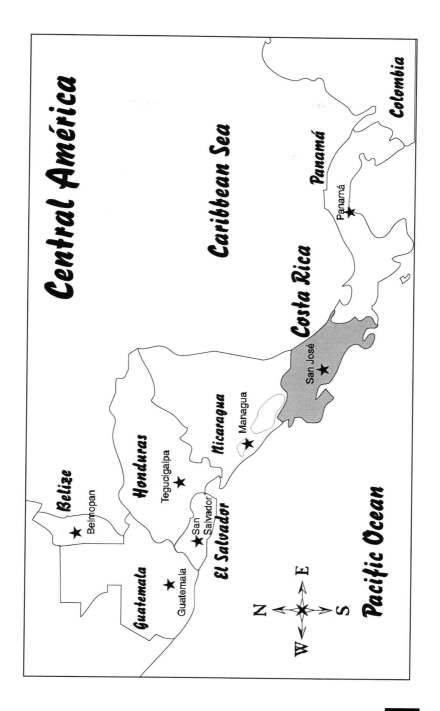

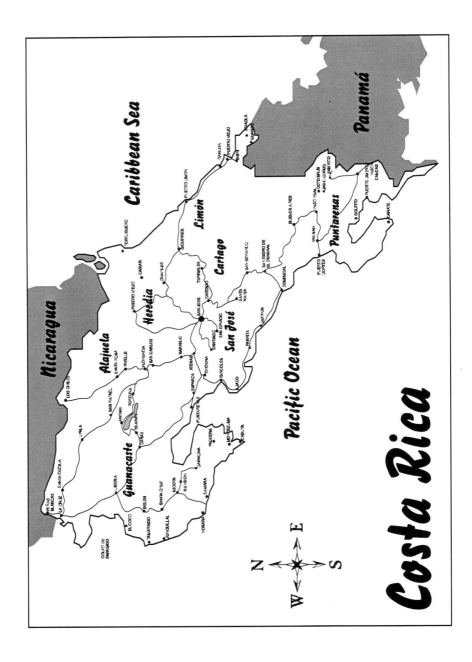

Weather

Costa Rica has a tropical climate since it lies so near the equator. The country is famous for having one of the best climates in the world. You dress in lightweight clothing year-round and a jacket may be necessary for higher elevations and cool nights. Don't forget your umbrella for the rainy season. U.S. style rain gear is too warm and cumbersome for the tropics.

Temperatures vary little from season to season and fluctuate with altitude. The higher you go the colder it gets, and the lower you go the warmer it is. In the Central Valley spring-like daytime temperatures hover around 72 degrees all year, while lower elevations enjoy temperatures ranging from the upper 70s to the high 80s. Temperatures at sea level fluctuate between the high 80s and low 90s in summer with slightly more humidity than higher elevations.

Like other tropical places, Costa Rica only has two seasons. The summer or *verano* is generally from late December to April with March and April being the warmest months of the year. The rainy season or *invierno*, runs from May to November. January is usually the coolest month. At times, there is an unseasonably dry spell or Indian summer in either July, August or September. The Costa Ricans call this pause in the rainy weather, *veranillo*. A relatively dry period at the end of July is referred to as *canícula* when there is a respite in the May to November rains. Light rains mixed with sunshine characterize this period, which can sometimes extend into August.

Unlike many of the world's tropical areas, almost all mornings are sunny and clear with only a few hours of rain in the afternoons during the wet season. Since the temperature varies little, the wet months are usually as warm as the dry months. It is unusual to have two or three days of continuous rainy weather in most areas of the country. October is usually the rainiest month of the year. However, the Caribbean Coast tends to be wet all year long. For this reason many foreigners choose to live on the west coast of Costa Rica. This climate, along with a unique geography, is responsible for Costa Rica's lush vegetation and greenness at all elevations especially during the rainy season.

Foreigners should not let the rain get them down since there are a variety of indoor activities available. San José's many museums, theaters, malls, casinos, roller skating rinks, Internet cafés and other indoor activities will more than keep you busy when it rains.

Where to Live in Costa Rica
The Central Valley

The Central Valley or *Meseta Central*, is the center of Costa Rica due to its geographical location, culture and economic activities. The altitude of the valley is between 3000 to 4000 feet above sea level. It is surrounded by mountains and semi-active volcanos such as Poás and Irazú. Its fertile volcanic soil make it ideal palce for growing anything, including some of the world's best coffee. It is not surprising that over half of Costa Rica's people live in this area because of its almost perfect year-round climate.

There is a wide range of housing in the Central Valley. Decent affordable housing ranges from $50,000 to $100,000 while medium prices range from $100,000 to $250,000. Recently, there has been a boom in the construction industry which has created a wide variety of affordable new homes from which to choose. However, older homes also abound and are sometimes a better deal beacause they often have larger parcels of land.

Deciding where to live in Costa Rica depends on your preferences. If you like the stimulation of urban living and spring-like weather all year, you will probably be happiest living in **San José** or one of the adjacent smaller towns and cities in the Central Valley.

As we mention later in this book, there are hundreds of activities for everyone in, around and near San José. The infrastructure is excellent and this area offers almost all of the amenities of living in the U.S.

A $200,000 + home in the upscale Rohrmoser neighborhood.

Retirement is a big change for many people because they find themselves with more free time than usual and sometimes get bored. This should be a problem if you reside in the San José area since there is a large North American community and it is always easy to find something to do.

The are a couple of drawbacks to living in San José proper. Like most cities San José is crowded, noisy and there is some pollution from buses and cars. There is also some crime in the downtown area. If you own a vehicle it is hard to find a place to keep it except for public parking lots. Despite these shortcomings, we do know quite a few Americans who live in the center of town because it is convenient and there is a lot to do to stay busy.

One friend from Florida loves this area because he is right in thick of the action in the Gringo Gulch area. Another American likes to spend all day in front of the Hotel Costa Rica seated at one of the tables talking with other expatriates and people watching. The latter is a favorite among foreigners in the downtown area. There are a couple of group of *gringos* who gather for coffee and conversation most days at McDonalds and The Grand Hotel Costa Rica next to The Plaza de la Cultura and National Theater. Newcomers can make some instant friends there.

Many North Americans, who do not want to live too far from town, reside around the Sabana Park. Most of them reside in nearby **Sabana norte** and **Sabana sur**. Restaurants, gyms, the new Más por Menos supermarket and a variety of stores and services are all found in this area.

Located at the west end of Paseo Colón is the sprawling **Sabana Park**. It is the largest of Costa Rica's urban parks and is within walking distance of San José and neighboring Rohrmoser. La Sabana was originally the site of the country's international airport. It is now covered with tall trees, a lake, jogging trails, an Olympic size-pool, recreational facilities and many more attractions for the general public. The fashionable suburb of **Rohrmoser**, on the west-side of Sabana Park, is very popular with people who want to live in a suburban area close to San José. Living in Rohrmoser is much like having a home near New York's Central Park or San Francisco's Golden Gate Park. The main tree-lined street or Rohrmoser Boleveard runs right through the center of this neighborhood, virtually bisecting it in half. Rohrmoser is bordered on the south by the Pavas Highway. Just about any type of store you might need is found along this busy thoroughfare as well as the US Embassy to the west.

Rohrmoser has many beautiful homes of wealthy Costa Ricans and is considered very safe, since a large number of well-guarded foreign embassies are there. Home prices start at around $80,000 on the low end, from

$80,000 to $125,000 for a mid range home and $250 for an upper end home. Rents begin at $500. When we lived there a few years ago we paid $600 for a three bedroom-three bath penthouse apartment with a panoramic view of the mountains.

Excellent supermarkets, boutiques, international restaurants, the Cemaco department store, pharmacies, bars, discos, doctor's offices, health clubs and the modern Plaza Mayor Shopping Center are also located in and around this upscale neighborhood.

For you nighthawks there is even a 24-hour mini-market at the Shell gas station. The only thing bad about Rohrmoser is that bus service to downtown San José is not good, but you can always take a taxi since they are so affordable.

About five minutes east of downtown San José, sits the residential neighborhood of **Los Yoses.** Like all areas east of downtown San José, there is a mixture of new and old homes and businesses. Many foreigners live in this area because it is only a short walk to downtown San José. The *Centro Cultural Costarricense-Norteamericano* is located in this area so there are interesting activities to keep a person occupied (There is also a smaller branch in Sabana Norte next to the American Chamber of Commerce). Los Yoses boasts a bowling alley, a supermarket complex, a bookstore and many bars and restaurants. The gigantic San Pedro Mall is found on the eastern edge of this neighborhood. **Barrio Escalante,** slightly to the north of Los Yoses, has many older homes and stately mansions. The area provides a glimpse of how the upper crust used to live in Costa Rica. Many foreigners prefer this area since it is so close to downtown and there is some reasonably priced housing available. Prices range from about $80,000 on up. Rents start at about $300 for a small apartment

Just east of Los Yoses is **San Pedro**—the home of the University of Costa Rica. The campus and surrounding area resemble many U.S. college towns with its many student hangouts, restaurants, bookstores, nightspots, boutiques and two large shopping malls. You can spend the day sitting at a table at one of the many sidewalk cafes and check out the passersby. A definite bohemian-like ambience fills the air. Some interesting event or cultural activity is always happening in or around the university. During April, the annual University Week celebration takes place. This spectacle includes floats and a carnival-like atmosphere. Low-priced student apartments are available within walking distance of the university.

Another place you might consider living is **Escazú** —a popular suburb where many North Americans reside and sometimes referred to as the Beverly Hills of Costa Rica due to its upscale cosmopolitan-like atmosphere.

Why I live in Costa Rica?
By Jo Stuart

The quality of life is not measured simply by efficiency nor by material things. For those of you who want to know why I live Costa Rica, here are my reasons why.

(1) I was originally drawn to this country because it has no army, and as a result has developed a peaceful mentality. Costa Ricans do not like confrontations and are not greatly into competition. Perhaps because of this, the minute I arrived, I felt comfortable here.

(2) I was charmed (and still am) because when *ticos* "Thank you," they don't say "*Gracias*." They usually *say"Gracias muy amable*," which means "Thank you, you're very kind." Being told I am kind often enough makes me see myself as kind and wanting to be more so.

My life here is enhanced each time a *tico* says, "You're welcome." Here they don't say, as they do in most other Spanish-speaking countries, "*No hay de que*" or "*De nada*" (For nothing). They say "*Con mucho gusto*" (Which much pleasure or, more loosely, The pleasure is mine). My friend Jerry has said more than once that giving and receiving are the same thing, and *Ticos* seem to have recognized this. I have been trying to remember to say both *Gracias, muy amable* and *Con mucho gusto*. Language is a powerful influence on attitude.

(3) Although I have learned that there is a downside to a peace-loving philosophy, a trait called passive-aggressive, I have decided that I can handle passive-aggressive better that I can the downside of a personal freedom-loving philosophy, which seems to be aggresive-aggressive.

(4) I enjoy walking in downtown San José in spite of the traffic and challenging sidewalks. When I first came here and mixed with the people on the streets, I thought there are as many pedestrians here as there are in New York at Christmas time but without the hostility. Instead, I find myself energized and uplifted.

(5) I also noticed that Costa Ricans as a rule have fine postures. It is a pleasure to see them, and seeing them reminds me to straighten up. It is surprising how much better you feel when you walk tall.

(6) I have on a number of occasions, experienced the health care system of Costa Rica, both private and public . The cost here for medical care is far less than in the United States, and I always have felt more cared for and cared about in my experiences here. Even in the overworked and under-supplied public hospitals, I have found attention and compassion. It outweighs the lack of Kleenex. The last time I was in Calderón Guardia emergency section, they passed out lunches at noon and coffee and snacks in the late afternoon to the waiting patients.

(7) Although business transactions are not always speedy here, how can you not like a country where it is the law that every public building must have a public bathroom? (That doesn't mean they must supply paper.) It is true one spends considerable time waiting in lines. This is where I get a lot of my reading done. I've waited in lines in many countries, and I'll take orderly, friendly queue of *ticos* any day.

(8) There is a custom here that many North Americans have picked up and that is the custom of brushing cheeks when seeing a friend or acquaintance. In the States, after an initial handshake following an introduction, I seldom touch that person again, certainly not my travel agent, my doctor or my landlord. Here, I do. Touching cheeks makes me feel a connectedness to others, and when you think about it, is much more sanitary than a handshake.

(9) On the comfort front, it is hard to beat the climate in the Central Valley of Costa Rica. I have lived where there were 15-foot snowdrifts and where I became accustomed to perspiration dripping down my neck all the time. Living where I need neither air conditioning nor a heater is such a pleasure, and I am sure, far healthier.

(10) Something that is changing here that I regret are the window displays in the stores. Once there was nothing that caught my attention, and I had no desire to buy. I was not lured into being a consumer. Now they are getting both more artistic and more products, and I have found myself stopping and thinking I would like that something.

(11) Because the growing season is so rapid, fresh vegetables and fruits are available most of the year. If one were a vegetarian, one could live very cheaply here.

(12) And finally, what clinched my love affair with Costa Rica was discovering that their national bird is the *yigüirro*. The *yigüirro* (which I can't even pronounce) is very similar to the U.S. robin but smaller, and even less colorful. The yiguirro neither threatens anyone's existence (it is certainly not a bird of prey nor is it a rare or endangered bird.) It is a common little dun-colored bird, an Every bird, if you will. I think people who choose the *yiguirro* as a national bird has something to say to the rest of the world about peaceful co-existence, humanity, self-esteem and equality.

*Jo Stuart is a regular columnist for the online daily *Am Costa Rica*. See **www.amcostarica.com** for more details.

Escazú is about five miles west of San José, 10 to 15 minutes driving time on the old two-lane road or new *autopista*, (highway). Since most of this town is located on hilly terrain, it is especially appealing to those people who like cooler temperatures. In fact, Escazú is one of the more popular places English-speaking foreigners live. Bus service is excellent to and from San José. You can catch either a micro-bus or regular bus in the park behind the church in downtown Escazú.

Despite being quaint and country-like, Escazú has all the amenities of any North American suburb: pharmacies, mini-malls, supermarkets, excellent English-speaking private schools, first-class restaurants, trendy shops, doctors, dentists, a post office and much more. The main entrance to Escazú has so many US franchises, you may find it hard to believe you're not in the States. If you reside here you won't have to go to San José for basic services unless you want to. There is even a beautiful private country club and golf course. Housing is plentiful, but expensive because Escazú is popular with wealthy Costa Ricans and well-to-do foreigners. You can find simple *tico*-style single family homes, condos, highrise penthouses and even country estates scattered around this area.

Trejos Montealegre is a neighborhood just off the highway which boasts many homes, condos and apartments from which to choose. Some upper-end homes in Escazú cost a couple of hundred thousand to one million dollars. However, if you are living on a budget or small pension you can find more affordable housing in San Antonio de Escazú. There are many affordable *tico*-style homes scattered around this area. Because this area is very exclusive, home prices start at around $100,000. Mid range homes and condos go for around $150,000 and upper end prices start at about $300,000. Rents range from $800 to $2,500 or more monthly.

Santa Ana, nestled in the "Valley of the Sun", is more rural than Escazú. This fast-growing village is about four miles west of Escazú and has a good mix of Costa Ricans and foreigners residing there. Santa Ana's warm climate makes it almost perfect place to live. At one time Santa Ana was a popular weekend retreat and summer home for well-to-do Costa Ricans. Many foreigners and ordinary Costa Ricans reside in this town of 2,500 inhabitants now. You can get to Santa Ana by taking the old scenic road from Escazú through the hills or by the new highway. We recommend checking out this town. Downtown Santa Ana retains a small town flavor. It is more rural and less developed than Escazú but there are good supermarkets and some shopping. You don't have to go to San José for your essential products. Lately there has been a building boom in the area. Homes here are more reasonably priced than in Escazú. Luxury homes in a secure gated community are a popular choice for middle-to-high income budgets. An upscale four-bedroom home in a gated community will cost between $200,000 to $375,000. Lots run between $50 -$75 per square meter.

Cuidad Colón, located about twenty minutes beyond Santa Ana, is the farthest western suburb of San Jose. Some foreigners live there. In a year a new highway extending from Ciudad Colón to the town of Orotina will reduce driving time to the beach from the Central Valley in half. Beyond Ciudad Colón is the mountain town of **Puriscal**. The cooler mountain climate makes this town appealing. This town is perfect for people who seek affordable housing, more land for their money and rural living. There are a few properties that have views of both the ocean and Central Valley. Many people who live in Puriscal commute daily to San José since bus service is good.

The town of **San Antonio de Belén,** a laid-back town behind the airport and just a couple of miles off the main highway west of the Cariari, is another good spot to live. This town has experienced a great deal of growth since INTEL's mammoth plant opened a few years ago and Marriot built a five-star hotel in the area. A couple of nice gated communities can be found there. Home prices, rents and land are lower than Escazú, Santa Ana and Cariari. The *Ojo de Agua* recreational complex is also in this area.

If you wish to combine an urban life and warmer weather, you can reside in San José's neighboring city **Alajuela**, Costa Rica's second largest city located almost next to the airport. This quiet city is about 20 minutes by bus from downtown San José and has everything you want in a city without the city feeling. The bus service is excellent during the day, so it is easy to commute to San José if necessary. Because of the warm climate, many Americans live in Alajuela, so you can easily make new acquaintances. Try the city's shady central park if you are looking to meet fellow expats. There are other nice parks, movies, restaurants, doctors, supermarkets and more in this city. Housing is also very reasonably priced when compared to San José and plentiful. Prices range from about $20,000 to $300,000 and rents begin at $300.

Ciudad Cariari, about 5 miles west of San José and about five minutes before the airport, is an upscale development of mostly newer homes and condos. Housing in this gated community ranges between $130,000 to $350,000. This area is perfect for those interested in country-club living. Within this area are the Cariari Hotel and Costa Rica's oldest golf course, the Cariari Country Club, the Los Arcos neighborhood and the American International School — one of the best English-language schools in the country. A couple of golfer friends of ours live in this area and really like living next to the golf course. Right across the main highway from Carari sits the Real Cariari Mall.

La Garita, a pleasant area west of the airport on the road to the Central Pacific beach areas of Jacó, Hermosa and Quepos, is said to have one of the best climates in Costa Rica. An average year round temperature of 72 degrees makes it hard to beat. There are many foreigners living in this town. Some large homes come with large parcels of land. We have a friend who rented a home with a pool, a couple of acres of land and a watchman for a very reasonable price. There is also a small zoo and an excellent restaurant called La Fiesta del Maíz .

Heredia, "The City of the Flowers" located halfway between San José and Alajuela at the foot of Poás Volcano, is very suitable for living. It is only a short distance from San José by car or bus. Not as many foreign retirees live in Heredia as in Alajuela, but it is still a good place to live. Here, you may find a lot of affordable homes for under $100,000. At present, there is a construction boom in small gated communities in all over the Heredia area.

The surrounding countryside is very beautiful, especially above the city. The hills overlooking the city offer some of the most spectacular views of the Central Valley. Heredia also has a university and a beautiful central park. There is a group of expats who hang out at the two restaurants on the southwest side of the park. They can be found sitting there every morning. You will find it easy to strike up a conversation. You can meet colorful local characters like "Mr. Goldman," "Search Engine" Bill, "Banana Bread" Steve or "Sweatshop" Bruce.

San Rafael de Heredia is in the hills above the city of Heredia. The most notable feature of this area is the climate, which is considerably cooler than that in San José. Wealthy Costa Ricans and some foreigners live there.   The town's most salient feature is a huge church which may be seen from many miles away.

If you prefer living in a cooler alpine-like setting, you can find nice homes and cabins all over the pine-covered mountains surrounding the Central Valley. **Los Angeles de Heredia,** to the north of San Rafael, is a favorite with foreigners because of its pastoral setting. The nearby areas around **Monte de la Cruz** and **San José de la Montaña** are all similar but sparsely populated and cooler because of their higher elevation. We have several friends who live near the mountain towns of **Barva** and **Birrí**.

San Isidro de Heredia is an absolutely spectacular area to the east of Heredia. Gentle rolling verdant hills and meadows surround this Swiss-alpine like town. This area remains green even during the dry season due to its cool climate. Many Americans live in the San Isidro area. Phil form San Diego just purcahsed a huge parcel of land with an unbelievable view of the Irazú volcano. He paid about $80,000 for the land with a farmhouse. He is presently refurbishing it and plans to build his dream home on another part of the property. Ana Brown and her late husband built a quaint home in the Calle Chavez area of San Isidro.

Another neighboring city, **Cartago**, "just over the hill" from San José, was the former capital of Costa Rica during the colonial period. The city lies 30 minutes to the east of San José, and became the capital after an earthquake destroyed old Cartago. Perhaps the cooler year-round temperatures, explain why fewer North Americans reside there. Many Costa Ricans live in Cartago work in San José since bus service between the two cities is excellent. The nicest thing about Cartago is its proximity to the beautiful **Orosi Valley**. The valley lies about 60 minutes east of San José. Viewed from above, this Shangrala-esque valley is breathtaking. The spring-like temperatures on the valley floor stay the same all year. On one end of the valley is a large man-made lake, **Cachí**, and a park where one can participate in many recreational activities from picnicking to water sports. The lake is fed by the famous **Reventazón** white-water river that runs through the Orosi Valley. The area's other main attractions are waterfalls, nature reserves and several hot springs. We consider the Orosí Valley one of the most beautiful spots in the country and are surprised not more foreigners choose to live there.

Grecia, known as the cleanest town in Costa Rica, is also a place worth investigating. This tranquil agricultural town, about 30 miles from San José, has a beautiful central park, a famous church made of metal panels and an ideal climate. On Sunday evenings many residents stroll around the park just like in the days of old. The rolling hills surrounding the town are full of nice spots to live. Grecia will soon be the home of Plaza Grecia. It will house over 75 shops and be one of the first malls constructed in the region. Nearby is the town of **Sarchí**, famous for its handicrafts and wood products. Other towns worth checking out for living in the west are **Naranjo**, **San Ramón** and **Palmares**. We know of a few Americans and Europeans who live in and around these laid-back towns and are very happy.

Nestled in the foothills at the far end of the Central Valley, the picturesque rural town of **Atenas** offers panoramic views of the Central Valley and nearby volcanoes. Athens has a friendly, small-town atmosphere, and — according to *National Geographic* — the world's best climate. Three bedroom homes range from $80,000 to $100,000. Land costs around $5 per square meter.

For those seeking a more relaxed life style, many other small towns and *fincas* (farms) are scattered all over the Central Valley. These places are ideal for people who can do without the excitement found in and around large cities.

The Northern Zone

The little mountain town of **Zarcero** is famous for the sculptured bushes. The park in front of Zarcero's church is full of shrubs that have been sculpted into the shapes of arches, animals, people and even an oxcart complete with oxen.

San Carlos, or Ciudad Quesada as it is sometimes called, is considered the "capital" of the country's northern zone. We know a few North Americans who own ranches in this area. Almost everything of importance is found within several blocks of the town's main square. San Carlos boasts a new mall with around 70 stores including a supermarket, movie theaters, travel agencies and much more.

Northwest of San Carlos is the beautiful man-made **Lake Arenal**. It is surrounded by rolling hills covered with pastures and patches of tropical forest. The "very active" Arenal volcano can often be seen smoking in the distance. This area is rapidly becoming popular with foreign residents. The lake has excellent fishing, sailing, windsurfing and other outdoor activities. Land around the lake is readily available. Land prices range from $7 to $15 per square meter depending on location and views.

There are several interesting towns in this area. Nearby **Tilarán** is the home to a number of foreigners, as are **Nuevo Arenal** and **La Fortuna**. The latter is a quiet town east of the volcano and a good place to view its activity. The Catarata La Fortuna is a spectacular waterfall that plummets some 100 feet into a deep pool surrounded by luxuriant foliage. We have met a few foreigners live in and around Fortuna.

At **Tabacón** you will find a hot spring in a lush valley at the base of the picture-perfect Arenal Volcano. This is the place to soak your tired bones after a day of participating in one of the many activities this area has to offer.

The Northern Pacific Zone

The northwest region is the driest area of the country. Nevertheless, lush vegetation and breathtaking views can be found here. The city of Liberia and the new Tempisque Bridge are the entry points to Guanacaste's beaches. The region has over 50 beaches of all sizes, shapes and colors.

The capital city of **Liberia**, located 125 miles north of San José on the Pan-American Highway, is considered the heart of Guanacaste and a full-service city. It is quickly becoming one of the country's largest and most important cities, offering restaurants, hotels, several museums, good shopping, a new mall with movie theaters, a public hospital and the Daniel Oduber International Airport. Liberia is a good place to visit while on your way to Guanacaste's many beaches. Our good friend Bud from Las Vegas owns a small farm and is one of the foreigners who live in the area around the city of Liberia.

The Guancaste area has experienced a building boom, especially around the **Gulf of Papaguayo**. The Four Seasons Resort chain just built a mammoth complex here. Numerous daily flight to Liberia's **Daniel Oduber International Airport** and better infrastructure than the beaches on the Southern Nicoya peninsula have contributed to the development of this area.

A wide range of condos may be found on both isolated and popular beaches prices go from $100,000 to $400,000 depending on location. A couple of nice gated communities and golf resorts are found in this section of the country. Undeveloped beach and ocean-view properties can still be found at about $35 to $55 per square meter.

Spectacular white and gray sand beaches and clear blue water are found all along the Pacific Coast in Guanacaste Province and are perfect for beach living. However, a few of the adjacent beach communities may have too much tranquility for some people or have too much of a resort atmosphere for others.

Playa Hermosa has some of the country's best diving. It lies in the center of a string of four major beaches, all within 30 minutes of each other: **Hermosa, Playa del Coco, Playa Ocotal** and **Playa Panama. Playa del Coco** is a colorful beach town with an active nightlife and a small international community. It is set in a deep cove with consistently calm waters, making it a safe swimming beach. This charming seaside community is surrounded by emerald colored hills and offers a variety of water sports, and various forms of entertainment including restaurants a disco, and casinos. You will also find a bank, post office and all kinds of shops.

Flamingo is one of the finest resort areas in Costa Rica and has the country's second best full-service marinas and a beautiful white-sand beach. It is Guanacaste's sport fishing capital and offers some of the best sail and marlin fishing in the world. There is an abundance of real estate, including condominiums which dot the surrounding hills. Three golf courses are located nearby. Flamingo attracts retired foreigners as well people with children because of all it has to offer. The Country Day School, one of the country's most prestigious private primary and secondary institutions, has just opened in the area. **Hospital Cima** of San José plans to open a state-of-the-art clinic in this area.

Neighboring **Portrero** and **Sugar** beaches offer calm waters, ocean views and breathtaking sunsets. Many foreigners reside in these neighboring areas.

Brasilito and **Conchal,** south of Flamingo, are other beaches worth checking out. Conchal is famous for its beach, made of small white seashells. It is also the home of the all-inclusive **Melía Golf Resort**. There are a lot of high-priced condominiums and townhouses for sale at the resort.

Tamarindo is a laid-back beach town overlooking a long stretch of beautiful beach and a popular spot among surfers. It has the most developed tourist infrastructure in Guanacaste. The small foreign community has given birth to many restaurants, hotels, as well as a variety of stores for all tastes. The town itself is very cosmopolitan with residents from all over the world which adds a very exciting cultural diversity to the area. Property along with everything else has become rather expensive in the Tamarindo area due to its popularity.

South of Tamarindo is **Hacienda Pinilla Resort** which has a championship golf course and offers every imaginable water sport. **Junqullial** is another fast-developing area and has a white-sand, blue-flag beach.

Nosara is an attractive area to live if you are a nature lover. A flourishing expatriate community gives the town a slightly California-like flavor. Small U.S.-style restaurants and services exist for this growing foreign community. A world-famous Yoga retreat is found just outside of town. The Nosara area is slowly developing and land prices are starting to rise.

Sámara and **Carrillo** to the south are really worth exploring. Both beaches are located on bays and good for swimming. Property is still affordable since the area is not as developed as some of the beaches to the north. Samara has a small village with a few good restaurants, hotels and nightlife. Carrillo, the southern most of the two beaches is an exceptionally beautiful, palm tree-lined, white-sand beach on a curved bay, yet lacks the development of Samara.

Mal País, immediately northhwest of Cabo Blanco near the southern tip of the Nicoya Penninsula, is a surfer's paradise. The word Malpaís means "bad country" in Spanish and is a misnomer. Nothing could be farther from the truth. There are several beaches to swim, dive and snorkel, though its main attraction is its unique conditions for surfing. This isolated area is becoming very popular with some foreigners because of its scenery and incredible sunsets. A few foreigners reside there full-time. To the north lies **Playa Santa Teresa**, one of the best beaches for surfing on the entire Nicoya Peninsula. Nearby **Playa Manzanillo** is also becoming popular with expatriates. We have a German friend who has lived there for several years and really loves the area.

Montezuma, a remote little fishing village near the southern tip of Nicoya Peninsula, has almost perfect beaches with clear-blue water just right for bodysurfing. There are miles of beaches and even a tropical waterfall. This cozy town is a magnet for the hip and Bohemian types interested in alternative lifestyles. European backpackers, yoga enthusiasts and people in search of something new visit this area. In this town one can either hangout at the beach or at a local restaurant. The Sano Banano is a vegetarian restaurant where many locals and tourists congregate. There is property available in the area. Jimmy, a 45-year old retiree from Boston, told us he moved there ten years ago and bought a small home because he found living in San José to be too expensive. He gets by on around $800 or less monthly—beer included.

Tambor is located on a deep circular bay and is good for swimming and other ourdoor activities. The Hotel Barceló Palaya Tambor resort is located here. We know a few Americans who reside here and there are some excellent real estate buys.

The Central Pacific

The closest and most accessible beaches to San José are found in this area. The beaches are sunny all year round, the weather is hot and the ocean warm.

The Central Pacific's largest city, **Puntarenas**, sits on a long, narrow peninsula or spit in the Gulf of Nicoya, a short 62 miles from San José. It is the capital of the province with the same name. Costa Ricans affectionately refer to Puntarenas as "*El Puerto*" or "port." For many years it was the country's main beach before the northern and other Central Pacific beach areas became accessible. The beach is far from being the country's most beautiful with its black sand and murky waters. However, this does not stop *ticos* from flocking there on weekends. The Paseo de los Turistas is a seaside walkway which has a series of open-air bars and restaurants that dot the waterfront and add to this city's atmosphere. This tourist walkway is also the place where huge cruise ships anchor. Puntarenas is one of the best places to savor fresh seafood. We know a few Americans who call this port city their home.

In the Central Pacific Coast region to the south of Puntarenas are superb locations for living. This area has something for everyone: swimming and surfing beaches, excellent sport fishing, developed and undeveloped beaches and natural parks. This area is a magnet for beach lovers due to its proximity to San José. Its attraction will increase when the new Ciudad Colón-Orotina-Caldera Highway is finished. The new highway should reduce the driving time from San José to any of the Central Pacific beaches by about an hour.

Just North of Jacó, at Bahía Herradura, is the new, upscale **Los Sueños Resort**. The largest full-service marina between Mexico and Chile is found here. In addition to the boat facilities, the marina offers restaurants, bars, a supermarket, gift shop, marine supplies and concessions for jet skis, kayaks, water skiing, scuba diving, snorkeling and other recreational activities. There is also an 18-hole golf course, a 212-room palatial Marriott Hotel, home sites and condominiums for sale and a number of nature walks. Condo prices start at around $350,000.

If you like a lot of action, good waves and partying, we recommend **Jacó Beach**. It is conveniently located just 72 miles from San José. This Key-West like town is a very popular weekend retreat with both *ticos* and foreigners since it is currently little less than two hours from San José and has excellent tourist infrastructure. Because of its fame, Jacó is usually packed on most summer weekends, holidays like Easter Week and special occasions such as surf tournaments. Boredom will not be a factor here. There are pizza parlors, international restaurants, handicraft shops, bars, discos, bars where you can party until the early hours of the morning. Water sports, especially surfing and sport fishing, attract scores of people to the area.

Just two miles down the coast from Jacó, lies **Playa Hermosa**. Do not confuse this idyllic surf community with the beach with the same name in Guanacaste. Because of good year-round waves, most people come to Hermosa to surf, however there is plenty to keep non-surfers busy, especially at nearby bustling Jacó. There has been a lot of building in this area, especially 10 miles south in **Esterillos Este** and near the town of **Parrita**.

The **Quepos-Manuel Antonio** area is one of the country's most popular tourist destinations and most beautiful beach resorts in the world. Few other places in Costa Rica offer so much in one spot. Some of the areas most prominent features are white sand, paradise - like beaches, abundant wildlife, world-class sport fishing, good nightlife, fine cuisine, unforgettable sunsets from many vantage points and even a chance to mingle with the Hollywood crowd at a 5-star hotel. The majority of foreigners live in and around the town of Quepos and along the road leading to **Manuel Antonio National Park** just a few kilometers south and over the hill. Despite its small size, the park receives more visitors than any other park or reserve in the country. If you are a nature lover you can always explore the national park or go to one of its pristine white-sand beaches. In Quepos there are bars, eateries, a mini-bookstore, and a whole lot more to keep local foreigners entertained. It comes as no surprise that the area's beauty and popularity have made real estate very expensive. Land prices start at about $75,000 an acre.

Matapalo, between Quepos and Dominical, is a little town with a laid-back beach community and virtually unspoiled beach. There is still a lot of beachfront property found in this area.

All of the property between Quepos and Dominical will increase in value when the last unpaved stretch of the costal highway is finally paved by 2005.

Dominical, located 46 kilometers (30 miles) south of Quepos, is a tiny laid-back resort town surrounded by some of the most breathtaking coastal scenery Costa Rica has to offer. The beautiful **Barú River** winds its way down from the surrounding mountains and empties into the sea at the north end of town. Dominical marks the border between the Central And Southern Pacific.

This area is reminiscent of California's Big Sur because of its spectacular coastline and towering mountains that meet the sea. Dominical is also famous for its long beach, spectacular shoreline, mountain backdrop, panoramic views, excellent surfing, and jungle waterfalls. One of the area's claims to fame is that it was used as a backdrop to shoot the 1996 Sport's Illustrated Swim Suite issue.

Dominical is less developed than the other beaches in the central area, but this is changing quickly. Land prices are lower than the Quepos-Manuel Antonio area but are rising fast. There are a few restaurants and some limited entertainment. Much like Montezuma, this town attracts those seeking an alternative lifestyle. It is not unusual to see people practicing the oriental art of tai chi or yoga on the beach. Dominical is a charming little town with freindly people who say hello and greet you with smiles.

There are large homes with views that cost in the hundreds of thousands of dollars dotting the steep hills above the beach. Many expatriates have started businesses or are buying land in the area.

Dominicalito Beach has calm water for swimming. Incedible views of the coastline may be seen from nearby **Punta Dominical**.

Just to the south of Dominical is **Punta Uvita.** It is a small town with good swimming. At low tide you can walk out to the point. Many foreigners live in the hills above Puinta Uvita just as they do in Dominical. The setting with mountains in the background is very similar to Dominical. The highway was just paved from Dominical all the way to Palmar Norte, making this once virgin part of the coast very accessible. Prices are still affordable and there are plenty of mountainside homes and lots with spectacular views. We have a friend who just purchased a beautiful mountaintop home overlooking the beach.

The **Tortuga/Ojochal/Cinco Ventanas** area is also suited for living. Ojochal, about 20 miles south of Dominical, is a quaint country village with a nice mixture of Ticos, French-Canadians and other foreigners. This area's popularity is growing as the word spreads about all the natural wonders it has to offer. The beach at Cinco Ventanas Beach got it's name because of five spectacular 50 foot tunnel-like blow holes in the rocks. This beach is truly a work of nature and has to be seen to be believed. **Playa Tortuga** and **Playa Ballena** are other spectacular beaches in the area.

San Isidro de El General, a half-hour inland from Dominical and located along the Pan-American Highway, offers a warm climate and inexpensive housing. It is considered to be the fastest growing city in Central America. San Isidro is off the beaten path but some foreigners make this small city their permanent home. Real estate is reasonably priced in comparison with some of the areas in the Central Valley. There are many ocean-view properties in the mountains along the highway between San Isidro and Dominical.

The Southern Pacific Zone

This is one of Costa Rica's least developed and remote regions. It extends all the way to the Panamanian border on the Pacific Coast. The spectacular Cocorvado National Park, Drake's Bay and Isla Caño are a few of this areas salient features.

Some expatriates live around the port of **Golfito** on the **Golfo Dulce Bay**. .Sometimes called the "armpit" of the country, this drab former banana town leaves a lot to be desired. The climate can also be oppressive due to the high humidity. However, there has been a lot of new development going on recently. Plans call for a world-class marina and condo ccomplex to be built in the next few years. The Free Trade Zone has helped the local economy to some extent. Many *ticos* make the long journey to Golfito since appliances and other items may be purchased for much less than in San José. There are several restaurants and *gringo* hangouts in Golfito.

Playa Zancudo ("mosquito" in Spanish), about 20 kilometers south of Golfito, is the home to some foreigners. Medium priced housing may be found in the area. **Pavones**, 40 kilometers south of Golfito, is a surfer's mecca and renowned for having the longest left-hand breaking waves in the world. Numerous North Americans and foreigners own large *fincas* (ranches, farms) in this area while others live in the more isolated areas around the gulf. Our Costa Rican dentist has a vacation home in Pavones

The Caribbean Zone

The 150-mile Caribbean coast extends from the border with Nicaragua in the North to the border with Panama in the south.

Puerto Limón is one of Costa Rica's two important ports. It is the cradle of the country's Afro-Caribbean culture and the local version of the English language. Few Americans live in this city.

The Caribbean coast below Puerto Limón has many places to live. This area particularly appeals to young people who like beautiful tropical settings, surfing, reggae music and the Afro-Caribbean culture. A large colony of foreigners from Europe and the United States live here.

The village of **Cahuita**, probably the most popular spot on the Atlantic coast, lies next to Cahuita National Park and has one of the best beaches in the world. Despite a rising crime rate, it is still considered one of the most laid-back places anywhere in Costa Rica. **Puerto Viejo**, a few miles to the south, is a great place for lovers of the Caribbean lifestyle and outdoor activites such as snorkeling and surfing. There are some lovely swimming beaches in this area and the water is crystal clear.

About nine kilometers down a dirt road are **Punta Uva**, with a gorgeous beach for swimming, and the fishing village of **Manzanillo**. This area is spectacular and undeveloped—but not for long.

The Caribbean coast sounds very enticing, however, the abundant year-round rainfall and humidity make most Americans, Canadians and other foreigners choose to live on the drier west coast.

If you live in a beach or rural area, life is generally less expensive and more tranquil than in San José. People living on a small budget might consider this factor before choosing a permanent place to settle.

In this section we have tried to give an idea of the more desirable places to live in Costa Rica. Since there are so many other great areas from which to choose—it is impossible to describe all of them here—we suggest you read some of the guide books listed in the back of this book to get a better picture of what Costa Rica has to offer. Then you should plan to visit the places where you think you may want to live. The best guidebook of the bunch is Moon Publication's *Costa Rica Handbook* by the award-winning travel writer Christopher Baker. We highly recommend this great book.

One-of-a-Kind Tour

"This was the tour of a lifetime for us -**Dan and Lani Curtis, Camarillo, California"**

One way to see Costa Rica that we highly recommend is to take one of the introductory tours operated by either **Live in Costa Rica Tours**.

What you learn from our unique tour:

*The best locations suited to lifestyle and personal needs.

*How it really is to reside in Costa Rica

*Detailed information on the legal system and residency

*Inexpensive health care and how to get it

*How the banking system will work to your advantage

*How to learn Spanish easily

*Cultural differences of the various areas

*What to expect when you first arrive

*Detailed appraisal of the growth areas that will drive growth and profit for year to come

*For the investor minded, clear investment opportunities that are can be compared to Hawaii 60 years ago

*The inexpensive and expensive things here

Below is a sample itinerary from their one-of-a-kind 5-day Central Valley tour.

Day 1:

Arrival

Ground transportation and orientation from the airport to the Hotel Presidente in downtown San José.

Day 2 :

Breakfast at the hotel

First day of Costa Rica Residents Association (ARCR) highly informative all-day seminar featuring:

8:10 Welcome by Robert Miller President of the Association

8:20 Real Estate - Buying, Selling & Renting by Mercedes Castro or Les Nuñez (Remax Reality)

9:00 Questions about real estate

9:20 Costa Rican Laws & Regulations by Lic. José Carter

10:00 Questions about Costa Rican laws

10:30 BREAK FOR COFFEE

10:55 Moving and Customs by Charles Zeller (ABC Mudanzas)

11:35 Questions about Moving and customs

12:05 BREAK FOR LUNCH (included in tour)

1:00 Investing in Costa Rica and Abroad by Alan Weeks Marketing Consultant

1:35 Questions about funds

1:45 Residency by ARCR Legal Residence Advisors

2:10 Questions about residency

2:30 About the Assocition of Residents by Ryan Piercy (manager)

3:00 Questions about the Residents Asociation (ARCR)

3:10 The Move to Costa Rica by Jerry Ledin (ARCR member)

3:30 Questions about moving to Costa Rica

4:00 HAPPY HOUR!

Day 3 :

Breakfast at the hotel

Second day of Costa Rica Residents Association (ARCR) highly informative all-day seminar featuring:

8:10 Welcome by Robert Miller President of the Association

8:20 CCSS Public Health System in Costa Rica by Ryan Piercy (ARCR)

8:40 Questions about the CCSS (Public Health System)

8:50 Health Care Quality by Dr. C. Alpizar (Cima Hospital)

9:20 Questions about health care

9:35 BREAK FOR COFFEE

9:50 INS and Insurance in Costa Rica by Representative from Garrett and Associates

10:20 Questions about insurance

10:30 International Health Insurance by Brad Cook (Clínica Bíblica)

10:40 Questions about Insurance

10:50 Learning Spanish by Christopher Howard (Author and Guide)

11:10 Questions about learning Spanish

11:25 Internet and Communication by Tim Lytle

11:45 Questions about internet

12:00 BREAK FOR LUNCH (included in tour)

1:05 Investing from Costa Rica by Silvia Carmona (Popular Valores)

1:20 Questions about services

1:35 Banking by Marietta Herrera (Elca Bank)

2:05 Questions about banking

2:10 Culture of Costa Rica by Eric Liljenstolpe

2:30 Questions about Culture

2:40 Living in Costa Rica by Ryan Piercy (ARCR manager)

3:30 Closing Remarks for the two-day seminar

6:00 Dinner at the world famous restaurants.

Day 4:

Tour of the city of San José including: Clínica Bíblica Hospital, markets, San Perdro Mall, University of Costa Rica, Hipermás mega superstore, neighborhoods where Americans live (Los Yoses, Barrio Escalante, Sabana Norte, Sabana Sur, Rohrmoser, and Escazú) Hospital Cima and Multiplaza Mall. Continue tour around the Central Valley to see the other choice areas where foreigners reside: Escazú, Santa Ana, San Antonio de Belén, Ciudad Cariari, Alajuela, Heredia and Moravia.

Lunch at La Cocina de Doña Lela where they serve authentic Costa Rican cuisine.

Free night

Day 5 :

Breakfast at the hotel

Tour the best areas for living west of San José including the city of Atenas famous, for having the "best climate in the world" according to National Geographic," the charming town of Grecia, known as the "cleanest city in Costa Rica , Alajuela, Costa Rica's second largest city with its thriving expatriate community and finally the area Santa Bárbara and San Joaquin de Heredia. You will view the inside of several homes and developments after a mouth-watering lunch at Costa Rica's best restaurant. Final questions, answers and other concerns.

Day 6:

Breakfast at hotel

Transportation to the airport

This is an excellent tour to meet the country and especially the inferstructure of the country. $1299.00 per person Airfare is not included. Discounts apply if you book 30 days in advance.

*The above itinerary is subject to change.

All trips are led by Christopher Howard the author of this guidebook and expert on living and investing in Costa Rica. For additional information contact **Live in Costa Rica Tours** toll free at: **800 365-2342**, e-mail: **crbooks@racsa.co.cr** or go to **www.liveincostarica.com.** In additon to the Central Valley Tours listed above, they offer their most popular 7-day **Central Pacific Beach Tour** for people interested in Costa Rica's spectacular beaches, their 10-day **Combo Tour** (Central Pacific Beach Tour and Inland Tour), the **Guanacaste Beach Tour** (only given twice a year and may also be combined with the Central Valley Tour as a combo tour) and Private **Consultations** or **Tailor-Made Tours** for individuals, couples and small groups short on time or whose schedule does not coincide with the regular fixed date tours. All tours include a **two-day seminar** given by experts in real esate, law, banking, health care, investing and more. Please see pages 296-298 in Chapter 10 for the complete itineraries for these tours.

Costa Rica's Unique History in Brief

Traditionally Costa Rica has been a freedom-loving country living by democratic rules and respecting human rights.

When Columbus set foot on the Atlantic Coast at a place called Cariari (Puerto Limón) he anticipated finding vast amounts of gold, so he named

Our Adventure in Paradise
By Carol Burch

"Oh that's far too beautiful to be real," I muttered to myself, while examining the photographs in Christopher Howard's latest book. "These photos can't be real, I'm sure," I commented cynically. It was October, a comfortable autumn day. But the days were getting shorter and the nights colder. Cold, windy, bleak, winter days were just around the corner. Summer and fall are enjoyable seasons in northeast Ohio. And then there's winter...my thoughts drifted to the ice storm of 1991. Downed trees and powerlines closed many roads. Driving was trecherous. Stores were closed, schools too, and cable TV was out. "How would you like to see Costa Rica?" my husband Jim's question interrupted my thoughts. "Christopher Howard is leading a tour in January," Jim remarked. "Do you think you could get time off? "What are Costa Rica winters like?" I asked. "January is their summer, and in the Central Valley it's 72 degrees year round," he replied. "If you like it we could live there comfortably on my pension. You wouldn't have to work, it would be optional." "Even with the two children," I asked. "Yes," was his reply.

We departed from Cleveland and had an enjoyable, uneventful flight to San José. Jim and I were weary of customs, but it proved to be easier than car trips to Canada. Costa Rican warmth and hospitality were immediately evident; we felt welcome. Someone from the tour company was expected to meet us, but we were flattered and amazed this it was Christopher Howard! Our Costa Rica adventure had begun.

On the way to our hotel Chris helped us get our bearings and was more than willing to answer our many questions.

I was immediately struck by the absolute beauty of the country. Such contrasts! It is even more beautiful that the photographs.

The Hotel Presidente was convenient and comfortable. The location was perfect for touring the city on our own. Meals were delicious and reasonable, and in close proximity to numerous "sodas" (small cafés), souvenir shops, a museum, the Central Market and casinos. Hotel security watched over us. We were able to mail our postcards and exchange money at the hotel. They also gave directions and called taxis for us. Imagine that at a Holiday Inn. The streets felt safe too, unlike big cities in the States.

The Irazú Volcano Tour and trip afterwards around the lake in the beautiful Orosi Valley had to be seen to be believed. The morning excusion to the CoffeeBritt plantation in Heredia to see how coffee is grown and processed was very educational.

We were especially enthralled by our catamaran boat ride to Tortuga Island. We lunched on the island with an iguana, saw a school of playful dolphins jump next to our boat. and marvelled at Costa Rica's spectacular scenery.

We also loved the Banco de Mariscos restaurant in Heredia. It is touted as the best seafood restaurant in the country. Their dishes are absolutely delicious and a bargain. Tiny's American Sports bar was great fun. We had a group luncheon there and enjoyed hamburgers and fries Costa Rica style.

The lectures and seminars were helpful and informative, especially the representative from the Residents Association of Costa Rica. We have been in touch with several speakers from the tour since our return to the States. Without Chris, we would have never met the realtors, movers, a business consultant, attorneys and other contacts.

The Clinica Bíblica Hospital offers great medical care. Not wanting to miss any of the tour, I saw a doctor there for a minor problem. The doctors and nurses speak great English. Bedside manner far exceeds what I'm accustomed to. The wait was short, care great and fee minimal.

When we departed paradise, our flight from New Jersey was cancelled due to the weather. The next flight was delayed for hours while all planes de-iced. Both at the airport and at home we shoveled snow. Sniff, sniff, good-bye for now, paradise.

Update: We are now in the process of selling our two homes in the States and plan to move with the kids to Costa Rica before the new millennium. It came down to a choice between Costa Rica and Florida and the former won out easily. Florida's sweltering summers cannot compete with Costa Rica's spring-like climate.

this area Costa Rica — "rich coast" in Spanish. However, unlike Mexico and Peru, Costa Rica had neither advanced Indian civilizations nor large deposits of gold. The small Indian population offered little resistance to the Spanish and was eventually wiped out by disease. Faced with no source of cheap labor, the Spanish colonists were forced to supply the labor themselves. Thus, a sort of democratic, equalitarian society developed with everyone doing their share of the work, and few becoming very rich or very poor.

For a long time Costa Rica was almost forgotten by Spain because she lacked trade and wealth. In fact, Costa Rica became so isolated and unimportant to the Mother country that there was no War of Independence from Spain in the early 1800s, as there was in the rest of Latin America. Costa Ricans learned of their newly won independence from a letter that arrived one month after it was officially granted. During this period, coffee became the leading export and the wealth it brought to the coffee growers allowed them to dominate politics.

Costa Rica's peaceful development continued well into the 20th century with only a few minor interruptions. The most notable achievement was the abolition of the army forever in 1948. The same year, a new constitution was drafted that laid the groundwork for the most enduring democracy in Latin America.

Although the military has constantly threatened democratic institutions throughout the rest of turbulent Latin America, this is not the case in Costa Rica. Costa Rica has a 5,000-man, non-political National Guard or police force under control of the civilian government. Like the police in the United States, they concentrate on enforcing the law and controlling traffic.

Due to a lack of large military expenditures that go with maintaining an army, Costa Rica has put its money into human development and been able to establish one of the best all-encompassing Social Security systems in the world. It also developed an excellent public education system, hospitals, housing, modern communication systems and roads. Every school now has at least one computer. As a result, Costa Rica has the largest proportion of middle class citizens in Latin America and a literacy rate of over ninety-percent. Furthermore, the prohibition of armed forces guarantees political stability and peace for future generations and reaffirms Costa Rica's dedication to a respect for human rights unequaled anywhere else in the world.

Government

Costa Rica's government has been an outstanding example of an enduring democracy for almost fifty years. This is quite an achievement when one looks at the rest of the world—particularly Latin America. In an area of the world noted for wars, political chaos and even dictatorships, Costa Rica stands out as a beacon of democratic tranquility.

Costa Rica is compared to Switzerland because of its neutral political posture, with one exception; Costa Rica has no army. As we mentioned earlier, in 1948 Costa Ricans did what no other modern nation has done — they formally abolished their army. That same year, they limited the power of their Presidents, began universal suffrage and dedicated their government to justice and equality for all, thus ending discrimination and making Costa Rica a truly unique nation. Consequently, in Costa Rica you do not see any of the racial tension so prevalent in the United States and some other parts of the world. Non-citizens have the same rights as Costa Ricans. Today there is even a growing women's- rights movement.

Costa Ricans set up the legislative, judicial and executive power structure to prevent any one person or group from gaining too much power in order to ensure the continuity of the democratic process. For example, to eliminate the possibility of a dictatorship, all presidents are limited to four-year non-consecutives terms. The members of the legislative assembly are also limited to a single four-year term and cannot be re-elected.

Costa Rica's government is divided into four branches: The Executive (the President and two vice presidents), the Legislative Branch (Legislative Assembly and 57 deputies), the Electoral Tribunal and the Judicial Branch (the Supreme and lower courts) .

The court is divided into four sections. The first court, called the *Sala Primera*, decides civil matters. The second court is called the *Sala Segunda*, and is the labor court. The third court, the *Sala Tercera*, is the criminal court. The fourth court is the Constitutional Court, called the *Sala Cuarta*, and by its name it is obvious that it decides constitutional issues and that its decisions can override law made by any of the lower courts.

The country's two main political parties are the National Liberation Party and the United Social Christian Party.

The Costa Rican National Assembly has just inaugurated a new Internet site **(www.asamblea.go.cr)** that you can visit to keep up on new laws and legislation as well as contact local legislators and politicians.

Since Costa Rica is such a small country, voters can participate more directly in the democratic process. Each vote carries more weight so politicians are more accessible and have more contact with the people. Costa Ricans approach the presidential elections with such enthusiasm that they celebrate Election Day as if it were a big party or national holiday. People wearing party colors, honking cars, bands playing Latin music all contribute to the festive atmosphere. For the 2002 presidential election the turnout was around 90 percent— numbers which dwarf the U.S.' meager 50-percent turnout.

In Costa Rica people settle arguments at the ballot box, not on the battlefield. A group of American Quakers established a colony because of this peaceful democratic tradition and the University of Peace was started and still exists near San José.

Costa Rica's former president, Dr. Oscar Arias Sánchez, was awarded the Nobel Peace Prize in 1987 for his efforts to spread peace and true democracy from Costa Rica to the rest of strife-torn Central America.

Much has been made about corruption in Latin America. According to the *Transparency International Corruption Perceptions Index,* Costa Rica is ranked third in all of Latin America in a list of least corrupt countries. As a whole Costa Rica is considered the 40th least corrupt country in the whole world. This is a very favorable ranking since there is currently a worldwide corruption crisis.

Economy

Costa Rica's reputation as the "destination of the 90s" has helped the economy. From 1993 to 1998 the tourism industry was the prime source of foreign capital. Due to its endless beauty, natural wonders and peaceful atmosphere, Costa Rica became very popular with nature lovers, adventurers and others. However the electronic sector, led by multinational microchip manufacturer Intel, became the country's top foreign currency earner by the end of 1998.

The new Intel plant has turned Costa Rica into a leading exporter of computer parts. In 1999, microchips exported by Intel continued to drive the Costa Rican economy and were responsible for about half of the country's booming 8.3 percent growth (GDP) which gave rise to some of the decade's best economic indicators. Hopefully this will lead to more foreign investment in this area.

Banana exports are the third major source of income. Due to ideal growing conditions, Costa Rica has produced some of the world's best coffee for over a hundred years. However, worldwide fluctuations in prices have affected this export in recent years. Other exports include electrical components, sugar, cacao, papaya, macadamia nuts and ornamental household plants. Some of these non-traditional export items are beginning to rival such traditional exports as bananas, coffee and sugar.

Recently new companies have invested in Costa Rica which should help the domestic and export economy. The California-based wholesale shopping chain Price Smart has opened three warehouse-style stores in San José during the last three years. The Price Smart concept has revolutionized shopping in other Central American countries as well. In the wake of this U.S.-style shopping craze, a local company constructed two Hipermás Mega Markets to rival Price Smart.

The Swiss pharmaceutical giant Roche announced it would build its operations center in Costa Rica to service its plants in Central America and the Caribbean. U.S. health products manufacturer Proctor and Gamble recently opened a business center in Costa Rica. Several U.S. pharmaceutical companies also have opened plants in Costa Rica.

U. S. all-night diner franchise Denny's opened its first restaurant and will open several more in coming years. The GNC Nutritional Chain opened its first store in the Multiplaza mall. Multinational tire manufacturer Bridgestone Firestone inaugurated a new plant in April of 1999, promising to double its exports. This wave of new foreign investment will create thousands of jobs for Costa Ricans.

Despite the new areas of investment and exports just mentioned, Costa Rica is still heavily dependent on foreign investment and loans to help fund its social programs and keep its economy afloat. However, the country no longer receives as much foreign aid as it used to and still has one of the highest per capita debts in the world. The government has, at times, been hard-pressed to meet loan payments from abroad, which take up most export earnings. Foreign debt has hindered economic development to some extent. Gradual currency devaluations have helped the country meet its obligations. Fortunately, these devaluations have been in small increments.

Hopefully the present growth in tourism and continued foreign investment will help the country's economic future. President Clinton's trip to Costa Rica in May of 1997 set the wheels in motion for a free-trade treaty with the Central American countries. It promises to be much like the NAFTA treaty between the U.S., Canada and Mexico. The good news is that The **Central America Free-Trade Treaty Agreement** or **CAFTA** will enter into effect on January 1, 2005 and promises to help all of the Central

American countries economies including Costa Rica. The general opinion is that Costa Rica came out significantly better than the rest of Central America.

The most salient feature of the new trade pact calls for the partial opening of the government-run telecommunications monopoly by 2007. After January 1, 2007, Costa Rican and foreign companies will be able to offer their telecomunication services, despite the seeming strangle hold of the Instituto Costarricense de Electricidad, know as ICE. Broadband Internet and cellular phone service will be affected by the opening up of telecommunications. The treaty also calls for the complete opening of the country's insurance monopoly or *Instituto Nacional de Seguros* or INS by 2011. Costa Rica must allow foreign companies to sell all types of insurance except mandatory policies by 2008.

Other sectors of the economy affected by the new treaty are rice, sugar, beef, chicken drumsticks, pork, oils, ethanol, dairy products, industrial goods, free zones, textiles and intellectual property.

According to the Central Bank, inflation was 22.56 percent in 1995, almost double what the government had hoped for. In 1996 inflation was about 14 percent, dropped to 11.2 percent in 1997, was around 12.6 percent in late 1998, 10 percent in 1999, 10.3 percent for 2000, 11 percent for 2001, 9 percent for the year 2002 and 9.4 for 2003. Gross domestic product (GDP) grew 3.2 percent in 1997, 4.5 percent in 1998, 8.3 percent in 1999, 2.2 percent in 2000, .3 for 2001 and 5.2 percent in 2003

Central Bank economic indicators and other financial information are available (in Spanish) on the bank's web site: **www.bccr.fi.cr.**

The People

Besides its excellent weather and natural beauty, Costa Rica's unique people are probably the country's most important resource and one of the main factors to consider Costa Rica as a place to live or retire.

Costa Ricans proudly call themselves *ticos.* They affectionately and playfully use this nickname to set themselves apart from their neighbors. This practice is derived from their habit of adding the ending *"tico"*to many words instead of *"ito"*, as done in the rest of Central America. For example, instead of saying *un ratito* (a little while), they say *un ratico*.

Foreigners who have traveled in Mexico and other parts of Central America are quick to notice the racial and political differences between Costa Ricans and their neighbors.

Costa Ricans are mostly white and of Spanish origin with a mixture of German, Italian, English and other Europeans who have settled in Costa Rica over the years. This makes Costa Ricans the most racially homogeneous of all the Central American people. Over 90% of the population is considered white or *mestizo*. Argentina and Uruguay are the only other countries in Latin America with similar racial compositions.

There is also a small black population of around 2%, mainly living on the Atlantic Coast, and a handful of Indians in the mountainous areas of the Central Plateau and along the Southeastern Coast. Costa Rica has never had a large Indian population cpmpared to other countries in the region.

In recent times the country's stability and prosperity have make it a type of melting pot for people from less stable Latin American countires such as neighboring Nicaragua, Colombia, Cuba and Agentina. Many Colombians have sought refuge in Costa Rica because of the strife at home and similarities between the two countries food, culture and language.

About 300,000 Nicaraguan immigrants make their home in Costa Rica. Economic hardship in their own country has caused them to flock to Costa Rica to find work. Most Nicaraguans work as domestics, in construction, picking coffee, cutting sugar cane and engaged in other menial jobs. As prosperity and opportunities have increased, fewer and fewer Costa Ricans will do this type of work.

A tightly-knit Costa Rican family.

Most of these new immigrants come to Costa Rica to seek a piece of the so-called, "*sueño tico*" or Costa Rican Dream. This phenomenon is the Latin American equivalent of the "American Dream."

Unofficially there are about 50,000 North American English-speaking residents residing in Costa Rica. Many more North Americans and Europeans live here illegally as tourists. Some are "snow birds" only spending part of the year in the country.

Politically, Costa Ricans have always been more democratic than their neighbors—especially during the last 45 years. Indeed they should be congratulated for being the only people to make democracy work in such a troubled region.

National Geographic reported several years ago that, when asked why Costa Rica isn't plagued by political instability and wars like her neighbors, a Costa Rican replied, in typical Costa Rican humor, or *vacilón*, "We are too busy making love and have no time for wars or revolutions."

Because they have the largest middle class of any Central American nation, Costa Ricans love to boast that they have a classless society. Most people share the middle class mindset and tend to be more upwardly mobile than in other countries of the region.

Although there is some poverty, most Costa Ricans are well to do when compared to the many destitute people found in neighboring countries.

Another thing setting Costa Ricans apart from other countries in the region is the cleanliness of its people. Costa Ricans take pride in their personal appearance. The people here are very style-conscious. We know a *tico* of modest means who dresses so well he is often mistaken for a millionaire. Men, women and children seem to be well- dressed. Above all, you don't see as many ragged beggars and panhandlers as in Mexico and many other Latin American countries.

Costa Ricans are healthy people and have a longevity rate on par with most first-world countries— 76.3. In fact, they have the highest life expectancy in all Latin America and just about the same as the U.S. This is primarily due to the country's excellent Social Security System that provides "cradle-to-grave" health care.

The people of Costa Rica place great emphasis on education. Education has been compulsory in Costa Rica since 1869, and the federal government currently spends about 20 percent of its budget on education. Costa Rica's 95 percent literacy rate is among the highest in Latin America. A higher

One View of Living in Costa Rica
by Martha Bennett

Costa Rica is, quite naturally, very Latin. The Ticos are fatalistic and live for the moment. They have extended families which often supply most of their social life. By and large they are a happy people, accepting their lot in life and finding a bright side to dark issues. Music and laughter are common sounds everywhere. For me, these are the positives.

Ticos do things that amuse rather than irritate me, such as shoot off fireworks to celebrate a Virgin's Day. Do virgins like fireworks? On the negative side, I must tolerate what appears to be a total lack of planning. Things happen when they happen no matter what promise has been made. It is not a place where"to do" lists get done. Long lines are common in banks, telephone offices or almost everywhere.

Costa Rica is caught between the old world where oxen still pull *carretas* (carts) and the new world of TV and computers. Because of this, there is apt to be confusion about what North America is like, and problems with computers that don't compute because there is a lack of training of the user.

Ticos seem to have a love-hate relationship with the U.S. They want to be like it, but resent it at the same time. This sometimes produces jaded dealings with *Gringos*, i.e.: special prices for blue eyes. But it doesn't happen all of the time and sometimes they cheat each other too. I am a guest in their country and don't try to tell them how to run it.

Since I used to live in Michigan, I find the climate in Costa Rica perfect. It's the same all year round. The sun shines daily and the rain keeps everything green. The countryside is outrageously beautiful .

Ticos are paranoid about crime and all houses in the cities have bars. Yes there is crime here, but I feel safer here than I did in Detroit.

Driving here can be a nightmare. This combined with some bad roads can ruin your day. Buses are cheap and go everywhere.

The cost of living is low if you don't buy a lot of imported stuff. A three-bedroom house can be rented for under $500 in some areas like Heredia. Utilities are a bargain. Food is cheap. Fruits and vegetables are almost free. However, appliances cost almost double. Books are expensive, so bring reference books. Cars are twice the cost to buy or bring in. Group health insurance costs around $600 a year per person.

Spanish is important. It allows you to make many friends.

I have been living here four years and never dream of returning to the States. But that's me. To know how it is for you, you'll have to try it.

percentage of the population is enrolled in universities than in any other country in Latin America.

Costa Ricans are friendly and outgoing and will often go out of their way to help you even if you do not speak Spanish. They are also very pro-American and love anything American—music, TV, fashion and U.S. culture in general. Because of these close ties to the U.S. and just the right amount of American influence, Costa Ricans tend to be more like North Americans than any other people in Latin America.

Surprisingly, Costa Ricans, especially the young people of the country, seem to have more liberal attitudes in some areas. Costa Rican women are considered to be some of the most sexually liberated females in Latin America. Their liberation is due in part to the fact that the Catholic Church seems to have less of a foothold in Costa Rica than in some other Latin American countries.

However, you should not get the wrong idea from reading this. The vast majority of the people are Catholic and can be conservative when it comes to such issues as movie censorship. Also, Costa Ricans don't miss the chance to celebrate the many religious holidays that occur throughout the year. (See Chapter 9 for a list of some of the most important holidays.)

Generally speaking, the people of Costa Rica love to have fun, to live with "gusto" and know how to enjoy themselves. One has only to go to any local dance hall on a weekend night to see *ticos* out having a good time, or observe entire families picnicking together on any given Sunday—the traditional family day in Costa Rica.

The people of Costa Rica, no matter what their station in life, seem to enjoy themselves with less and do not give as much importance to materialism as do North Americans. Even people who can't afford to, seem to be able to eat, drink, be merry and live for today.

Recent polls indicate that the majority of Costa Ricans are happy with their quality of life. Out of 162 countries polled, Costa Rica was in the top 40 when it comes to quality of life. More and more job opportunities, the accessibility to education and a state-run health care system are cited as the prime reasons for the country's excellent quality of life.

Basic old-fashioned family values and unity are very important to Costa Ricans. Just as in the rest of Latin America, a strong family unit seems to be the most important element in Costa Rican lives. Social life still centers around the home. Much of one's leisure time is usually spent with family. Mother's Day is one of the most important holidays. Parents and relatives go to almost any length to spoil and baby their children. Elderly family members are revered and generally treated better than their counterparts in the U.S. or Canada. Most are not sent to nursing homes as in the U.S. Young, adult, singles, especially women, tend to live with their families until they marry.

Costa Rican families will help each other through hard economic times and in the face of poverty. Some foreigners complain that it is difficult to develop deep friendships with Costa Ricans because the family unit is so strong and predominant.

Nepotism, or using relatives and family connections to get ahead, is the way things work in business and government in Costa Rica. In many instances it doesn't matter what your qualifications are but who your family knows that helps you.

Despite all their admirable qualities, there is a negative side to the character of the Costa Rican people. While similar to North Americans in many ways and with a fondness for some aspects of *gringo* culture, Costa Ricans are distinctly Latin in their temperament. They suffer from many of the same problems endemic to all Latin American societies.

Corruption and bribery are a way of life; bureaucratic ineptitude and red-tape thrive; the concepts of punctuality and logical reasoning are almost non-existent by North American standards, and the "Mañana Syndrome"—of leaving for tomorrow what can be done today—seems to be the norm rather than the exception.

Soccer is the most popular sport among Costa Ricans.

Unfortunately, as in most Latin American countries, *machismo* (manliness) is prevalent to some degree among Costa Rican males. *Machismo* is the belief in the natural superiority of men in all fields of endeavor. It becomes the obsession and constant preoccupation of many Latin men to demonstrate they are *macho* in a variety of ways. Fortunately, the Costa Rican version of *machismo* is much milder than the type found in Mexico but it nevertheless exists.

There is no telling to what lengths some men will go in order to demonstrate their virility. A man's virility is measured by the number of seductions or *conquistas* he makes. It is not unusual for married men to have a *querida* or lover. Many even have children with their mistresses. Since many married men do not want to risk having a lover, they sleep with prostitutes or loose women called *zorras*. For this reason many Costa Rican women prefer American men to Costa Rican men. As the Costa Rican women say, "Costa Rican men are *machista* and always have to prove it. You marry a Costa Rican man today and tomorrow he is out chasing other women and drinking!"

Costa Rica is said to have the highest rate of alcoholism in Central America — an estimated 20% of the population are problem drinkers. This should come as no surprise, since drinking is part of the *macho* mentality. Making love, drinking and flirting are the national pastimes of most Costa Rican men.

As we discuss in Chapter 5, foreign women walking along the street will be alarmed by the flirtatious behavior and outrageous comments of some Costa Rican men. Many of these flirtations or *piropos*, as they are called in Spanish, may border on the obscene but are usually harmless forms of flattery to get a female's attention . Foreign women are wise to ignore this and any other manifestations of Costa Rican men's efforts to prove their manliness *or machismo*.

Sadly, many Costa Ricans have misconceptions about North Americans' wealth. A few people seem to think that all Americans and Canadians are millionaires. It is easy to understand why many *ticos* think this way because of the heavy influence of U.S. television and movies that depict North Americans as being very affluent. Also, the only contact many Costa Ricans have with Americans is primarily with tourists, who are usually living high on the hog and spending freely while on vacation.

It is therefore not surprising that some individuals will try to take advantage of foreigners by overcharging them for services and goods. Others will use very persuasive means to borrow amounts of money ranging from pocket change to larger sums of money and have no intention

Retirement in Costa Rica Is It For You?
By Shirley Miller

There is a great deal of interest in retirement in Costa Rica, and it grows yearly. Would we like to retire in Costa Rica? Sure we'd like to settle down on a secluded farm just outside of San José, Costa Rica, and relax for the rest of our lives, but we're not quite ready for that. Only time will tell.

We've encountered numbers of retirees during our Costa Rica travels. They all have one thing in common: they fell in love with the country and wanted to spend their remaining "good" years enjoying the weather, natural beauty and friendliness of the people.

Former San Diego dentist, Chuck Miller, entertained us in his home at Tango Mar Resort at the base of the Nicoya Peninsula. His penchant for creativity is being fulfilled through active projects such as building two homes, landscaping them, then designing and constructing the furniture, cabinets,etc. The monkeys are his neighbors, while the beautiful flowers he cultivates in his environment enhance the jungle.

Toni and Dan Daniel originally discovered Costa Rica 38 years ago. Their demanding and active lifestyle in Sacramento, California, provided sufficient funds for travel, but they needed more time to themselves. After 12 years of "visits only" the Daniels returned to Costa Rica for a permanent stay. It was a big step, but one they've never regretted.

Their three-bedroom home is on a secludeded section of land overlooking Lake Arenal, the largest lake in Costa Rica. They enjoy the peace and quiet and the guapote bass fishing in the summer, while Arenal Volcano's bursts of life add mystique to the adjacent countryside.

I'm sure retirement anywhere in the world isn't perfect, including our own back yard. But each person must decide what they are looking for, and the best way to find it is to spend time researching.

If you can afford it, visit several areas—there is no one area of Costa Rica where retirees congregate. Meet with others who live there. Ask how and why other retirees enjoy the lifestyle. Get acquainted with your potential neighbors, as well as yourself. Learn the language. Join organizations. Keep active. Give of your time to others. Take the hand of friendship that is offered—that's easy in Costa Rica. Maintain an attitude of openess. Become part of your new world and give something back to the country, the people and the land. You'll have a richer and fuller life.

of ever paying the debt. Please, take our advice: do not lend money to anyone, however convincing their sob story.

Another thing to be wary about is the *"regálame* mindset" of a few Costa Ricans. Basically this term comes from the Spanish verb, *regalar,* which means to give something as a gift with no intention of repayment. The verb, *dar,* is the correct verb to use when requesting something. People here use *regalar* in a figurative way in everyday conversation when asking for everything from small items in stores to ordering a beer in a bar.

Unfortunately, too many people take this verb literally and expect something for nothing. We know of many instances where foreigners have been overly generous to locals. As long as they continued their altruistic ways they were liked. Once they got wise or decided to curtail their generosity, they were considered cheapskates. The bottom line is not to be too generous or spoil people here. Some people will take advantage of your generosity and misunderstandings inevitably will arise.

There have ben cases of foreigners who have married Costa Rican women being "taken to the cleaners." Because family ties are so strong in Costa Rica, you can end up supporting your spouse's whole family. We talked to one retired American who could not live on his two thousand dollar a month pension because he had to support not only his wife and stepchildren, but his wife's sister's children as well. Furthermore, he had to lend his father-in-law money to pay off a second mortgage because the bank was going to repossess the latter's house. This is an extreme example, but we have heard many similar stories while living in Costa Rica. Not all Costa Rican families are like this one,

When doing any business with Costa Ricans, you should exercise extreme caution. A few years ago we had the pleasure of dining with a prominent Costa Rican banker who is presently the country's Minister of the Interior. We mentioned that we wanted to start a business in Costa Rica. He replied, "Be very careful when doing business with Costa Ricans. This is not to say that all people are dishonest here. Just be cautious who you deal with."

We suggest that you do not dwell on these negatives and hope you realize how difficult it is to generalize about or stereotype any group of people. After you have resided in Costa Rica and experienced living with the people, you will be able to make your own judgments.

The good qualities of the Costa Rican people far outweigh any shortcomings they may have.

SAVING MONEY IN COSTA RICA

How Much Does it Cost to Live in Costa Rica?

An important factor that determines the cost of living for foreigners in Costa Rica is their lifestyle. If you are used to a wealthy lifestyle, you'll spend more than someone accustomed to living frugally. Either way, you will still find Costa Rica to be a bargain.

Despite having one of the highest standards of living in Latin America, purchasing power is greater in Costa Rica than in the United States or Canada.

San Jose's cost of living ranks close to the middle when compared to 118 cities worldwide. The cost of living in Guatemala City or Panama City is about 14% higher than in San José. Corporate Resource Consulting firm that compares costs of goods and services rates San José among the least expensive coast-of -living cities in the world. It is second to Quito, Ecuador in the Americas in terms of affordability.

In most areas housing costs less than what it does in the U. S. and hired help is a steal. Utilities (telephone service, electricity, and water) are cheaper than in North America. You never need to heat your home or apartment since Costa Rica's climate is warm. You need not cook with gas, since most stoves are electric. These services cost about 30% of what they do at home. Bills for heating in the winter and air conditioning in the summer can cost hundreds of dollars in the States. Public transportation is also inexpensive. San José and surrounding suburbs occupy a very small area. A bus ride across town or to the suburbs usually costs from 25 -50¢. Bus fares to the provinces cost no more than $10 to the farthest part in the country (see Chapter 8). Taxi travel around San José is also inexpensive.

A gallon of regular gasoline costs about $2.00, making Costa Rica's gasoline prices among the lowest in the Americas. Only oil-exporting countries like Mexico and Venezuela have cheaper gasoline. However, you do not really need a car because public transportation is so inexpensive and accessible. If you must have a new car, remember that new cars are very expensive due to high import duties. In Costa Rica people tend to keep their cars for a long time and take good care of them. We recommend buying used cars since they are usually in good mechanical condition and their resale value is excellent. Food, continuing education, entertainment (movies cost about $3.00) and, above all, health care, are surprisingly affordable. Both new and second-hand furniture is priced very low. You will find more about these benefits later on.

When you have lived in Costa Rica a while, learned the ins-and- outs and made some friends and contacts, you can cut your living costs more by sharing a house or apartment, house-sitting in exchange for free rent, investing in high-interest yielding accounts in one of Costa Rica's many banks, working full or part-time (if you can find legal work), starting a small business or bartering within the expatriate community. Doing without packaged and canned imported brand-name foods and buying local products, eating in small cafes or *sodas* instead of expensive restaurants, or buying fresh foods in bulk at the Central Market like Costa Ricans do can also reduce your living costs. You can also help yourself by learning how to get a better rate of exchange on your money and by learning Spanish so you can bargain and get lower prices when shopping.

If you take lessons from the locals and live a modest *tico* lifestyle, you can save a lot of money and still enjoy yourself. By not following a U.S.-"shop-till-you-drop" mentality you can live reasonably. Taking all of the aforementioned and personal lifestyles into consideration, the minimum needed for a decent standard of living for a single person ranges from $1200 to $1500 monthly. A person can indeed live for as little as $35 a day excluding housing. Some single people scrape by on considerably less and others spend hundreds of dollars more, again depending on what one is accustomed to. A couple can live well on $1500 per month, and live in luxury for $2000. Couples with husband and wife both receiving good pensions can live even better. Remember, two in Costa Rica can often live as cheaply as one. Any way you look at it, you will enjoy a higher standard of living in Costa Rica and get more for your money. Consider that the average Costa Rican earns only $250-$350 a month.

When you take into account all these factors and such intangibles as good year-round weather, the friendly Costa Rican people, the lack of political strife and a more peaceful way of life—no price is too high to pay for living in a unique, tropical paradise like Costa Rica.

Before closing this section we want to emphasize that you should not be alarmed by high real estate prices you may hear about or see advertised in English publications such as *Costa Rica Today* or the *Tico Times* . This recent rise in land prices results from the current land boom and increasing popularity of Costa Rica. Inflated real estate prices do not reflect the real cost of living in Costa Rica, which is still relatively low when compared to Canada, Europe and the U.S. Even more important, the Costa Rican government must keep the cost of goods and services affordable for the Costa Rican people in order to avoid the social problems found in most other Latin American countries.

Approximate Cost of Living and Prices as of June 2004 in Dollars*

Rentals - Monthly

House (small, unfurnished) $400

House (large, luxurious) $1000–1500

Apartment (small, 1–2 bedrooms, unfurnished........................$300+

Apartment (large, luxurious)...$700+

Property Taxes...............................$100 a year on a small home

Home Prices

House (small) ....$50,000+

House (large)..$85,000+

Miscellaneous ....**Monthly**

Electric Bill (apt.)...$15–25

Water-Sewage (apt.)..$8

Telephone (calls within the country) $10
Cable TV...$30
Taxi...₡265 first kilometer, and ₡150 thereafter per kilometer
Bus Fares (around city) ....$.45
Gasoline (regular gas) ....$2.00 per gallon
Gasoline (super) ....$2.25 per gallon
Gasoline (diesel) ....$1.75 per gallon
Maid/Gardener ....$1.25 per hour
Restaurant Meal (inexpensive)..$5.00+
Soda (a diner or coffee shop) Meal $2.00
Restaurant (mid-range)..$10.00

Banana ....$.05
Soft drink...$.50
Pineapple...$1.00
Papaya ....$.70
Avocado (large) ....$.50
Lettuce ....$.30
Cereal (large box of corn flakes) $3.50
Bread (loaf) $1.00
Tuna (small can)...$.75
Orange ....$.08
Rice (1lb.)...$.45
Steak ....$4.60 lb.
Quart of Milk...$.95
Beer ....$.85
Airmail Letter..around $.33 to the U.S.

Doctor's Visit...$25–35
National Health Insurance ....$450.00 yearly for permanent residents
New Automobile..$15,000–$50,000

* These prices are subject to fluctuations.

How to Get By on a Shoestring in Costa Rica: The Story of Banana Bread Steve
By Christopher Howard

This purpose of this article is to show one person's resourcefulness and courage in the face of adversity. The author is not advocating moving to Costa Rica with little or no money.

About three years ago I met Steve who had lived in Hawaii for many years. He moved here because Hawaii had become very expensive and he wanted to make his early retirement "nest egg" go farther. Steve had always been used to living frugally and in the process amassed a few hundred thousand dollars.

Within a few months of moving here Steve invested his life savings in two high interest -yielding investments with the idea of doubling his money in a few years. This was his game plan but unfortunately both of his investments went "belly up." Steve was left with only a few thousand dollars to his name. As we mentioned Steve had mastered the art of living on very little money but had never been faced with having no resources and living in a foreign country. He knew that he would not be able to draw his pension for four more years. Steve thought of returning to the States to work and then moving back to Costa Rica when he got back on his feet. However, he became involved with a nice Costa Rican woman and had also fallen in love with the country.

His close friends provided him with a place to live for free, but he still had to find a way to generate and income. Since he was born with the ability to repair almost anything, he did odd jobs in exchange for small sums of money and food.

After a while he figured that the only way he could continue to live in Costa Rica was to start a business. Steve had one big problem; no money with which to start a business. His pride kept him for asking for a loan from friends. He started to look at local small business and do research on the Internet. It did not take him long to come up with a good idea for a small business. He came across a good recipe for banana bread and his business was born.

At present he sells he bread to tourists and his many friends in the city of Heredia where he lives. He has purchased a mixing machine, an oven and his lady friend is helping him.

Steve is a born survivor. All of his friends are sure he will continue to do well and continue to enjoy living in the country he has adopted as his home.

Money

The *colón*, named for Christopher Columbus, is Costa Rica's official currency. One of the most stable currencies in Latin America, the *colón* has recently been somewhat shaky because of devaluations. Fortunately, the devaluations are relatively small when compared to the mega-devaluations and run away inflation rampant in other Latin American countries. Since your main source of income will probably be in dollars, you should not worry too much about devaluations unless you have large amounts of money in *colones*, which is not advisable for long-term investments. Devaluations can be good because they increase your purchasing power until prices catch up.

Coins come in denominations of 1 *colón*,2, 5 10, 20, 25, 50 and 100, bills in 1000 *colones*(called *rojos* in slang) and 5000 (called *tucanes* in slang). At the end of 1998 2,000 *colónes* and 10,000 *colónes* bills were introduced. The rate of exchange, which is set by the Central Bank, was around 440 *colones* per dollar as of June 2004. New ¢5, ¢10, ¢25, ¢50, ¢100 and ¢500 *colón* gold -colored coins have been issued to replace Costa Rica's lowest denomination bills. The older silver colored coins are the only ones you can use for coin-operated public pay phones. They are available in ¢1, ¢2, ¢5, ¢10 and ¢20 denominations.

You can exchange money at most banks between 9 a.m. and 4 p.m. Monday through Friday. When you exchange money at a bank, do so early in the morning because lines can be long later in the day and you can wait for what seems to be an eternity. You should always carry your passport, certified copy of your passport or *pensionado* or resident I.D. when exchanging money or for other banking transactions.

Money can also be changed on the street, where you get the same rate of exchange than in the banks. Street money changers operate along Avenida Central between Calles 2 and 4, in the vicinity of the Post Office. You don't have to look for these money changers since they usually approach you. Many people prefer to change their money this way because all transactions are quick and there are no lines as in the banks. Once you have been in Costa Rica for a while some of these money changers will get to know you and may do the majority of your transactions. Most hotels can change traveller's checks or dollars when banks are closed.

Be careful of slick change artists who may be distributing counterfeit bills or attempt to shortchange you.

Banking

Before selecting a bank it is necessary to decide what services you will need.

There are branches of Costa Rica's state-owned banks in San José and in other large cities and towns. The headquarters of Costa Rica's largest banks: **El Banco Nacional, El Banco de Costa Rica** and **El Banco Crédito Agrícola** are in downtown San José near the Central Post Office. The government guarantees all monies deposited in these state banks. **BISCA** or the **Banco Internacional de Costa Rica** (506) 257-0885 is a special international bank with an office in a Miami bank.

When making deposits in national banks you should consider the following. Checks from outside Costa Rica, including bank cashiers checks, require 30 working days minimum before funds will be usable after they are deposited. Checks issued on Costa Rican private banks will usually take a couple of working days before the funds will be available. Checks deposited from the same bank and branch are usually available the same day. Wire transfers are available as soon as they arrive.

There are also numerous private banks affiliated with international banks. In the last few years there has been a trend towards privatization. Now private banks can offer many of the same services the state banks do. When the minimum deposit is not maintained, service charges for account operations at private banks can sometimes be higher that at the national banks. Many private banks pay higher interest than state banks but cannot guarantee your deposits as the government banks do. Remember the higher the interest the more the risk. In the mid-1980's private finance companies were offering up to 45% interest in *colones*. As recently as 2002 several other companies were paying as much as 3% monthly. Needless to say they all failed and the investors lost everything.

Some of the better private banks are **Banco de San José, Banco Elca, Scotia, Banco Interfin, Bancrecen, Cuscatlán** and **BANEX**. Check the yellow pages for more private banks. It is advisable to open an account at one of these banks or state banks so you can have a dollar account to protect against unexpected currency devaluations, cash personal checks, obtain a safety deposit box for some of your valuables and facilitate having money sent to you from abroad.

Regarding the latter, you should make sure that the bank you choose works with a U.S. correspondent bank to avoid untimely delays in cashing checks.

Warning: Be carfeful of Scotia Bank. We have heard many foreign residents complain about unfair treatment at this bank. They complain

about having to open their safety boxes for random inspections (which is illegal without a court order) and general lack of privacy at this overly intrusive bank.

We have a safety deposit box in the Banco Nacional that is readily accessible during working hours. We also have a dollar account, certificates of deposit, and an ATM card. Our only complaint is that service in state run banks tends to be very slow. You can spend up to an hour in the bank waiting to make a simple transaction.

Automated Teller Machines or ATMs are found all over the country in banks, supermarkets and other convenient locations. These 24-hour automated tellers that disperse a few hundred dollars at a time from your account, cash advance in *colones* only. When using one of these machines be sure to exercise the following precautions:

(1) Use ATMs located in well-lit area with good visibility.

(2) Use an ATM that allows you entry and a door to lock rather than one on a open sidewalk.

(3) Cancel the transaction at the first sign of suspicious activity.

(4) Take all paperwork with you and do not throw away anything that has your account number imprinted.

(5) Do not carry your ATM card with you unless you are going to use it.

Costa Rican Banks offer a full-range of services.

Other banking services are high-yield certificates of deposit in *colones*, certificates of deposit in dollars on par with U.S. interest rates and credit card related services.

All banks have different requirements for opening accounts or obtaining credit cards, possibly entailing banking or personal references, identification and most certainly minimum deposits. Requirements will vary slightly from bank to bank, so check with the banking institution of your choice.

Permanent and non-residents may open a savings account in state and private banks. All that is needed is a minimum deposit, in some cases a letter of reference and a passport or *cédula*. To open a local checking account you have to be a resident and may be asked to provide a Costa Rican ID card or passport as a means of identification.

You may be asked to show your water, telephone and electric bills in your name to prove you live here. If you cannot provide these documents you will need two references from banks in the U.S. or from two account holders in the same bank where you wish to open your account. If opening a checking account in local currency you will need an initial deposit of around $500.00. A local dollar checking account may require an initial deposit of $2000.00.

If you have a Costa Rican corporation you may also open a local corporate checking account, or *Cuenta Corriente Empresarial*. You'll have to provide the following: Passport or *cédula* (Costa Rican ID), the name of the corporation or *Personería Jurídica*, proof that it is active, a letter from the person who has general power of attorney of your corporation authorizing those people who can sign on the account along with their ID numbers and an initial deposit of around $1,000.00 for an account in local currency or $2,000 for a local dollar account.

International dollar checking accounts are offered through Bicsa and the Banco de San José. Individuals and corporations may open these accounts but their are specific requirements which must be complied. Check with the bank of your choice.

Most banks are normally open from 9 a.m. to 5 p.m., Monday through Friday. Two branches of the Banco Nacional in dowwntown San José open at 7:30 a.m. A few branch offices like the one in Plaza Mayor in Rohrmoser don not open until 10:30 p.m. The Banco Nacional in the San Pedro Mall and a few of the private banks open on Saturdays.

Warning: Never plan to do any banking on the second or last Friday of the month since it's payday for most Costa Rican workers and lines sometimes extend outside the bank.

The state banks are also very crowded after holidays and on Monday mornings. It is always best to get to the bank at least a half-hour before they open to get a good place in line. Bring some good reading material since the lines often move at a snail's pace.

Tipping

A 15 % sales tax, as well as a three percent tourist tax is added to all hotel bills. Cafes and restaurants include a 10 % service charge or tip, so tipping above that amount is optional. Employees such as bellhops and taxi drivers are appreciative of any additional gratuity for excellent service. It is also customary to give a small tip to the parking attendants who watch your car on the street, called *cuidacarros*. One hundred *colones* is usually sufficient.

Supermarket box boys should be tipped for carrying groceries to your car since they do not receive a salary. If you live nearby, they will even take your bags to your home. We used to live four blocks from the supermarket at Plaza Mayor in Rohrmoser and like to walk to the market. Our favorite box boy delivers our food to our front door for about 75 cents.

Paying Bills

Although your bills are sent to your home or post office box, the procedure for paying bills is different than in the United States and Canada. In Costa Rica you may pay your phone, electricity, water and cable TV bills at any supermarket, some banks or by going directly to the company that issues the bill. Nobody sends a check by mail to pay bills in Costa Rica. Some banks now starting allow you to pay bills online. Check with your local bank to see if they offer this service.

Housing and Real Estate Investments
Rentals

Housing is affordable and plentiful in Costa Rica. With the exception of downtown San José, rent for houses or apartments are reasonable (half or less the cost in the United States). Depending on location and personal taste, a small house or large apartment usually rents for a few hundred dollars per month. A luxurious house or apartment will go for $800 to $1500 per month or more. Most of these upper-end houses and apartments have all the amenities of home: large bedrooms, a spectacular view, pools, gardens with fruit trees, bathrooms with hot water, kitchens, dining rooms, a laundry room and even maid's quarters, since help is so inexpensive in Costa Rica.

In the lower range— from $300 to $700—you can expect to find a two to three bedroom house or apartment in a middle class neighborhood. Since the majority of Costa Ricans pay less than $150 monthly for rent, a few hundred dollars should rent a nice place to live. Most affordable houses and apartments are unfurnished. However, you can usually buy a complete household of furniture from someone who is leaving the country. This way you can save money. Most of these cheaper places will not have hot water. In the shower there will probably be an electric device that heats the water. If there is not one of these devices, you can buy one for about $30 and have it installed for a few dollars.

When looking for a place, remember to check the phone, the shower, the closet size, kitchen cabinets, electrical outlets, light fixtures, the toilet, faucets and water pressure, locks, general security of building, windows and the condition of the stove, refrigerator and furniture, if furnished. Look at ceilings for telltale leaks and stains.

Also, check for traffic noise, signs of insects and rodents and what the neighbors are like. Ask about the proximity of buses and availability of taxis. Have anything you sign translated into English before you sign it. **Don't sign anything you don't understand based on the landlord's word of honor.** You should be aware that by law landlords could raise rents where the contract is in *colones* a maximum of 15% annually. On the other hand, contracts in dollars may only be raised once every three years. There is a publication that you can purchase which explains in detail how the country's rental laws work (*La Ley General de Arrendamientos Urbanos y Suburbanos Ley 7527*). A SPanish version is available at www.asamblea.go.cr. You can soon find an English version at **www.rent.co.cr**.

Principal points of the rental law:

1.) A rental contract can be either verbal or written.

2.) No matter what a contract says, a renter who duly accomplishes the terms of a rental agreement, can stay for three years minimum, no matter what. If the period of the contract is more than three years, the higher term takes priority.

3.) At the end of the term, if the landlord wants the rental property back, he or she needs to notify the tenant at least three months before the term expires. Otherwise the term is automatically renewed for another three years or whatever the original term of the contract states.

4.) When property is rented to an individual as a home and in colons, Costa Rica's currency, the rent amount increases automatically 15 percent every year. When the rental price is agreed to in any other currency, the automatic increase does not apply. Usually rents are stated in colons or U.S. dollars in Costa Rica but can be negotiated using any worldwide currency. Businesses can negotiate any payment method and/or yearly adjustments agreeable to both parties.

5.) Public services and utilities are to be paid by the tenant except for property taxes, which are the responsibility of the landlord.

6.) If a property is sold or otherwise transferred it should not impact on the tenant's rights and the new landlord must respect any existing contract.

7.) Any improvements made by a tenant automatically become the property of the landlord.

8.) A tenant can not change the original agreed upon use of a property. For example, a home cannot be turned into a pet store nor a pet store into a bar.

9.) Landlords have the right to inspect their property once a month.

10.) Tenants have the legal right to pay rent up to seven days after it is due.

11.) In negotiating a rental contract, a landlord can request any guarantee deposit they see necessary to protect their interests.

12.) Tenants can not sub-rent/lease a property.

Rooms in homes usually rent for around $100 monthly. We know of several foreigners who live this way to save money.

As we mention later on, before deciding to live in Costa Rica permanently, it is a good idea to rent a place first or find a real estate agent who can show you around and guide you through the buying process. As you have just seen there are a variety of rental options and price ranges to match almost any taste or budget. However, for *gringos*, the prices are generally much higher.

You will need a map of San José and the suburbs. The *Tico Times* and *Costa Rica Today*, are two places to start looking. *La Nación* is the Spanish language newspaper with ads. They have an excellent real estate section on Saturdays. However, relying solely on classified ads in newspapers is a mistake and can prove to be misleading. Some places are outright disappointing when compared to the way they are described in ads.

Opening a Real Estate Company in Costa Rica
By Lester Núñez

I originally came to Costa Rica from Victoria, British Columbia where I was licensed as a broker and worked both residential and commercial real estate sales for over fifteen years. My interest grew in Costa Rica because of the country's weather and culture. Bascially, I guess I just wanted to seek my Hispanic roots.

My plan was to open a real estate office in Costa Rica. Shortly after arriving I met my present partner, Mercedes Castro, who had been working as an independent real estate agent here. My goal was to provide excellent service combined with professionalism and integrity, just like North Americans are accustomed to back home. However, much to my surprise I soon discovered that the local real estate scene was very disorganized. There was no licensing of agents, no formal training and little regulation. Anyone was permitted to sell anything. Now all of this has changed.

I quickly aligned our RE/MAX franchise with the Costa Rican Chamber of Real Estate (CCBR). My partner and I have worked very closely with them over the last five years to formalize real estate training and licensing as in the States and Canada. This has mainly been achieved by educational courses, creation of an Internet-based multiple listing system and licensing requirements.

The Costa Rican Chamber of Real Estate in conjunction with UNED University have created a twenty-two unit course which takes six months to complete and trains future agents.

Multiple listings were also created to further modernize the local real estate profession. The local multiple listing system is now affiliated with MLS Today which has its base in the U.S. and Canada. Combine this with RE/MAX'S worldwide multiple listing system and both the agent and client are now better off. Also, there is legislation pending to regulate the real estate business. All the government has to do is give its approval.

It initially took us a couple of years to get our business off the ground. Our international listings and advertising have been our "bread and butter." It is well-nigh impossible to make a living off the local market alone.

I love Costa Rica because of the climate, inexpensive health care, tax benefits for foreign residents, Spanish culture and much more. You really couldn't get me to return to Canada for anything in this world.

Other sources for finding an apartment are supermarket bulletin boards and word of mouth. Tell everyone you know you're hunting, and ask them to tell every one they know, and so on. The Blue Marlin Bar, in the Hotel Del Rey, MacDonald's in San José, around the Central Park in Heredia and other *gringo* hangouts are other places to inquire about rentals.

When hunting for an apartment or house to rent contact the **Association of Residents of Costa Rica ARCR**, Tel: (506) 233-8068/ 221-2053, Fax: (506) 255-0061, arcr@casacanada.net. They will help you look in those areas that suite your personal needs and take the headaches out of finding a place to live. Howver, the best source for rentals is **www.rent.co.cr Tel: 355-6820**.

When reading the ads in the Spanish newspapers you should be familiar with the following words: *Se Alquila*-for rent, *agua caliente*-hot water, *alfombrado*-carpeted, *amueblado*-furnished, *sin muebles*-unfurnished, *baño*-bathroom, *cocina*-kitchen, *cochera* or *garaje*-garage, *contrato*-contract, *depósito*- deposit, *dormitorio*-bedroom, *guarda*-guard, *jardín*-garden, *seguro*-safe, *patio*-patio, *parqueo*-parking, *verjas*-bars, *zona verde*-grassy area, ¢ = *colones* (Costa Rican money).

finding a Temporary Place to Stay

While exploring Costa Rica or looking for an apartment, house or another type of residence in the San José area, you may choose to stay at one of the many accommodations listed below.

If staying in downtown San José, we recommend the **Dunn Inn** (222-3232). It is run by North Americans and very popular *gringo* hangouts. The service is excellent and you can make some good contacts. **The Hotel Presidente** (222-2034) has reasonable rates, good service and a free breakfast included. We book many of the participants on our tour groups there because of its convenient downtown location. **The Hotel Grano de Oro** (255-3322) is another gem you should check out. Their excellent restaurant serves mouth-watering cuisine including great desserts.

In the beautiful city of Heredia we highly recommend the **Hotel America** (Tel:260-9292) E-mail: info@hamerica.net or see www.hamerica.net. The owners also operate three other quaint and affordable in the same area: **Hotel Ceos** (Tel: 262-2628), **Hotel Heredia** (Tel: 238-0880) and **Hotel D'Cristina** (Tel: 237-3036).

There are other accommodations for all tastes and budgets located in the metropolitan area. The price range is from a few hundred dollars at the top end to less than twenty dollars at the lower end of the scale. We don't have the space to list every hotel, motel, pensión, aparhtotel or bed and breakfast in the section below. If you want a more extensive list we suggest you purchase Christopher Baker's *Cost Rica Handbook* or any of the guides listed in the last chapter of this book.

Aparthotels

Aparthotels, a cross between an apartment and a hotel, are a good first option because they are furnished, completely equipped and have phone access as well as bilingual management. From there you can comfortably survey the market. If you are living in Costa Rica only on a seasonal basis, one of these aparthotels is probably your best bet. Most have a kitchenette or other cooking facilities. Usually they are less expensive than hotels with similar amenities, but more expensive than apartments. **The Don Carlos** and **Los Yoses** are also centrally located and have nice accommodations. **Aparthotel Castilla** (222-2113), **Aparthotel La Sabana** (220-2422), **Aparthotel El Sesteo** (296-1805 round out the list.

Bed & Breakfasts

Bed and Breakfasts, or B & B's as they are sometimes called, have sprouted-up all over Costa Rica in recent years. Most of these establishments are smaller and in many cases less expensive than hotels. What sets them apart from other lodging is their home-like, quaint ambience. Many have a live-in host or owner on the premises and some are downtown. Most B & B's advertise in the local English newspapers, but there is now a service to help you find the "right" B&B for you. Call or fax the **Bed and Breakfast Association** at 011-(506) 228-9200. To make a reservation call, 011-(506) 223-4168.

Homestays

Homestays provide a great introduction to the Costa Rican way of life and provide the opportunity for you to improve your Spanish. We highly recommend **Bell's Home Hospitality,** 011-(506) 225-4752, Fax: 011-(506) 224-5884, e-mail: home-stay@racsa.co.cr.

Apartments

Here are three apartments that cater to foreigners, are located in or near downtown San José and offer kitchens, a telephone, cable TV and are furnished. **Apartments Scotland** 011-(506) 223-0833 Fax: 011-(506) 2575317, **Apartments Sudamer** Tel: 011-(506) 221-0247 Fax: 011-506-222-2195 and **Apartments Van Fossen** Tel: 011-(506) 253-9586.

Buying Real Estate

If you can't afford to buy a house in the U.S. or Canada, prices of decent homes in Costa Rica begin at around $50,000 with financing available for new homes if you become a resident. In 1999 we purchased a new $65,000 home in Heredia with 80% financing. Our payments are $452 monthly on a 15-year, 9.0% loan—$150 less than we used to pay for rent in Rohrmoser. The monthly payment includes a life insurance policy that pays off the loan in full in the event of death of the owner.

You do not have to be a resident of Costa Rica to own property and you are entitled to the same ownership rights as citizens of Costa Rica. Ownership of real estate in Costa Rica is fully guaranteed by the constitution to all foreigners. This means your purchase here can be fully secured and safe.

The value of beach property has skyrocketed over the last decade due to the country's increased popularity. Many people want to realize their dream of owning a beachfront lot in a tropical paradise.

For most foreigners the main beach development areas that are worth considering for retirement and/or vacation homes can be found in Guanacaste areas such as Flamingo, Junquillal, and Tamarindo. The Central Pacific beach areas around the towns of Jacó Beach, Quepos and Manuel Anotonio are also attractive. This Central Pacific area has great potential, as it is much closer to the Central Valley and San José. The new Villa

A $50,000 + home in a middle-class neighborhood.

Colón-Orotina and Quepos-Dominacal highways will have a huge effect on real estate values in this area, as it will reduce driving time to the Central and South Pacific areas.

Unlike Mexico, some beachfront property may be purchased. However, the 200-meter strip of land along the seacoasts is owned by the government and for public use. It is prohibited to build anything within the first 50 meters of the high tide line.

This zone is for the public and cannot be turned into a private beach. Also, you can no longer build within the next 50 to 200 meters of the high tide line—this is called The Maritime Zone, or *Zona Marítima*, — unless there is existing housing or a new tourism project involved. If this is the case, you can lease the land from the municipality, which is overseen by the Costa Rican Tourism Institute.

In theory foreigners cannot lease this land, but there are loopholes in this law. One of the ways to circumvent this regulation is by obtaining a lease through a corporation that is owned mainly by a Costa Rican. Check with a lawyer to find out how this works.

For your information, beachfront property is being bought-up fast, and the price of this and other prime real estate is soaring.

Before you move to the beach, you should know that for some people the novelty of living at the beach wears off fast. Visiting the beach for a few days or weeks is very different from living there full-time. The

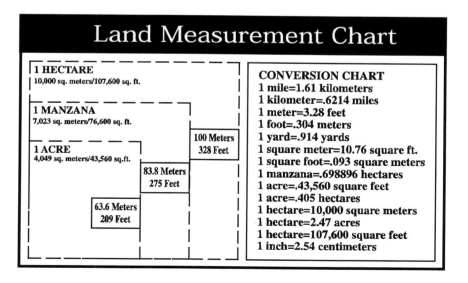

Land Measurement Chart

1 HECTARE
10,000 sq. meters/107,600 sq. ft.

1 MANZANA
7,023 sq. meters/76,600 sq. ft.

1 ACRE
4,049 sq. meters/43,560 sq.ft.

100 Meters
328 Feet

83.8 Meters
275 Feet

63.6 Meters
209 Feet

CONVERSION CHART
1 mile=1.61 kilometers
1 kilometer=.6214 miles
1 meter=3.28 feet
1 foot=.304 meters
1 yard=.914 yards
1 square meter=10.76 square ft.
1 square foot=.093 square meters
1 manzana=.698896 hectares
1 acre=.43,560 square feet
1 acre=.405 hectares
1 hectare=10,000 square meters
1 hectare=2.47 acres
1 hectare=107,600 square feet
1 inch=2.54 centimeters

humidity, boredom, bugs, lack of emergency medical facilities in a few areas and the occasional inconveniences of living in an often out-of-the-way area are factors which might deter some from moving to any beach area. However, in general the positives in beach living far outweigh any negatives. Due to Costa Rica's increasing popularity and improving infrastructure, beach property can be an excellent investment.

Besides homes and beach property there are also condominiums, farms, lots and ranches for sale at reasonable prices, depending on their location. See the section titled, "Where to Live" in Chapter 1 for a description of the areas where many foreigners reside.

You will be pleased to know that no capital gains taxes on real estate exist in Costa Rica, so it is an excellent investment. You do have to pay yearly taxes, but they are low by U.S. standards. Yearly property taxes are on a sliding scale up to .25 percent of the stated value of a particular property.

Purchasing property in Costa Rica is very different than making a similar purchase in your home country. The laws of Costa Rica and property registration process can be somewhat confusing to a foreigner. Your best bet is to work with a broker (not all brokers are licensed in Costa Rica) or real estate consultant when looking for property like the people we recommend in the section "Finding a Broker". When you find a property your broker can help you negotiate the price and explain your financing options.

If you decide to buy real estate, an attorney is absolutely necessary to do the legal work. We strongly recommend that your lawyer do a thorough search of all records before you make your purchase and make sure there are no encumbrances (*gravámenes*) on it. One of the biggest errors made by foreigners buying real estate is not properly researching the title for liens. You can obtain information about property at the **Registro de Propiedades** (like our land title office) in the suburb of Zapote, about five minutes from downtown San José by car or taxi.

You can also find the status and ownership of a piece of property and get any title documents and surveys you may need at this office. If the property is registered in the name of a corporation, the legal representatives must be verified, since they have power of attorney to make the sale. Information may also be obtained from the registry's website at: **www.registronacional.go.cr.**

If the property appears free and clear of encumbrances, the lawyer can then proceed. Your lawyer should then draft a transfer deed or *escritura* to move the ownership from seller to buyer. In Costa Rica the buyer and

Buying or Building a House in Costa Rica is Different
By Rudy Matthews

Having said that - Should you buy? Absolutely!

If you have a serious interest or have definitely already decided   to invest in Costa Rica real estate, go ahead and do it! Costa Rica is a remarkably beautiful country. The beaches and mountains would be hard to duplicate anywhere in the world. I really love it here.

My name is Rudy Matthews, I have a home in Heredia which is just north of the capital city of San José. Thanks to successful real estate investing in the United States I am able live here in Costa Rica.

After dealing with a variety of lawyers, construction companies and banks in Costa Rica I am on a mission to inform and advise anyone thinking of , or in the process of buying Costa Rican real estate.

You may have heard of a horror story or two about Costa Rica real estate and some people who have been taken advantage of. There is no need to dwell on the negative. Instead you should become an educated, well-informed person who learns how to make intelligent decisions before and during a real estate transaction.

You should gather as much information as you can, become informed and if you wish, talk to me. preventative knowledge is better than remedial. Remedial is where you lose your money.. as I stated above, if you are seriously thinking about purchasing real estate in Costa Rica - do it carefully.

I have more than twenty years experience buying, selling, managing and building houses and apartments. As an independent personal consultant, my main objective is to protect you, save you money and eliminate frustration. My knowledge of negotiation, contract clauses that protect you, construction and improvements will be an invaluable service . My understanding of Costa Rican real estate will protect you.

Hard work, honesty and integrity are virtues I have lived by and will maintain for my clients in Costa Rica.

I am **NOT** a broker nor do I sell property, so I have **NO** hidden agendas. I am paid by my clients and **NOT** by realtors or sellers. My fees are reasonable.

You may contact me at: **Tel: (506) 262-2083, Cell: (506) 839-6961, E-mail: rkmno@aol.com.**

the seller usually share the closing costs which normally run about 4-5% of the total purchase. A small real estate transfer tax or 1.5% of the actual value is included, a registration fee, stamps, notary fees, which vary and depend on the price of the sale. Title insurance is optional but advisable. It is common practice with many lawyers in Costa Rica to lower the actual amount paid on a sale to a much lower sum on paper to reduce land transfer tax. This can be risky and problems may arise later on.

Buying and registering a property in a corporation has many advantages, mainly, asset protection in the event of a divorce or a lawsuit. When a corporation owns the property, the sale or purchase of the company can be negotiated so you don't have to pay property taxes or stamp fees. All you have to do is change the Board of Directors, the legal representatives of the corporation and transfer the shares.

Do not hire the same lawyer used by the seller of the property. Also, don not forget to check that you are buying the land from its rightful owner. Some owners have sold their land to several buyers. You can protect your real estate investment further if you talk with neighbors about water shortages, safety and burglaries in the area.

Remember, always see the property in person and never buy sight unseen. Don't forget to see if you need special permits to build. Be sure to check the comparative land values in your area to see if you are getting a good deal. If you are thinking of living in a remote area, check to be sure that roads, electricity and telephone service are available.

If you cannot live on your property year-round, then you will have to hire a guard, caretaker or a reliable housesitter to watch it for you. Make sure boundary fences and limit signs are well maintained and visible. Visit the land periodically to check for squatters. They can be a real problem.

Undeveloped land is a prime target for squatter invasions. Once they establish themselves on your land it is difficult to get rid of them. If they occupy the land for a certain period of time they can claim it as their own. The sooner you get them off the land the fewer problems you will have. If you have to be an absentee owner, you can also have a friend or attorney stop by to check your property periodically. There is a trustworthy professional housesitting agency in San José which will watch your home while you are away. They are bonded and will provide references upon request. You may contact them at 256-7890.

We suggest that in some cases you rent for at least six months. However, whether you rent or buy first really depends on your comfort level. Make sure to buy where it's easy to rent or sell your home or condominium in case you change your plans or in the event of a personal emergency.

To find a house or land to purchase look for a well-recommended realtor who can identify true market value like the real estate agencies we list in this section. You may also want to see the listings in the back of the *Tico Times*. If you want to save money, look in the local Spanish newspapers *La Nación* or *La República* because prices are more realistic. Also, look around; go door-to-door in areas you like; and talk to other expats. Keep in mind that housing costs are much higher in *gringo* enclaves like Escazú and Rohrmoser. Be sure to remember that the farther away you live from San José and other cities the more you get for your money.

To find a good buy you should study the market. It is also a good idea to negotiate in *colones* since you will come out ahead in the long run as the *colón* continues to devaluate. This will make your home appreciate over time. Don't depend too much on the newspaper. Talk to as many people as you can. Nothing works better than word of mouth for finding good deals. Practice your negotiating skills. *Ticos* love to haggle. You may be better off having a trustworthy, bilingual Costa Rican search for you and do your negotiating. Your realtor or lawyer should also be able to assist you.

Stewart Title (Tel: 258-5600, Fax: 222-7936 or see www.stewarttitle.com) can assist you with title searches and full title guarantee. **American Title** also has a representative in Costa Rica.

Recently the **Costa Rica Realtors' Chamber** opened the country's first out-of-court conflict resolution center specializing in property disputes. They specialize in solving property disputes for both sellers and buyers within six months. The same process in the courts can often take up to 10 years or more to get to trial. Anyone in need of their services may contact them at Tel: 011-(506) 283-2891, Fax: 011-(506) 283-0347, or E-mail: caccbr@racsa.co.cr.

financing

Until about 10 years ago it wasdifficult for anyone to obtain financing The only thing available was owner financing. Now all of that has changed. In Costa Rica Costa Ricans as well as foreigners may now apply for loans from public and private banks. However, foreigners need to have a residency permit and/or a job are usually required. Interest on the loan and requirements may vary slightly from bank to bank. Please see the next page for details about financing.

Requirements for Obtaining a Loan

Private Banks

Banco Interfin

www.interfin.fi.cr
INTEREST RATES IN DOLLARS $9
INTEREST RATES IN COLONES .... ¢22%
TERM ....15 years
MINIMUM LOAN AMOUNT $30,000
MAXIMUM LOAN AMOUNT (% OF APPRAISAL VALUE) $70%/¢80%
COMMISSION FEES: 3.5% commission; 1.69% legal fees; appraisal fees
WHO QUALIFIES: Residents and non-residents who have lived in the country for at least a year*

Banco Banex

www.banex.co.cr
INTEREST RATES IN DOLLARS ....$8.5% revised
INTEREST RATES IN COLONES ....¢25%
TERM ....20 years
MINIMUM LOAN AMOUNT $30,000
MAXIMUM LOAN AMOUNT (% OF APPRAISAL VALUE) 80%
COMMISSION FEES: Approximately 6% including legal fees, bank commission and first month's insurance.
WHO QUALIFIES: Residents and non-residents who have lived in the country for at least a year

Banco San José

www.bancosanjose.com
INTEREST RATES IN DOLLARS ....Prime rate or 8% minimum, revised quarterly
INTEREST RATE IN COLONES ....Not available
TERM ....15 years
MINIMUM LOAN AMOUNT $30,000
MAXIMUM LOAN AMOUNT (% OF APPRAISAL VALUE) 70%
$400,000 maximum

COMMISSION FEES: Approximately 10%
WHO QUALIFIES: Residents only

Scotiabank
www.scotiabank.com
INTEREST RATES IN DOLLARS ....From 7.25% for residents.
From 8.25% for non-residents.
INTEREST RATES IN COLONES ....19.95% 1st year,
options start at 22.5%
TERM ....Up to 30 years
MINIMUM LOAN AMOUNT ....None
MAXIMUM LOAN AMOUNT (% OF APPRAISAL VALUE) ......75% for
living purposes / 65% recreational or rental purposes
COMMISSION FEES: From 5 to 10%
WHO QUALIFIES: Residents and foreigners/non-residents who must
have two types of ID (including passport),SSN, income tax statements
from last three quarters, last bank and credit card statements certification
of ownership of house, car, etc. Legalized by the Costarican Consulate
or Embassy in US (or Homeland)

Public Banks

Banco Nacional
www.bncr.fi.cr
INTEREST RATES IN DOLLARS ....$7,5% fixed first year, variable
from 9% minimum subsequent years (currently 9.25%)
INTEREST RATES IN COLONES ....¢20% fixed first years,
periodically adjustable subsequent years (currently 24,5%)
TERM ....$Up to 20 years / ¢Up to 30 years
MINIMUM LOAN AMOUNT ....$10,000 / ¢ No minimum
MAXIMUM LOAN AMOUNT (% OF APPRAISAL VALUE) $80%/¢90%
$200,000 maximum
COMMISSION FEES: 2% Comission: appraisal fees (vary with amount);
various other fees.
WHO QUALIFIES: Residents Only

Banco de Costa Rica
www.bancobcr.com
INTEREST RATES ....$9,5% / ¢23.5%
TERM ....15 years
MINIMUM LOAN AMOUNT $40,000
MAXIMUM LOAN AMOUNT (% OF APPRAISAL VALUE)........$70% / $80%
COMMISSION FEES: Approximately 10%
WHO QUALIFIES: Residents Only

Banco de Crédito Agrícola
www.bancocreditocr.com
INTEREST RATESIn DOLLARS $9,5%
TERM...20 years
MINIMUM LOAN AMOUNT $30,000
MAXIMUM LOAN AMOUNT(% OF APPRAISAL VALUE) ....$75% / ¢80%
COMMISSION FEES: Aproximmately 9%
WHO QUALIFIES: Residents Only

A well kept secret is that foreigners may use the pre-tax IRAS from the States to purchase property here. This procedure is perfectly legal. They can also take out a line on credit on the equity of their home in the States. We also know of some people who have obtained financing in Costa Rica without being residents as long as their credit rating is good in their home country. For information about financing, contact **Costa Rica Retirement/Investment Properties TOLL FREE 1-888-581-1786** E-mail:christas@racsa.co.cr or **costaricaretirementproperties@yahoo.com** or **see: www.primecostaricaproperty.com.**

Building A Home

In Costa Rica you can build your retirement dream house since land, labor and materials are inexpensive. However, think twice about undertaking such a project because you could be flirting with disaster. Many foreigners who have built homes complain that it sounds easier than it really is. They would not do it again because of costly delays, unreliable labor, fussy building inspectors, different laws and building codes and many other unforeseen problems. Be sure to talk with foreigners who have built homes to see what obstacles they encountered. Costs depend on location, materials and the size of the home you want to build. You generally pay between $500to $1000 a square meter or $45 to $90 a square foot.

One common mistake some newcomers make is to hurry to build their dream home while they are still on their "honeymoon" with the country. Many have been shocked by substantial cost overruns. Months or years later, they realize too much of their capital has been spent on their new home.

If you do decide to build a home on your land, there are several steps required. First, conduct a preliminary study, which should be completed before you buy the land. Also, be sure to see if your lot has access to water, drainage, electricity and telephone services.

The law says you have to hire an architect or civil engineer to file all of your construction permits.

A building permit must be obtained from the municipality where you plan to build. An architect can usually handle building permits and work jointly with the contractor to supervise the construction. It may take a couple of months or longer to get all of the permits in order. A reliable contractor will also have to be hired. You should get several bids and ask for references. Expect to visit the construction site almost everyday to ensure things are getting done. If you cannot be there have a reliable person inspect the construction site for you on a daily basis.

Finding a Broker

You are advised to use the services of a real estate broker to buy or sell property in Costa Rica. Real estate agents normally collect a 5% commission or higher. In order to find a competent, honest broker, it is wise to talk to other expatriates or contact the local Chamber of Real Estate Brokers or *Cámara Costarricense de Bienes Raíces*.

Be careful because the real estate industry is not regulated as in the U.S. Therefore, we recommend contacting **Costa Rica Retirement / Investment Properties TOLL FREE 1-888-581-1786 or 1-877-322-4690.** e-mails: **robert@costaricaretirementvacationproperties.com** or **costaricaretirementproperties@yahoo.com** or **see: www.primecostaricaproperty.com.** They have over 30 years combined experience in the retirement/investment market, and they have helped 1000s of people make their retirement and investment dreams come true.

Commercial Real Estate

There is commercial real estate for anyone thinking of starting a retail business or looking for office space. Office space in and around San José can be leased from anywhere between $7 to $20 per square meter, depending on the location. Downtown San José has outgrown itself. The majority of office space is now found west of the city. More and more tenants are moving into new buildings on the outskirts of town. The new Torre Mercedes and Centro Colón are huge office buildings west of downtown. Oficentro is a huge complex of 5 office buildings, to the south of Sabana Park. About 5 minutes to the west is Plaza Roble located next to the Multiplaza Mall. In Santa Ana, the newly constructed Plaza Forum Center has abundant office space.

Many large homes in the Rohrmoser area have been turned into businesses because of the lack of adequate space and office facilities in San José. All of the growth towards the west has happened because many Costa Rican landlords have not refurbished buildings in the downtown area.

Speculating

If you are interested in purchasing real estate for investment purposes, you will be pleased to know that the government welcomes your investment. If you choose to speculate in real estate, there are some prime areas to choose from in the Central Valley. This area offers a lot more potential due to its proximity to San José, the large number of services available and excellent infrastructure. The towns of Escazú, San Rafael de Heredia, Santa Ana/Ciudad Colón, Alajuela (Costa Rica's second city) and San José's suburbs of Rohrmoser, Los Yoses and San Pedro are all hot spots.

Homes range from about $30,000 in some *tico* neighborhoods to a couple of hundred thousand dollars in high-scale areas like Rohrmoser and Escazú. It is best to speculate in middle and lower-end properties since they are more affordable for the average Costa Rican and financing is available. A standard rule of thumb is the farther away from town you go, the lower the price.

The current housing shortage, the popularity of Costa Rica and Central Valley's weather assure excellent investment opportunities. Whether you are buying a home or an investment property, you are bound to make money if you hang on to your property. Real estate values are expected to double over the next decade or two. During the last ten years some property values have risen ten times. There is limited land in some urban areas, so the resale value goes up as population grows. Beach property will be a good investment because of the demand.

Presently there is a building and investment boom in Costa Rica's Central Pacific and Guanacaste beach areas. Infrastructure continues to improve in these once inaccessible areas. The Central Pacific area is like Hawaii or California, but only a fraction of the price. If you cannot afford to live in a prime costal area in the States, you may be able to find the property of your dreams in Costa Rica in a much more spectacular setting.

Another excellent investment is Costa Rica's nascent Real Estate Investment Trust Market. Briefly a Real Estate Investment Fund (*fondo inmobilario*)or REIT is a type of public investment fund that buys and rents out real estate and distributes the profits among investors. Depending on the fund, dividends are paid on a monthly, quarterly or yearly basis. Revenues for these types of funds depend mainly on the price at which the property was bought and the price at which it rents. For more information contact **Central American Consultants** at: **E-mail: costaricaretirementproperties@yahoo.com** or call toll free 1-877-815-1535

Banks offer properties which were collateral for a mortage loan and were legally repossessed by the bank after the client defaulted on the loan. Properties are awarded to the highest bidder. Most banks require a 5% security deposit when making a bid. Some good deals may be found by checking with a local bank.

Property management companies are available to take the hassles out of home ownership. Most property management companies charge a monthly fee to cover general maintenance, security and upkeep costs. The fee ranges from $50 to $150 monthly. If you have a rental in the Central Pacific or Guanacaste beach areas, one of these companies is essential. A list of property management companies can be found in the local Yellow pages under "*Administración de Condominios.*" In addition, many real estate companies have partnershpis with property management companies. We have friends who own a rental property in an exclusive gated community in the Central Pacific area who use a local realtor to manage their condo. They are very pleased with this service.

Before buying a home or making any other real estate investment, we suggest you educate yourself by studying the Costa Rican real estate market. Fortunately, there are two excellent guidebooks available to assist you and answer most of your questions.

Bill Baker's, *The Rules of the Game: Buying Real Estate In Costa Rica*, is a good source of information. Anyone considering purchasing real estate in Costa Rica will find this book extremely valuable. It is full of useful information and contains samples of standard real estate forms used to make most transactions. You should not consider making any real estate investment without reading this great book. (If you are interested in obtaining this one-of-a-kind book, see Chapter 10 for details.)

Purchasing Real Estate in Costa Rica, by Alvaro Carballo, a noted Costa Rican attorney and real estate specialist, is intended to reduce the anxiety of buying real estate in a foreign country. It is very informative and complete.

An excellent source of information is the *Tico Times* annual *"Real Estate and Investment Supplement."* It is packed with useful articles and advice. Reading this guide will keep you up on the local real estate scene. It is also filled with ads from local real estate brokers.

Costa Rica Real Estate Magazine is an informative publication which lists numerous properties for sale and brokers. To subscribe see, www.thecostaricaguide.com.

Affordable Hired Help

As you know, full or part-time domestic help is hard to find and prohibitively expensive for the average person, not to mention a retiree, in the United States. This is not the case in Costa Rica. A live-in maid or other full-time help usually costs between $150 and $200 per month. Often you can hire a couple for a bargain price with the woman working as a maid and the man working as a full-time gardener and watchman.

In Costa Rica, a maid usually does everything from washing clothes to taking care of small children. You can also use your maid to stand in line for you or run errands and bargain for you in stores, since foreigners often pay more for some items because of their naiveté and poor language skills.

After you have had an employee for a number of years, they begin to think of you as a father figure. As a result it is not unusual for an employee to ask for loans, advances, help with money for family members who wissh to build a home, furnish their house, provide school clothes for their children, or provide medical care and medications for family members.

General handymen and carpenters are also inexpensive. If you are infirm, one of the above people can assist you with many daily tasks. To find quality help, check with other retirees for references or look in local newspapers (*The Tico Times*, La *República* or La *Nación*).

Costa Rica's labor laws for domestic workers are strict and difficult to interpret. All full time domestic employees have the right to social security benefits from the **Caja Costarricense de Seguro Social** (roughly the equivalent of our Social Security System). This important institution pays for sick leave, general health care, pension fund, disability pensions and maternity care.

It is the employer's responsibility to pay monthly social security payments for each employee. The employer must make monthly payments of about 22 percent of the worker's monthly wage, and an additional 9 percent is deducted from the employee. In return, the worker is entitled to social security services mentioned above.

New employees must be registered with social security within a week of being hired. All new employees must register in an office in downtown San José (Tel: 223-9890). There is an automatic trial period of one month for domestic help, during which time an employee may be released without notice or termination pay.

It is also mandatory to insure employees against work-related accidents (*seguro contra riesgos de trabajo*). This type of workman's compensation costs 8,000 *colones* monthly for domestic employees and must be reapplied for annually.

Employers must also pay minimum wage to employees. This wage is set by the Ministry of Labor (Tel: 223-7166) and depends on the job and skills required. Average wages for unskilled workers start at about $120 per month. Live-in help can receive an additional 50% more that is not actually paid to them but is used when computing certain benefits and bonuses.

Live-in domestic help cannot be required to work more than twelve hours a day, although few expect this. Live-in workers usually work eight hours a day like other workers. Most regular employees work an eight-hour day, five days per week. Live-in employees can work more than this but have to be given some time off.

Furthermore, employees are entitled to a paid vacation depending on their length of employment and whether they are full or part-time. The law requires one day of vacation for every month of employment. A two-week vacation is due after fifty weeks of work. The employer can choose the time the vacation is taken and can require that half be taken at two different times, but they must be granted within fifteen weeks of the time when they were due.

Employers must also pay *aguinaldo* or Christmas bonus if an employee has worked from December 1 through November 30. It is the equivalent of one month's salary. This Christmas bonus should be paid in early December. Do not forget that live-in employees receive an additional 50 percent Christmas bonus. Employees must also be paid for five official holidays.

Paid holidays are January 1, Thursday and Friday at Easter, April 11, May 1, July 25, August 15, September 15, and December 25th.

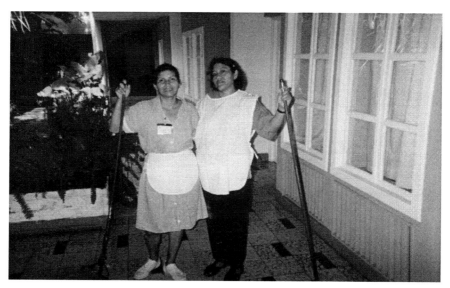

Domestic help is very affordabe in Costa Rica

A maternity leave of one month before a baby's birth is required; the employee receives 50% of her normal salary.

In some cases when a worker is terminated, it is the employer's responsibility to pay severance pay, all unused vacation time, the proportionate *aguinaldo*, and any wages due.

An employee must be given notice prior to being laid off. Severance pay, or *cesantía*, is usually one month's salary for each year worked. If an employee resigns voluntarily, the employer does not owe severance pay.

We have touched only briefly on the main points of Costa Rican labor law because it is **very complex**. If you have any questions, we advise you to contact the Minister of Labor (223-7166) or better yet your attorney. Have your lawyer help with any labor related matters to avoid unnecessary problems arising between you and your hired help.

There are two new books to help you communicate better with your hired help: Crown Publishers *Home Maid Spanish* and Barron's *Household Spanish*. Both books enable you to converse with your Spanish-speaking help without being fluent in the language. They are filled with all of the essential words and phrases you need to know.

Monthly minimum salaries are unskilled workers $230, semi-skilled workers $260, skilled workers $285, technicians $290, technicians with higher education $450 and employees with a university degree $530. To give you more of an exact idea of what salaries are like in Costa Rica, here are some samples of the approximate starting minimum monthly wages as established by the Labor Ministry or *Ministerio de Trabajo y Seguridad Social*: Accountant $400.00, bus driver $200.00, chauffeur $175.00, clerk $175.00, computer operator $300.00, dentist or doctor $1000.00, other professionals $430.00, farm hand $125.00, domestic worker $120.00, executive bilingual secretary $375.00, guard $180.00, journalist $550.00, messenger $175.00, nurse $375.00, plant supervisor $400.00, phone operator $170.00, secretary $200.00, and unskilled laborer $120.00.

Only inexperienced workers receive these starting salaries. Experienced workers command higher wages. However, keep in mind that these figures vary and are subject to change at any time. Such factors as bonuses and other perks also increase actual salaries.

Health Care
Staying Healthy

Unlike other countries in Latin America, especially Mexico, Costa Rica's water supply is good and perfectly safe to drink in San José and in the majority of small towns. In most places you can drink the water without fear of Montezuma's Revenge (diarrhea) or other intestinal problems. However, be careful when you drink water in the countryside. We have lived in Costa Rica for years and have not heard many people complain about the quality of the country's water. If you prefer, bottled water is available. Just as in the U.S., there are about twenty brands of bottled water in different size containers sold at the supermarkets. You will be pleased that Costa Rica's water is soft for bathing and washing your hair.

Although the Costa Rican government takes precautions to monitor the quality of the water and the country has high standards of sanitation, there are some precautions you should take. Wash and peel all fresh fruits and vegetables. Avoid drinking fruit drinks made with water that are sold in stands on the street. You should also watch out for raw seafood dishes, like *ceviche*, served in some bars and restaurants. This type of seafood is soaked in lemon juice and not cooked with heat.

Costa Ricans are proud of their nation's achievements in the field of health care. Their up-to-date, affordable state-run "cradle to grave" health care system reaches all levels of society by offering the same medical treatment to the poor as those with greater resources. Hospitals, clinics and complete medical services are available in all major cities and some small towns. Over 90% of the population is covered the Costa Rica Social Security system.

Many international medical authorities rate Costa Rica as having one of the best, low-cost medical care systems in the world when preventive and curative medicines are considered. The United Nations consistently ranks Costa Rica's public health system as the best in Latin America and one of the top 20 in the world.

Costa Ricans are a healthy people. The infant mortality rate of less than 11 in 100,000 live births in Costa Rica is lower than that in the United States. This figure is on par with any industrialized country in the world. Life expectancy is 76.3 years for men and 79.8 years for women. Today, an 80 year old man has a life expectancy of at least 8 years more. This puts Costa Rica in *first* place in the world for life expectancy from this age forward. Actually it's 8.4 years. Iceland and Japan follow with 7.7 years. The Costa Rica women at age 80 are actually expected to live longer than the men of the same age, 9.5 years slightly behind the women of Japan and France.

Hospitals have the latest equipment, and laboratories are excellent. You can feel safe having most operations without returning to the U.S. or Canada. Most surgical procedures cost only a fraction of what they do in the U.S. For example, a heart bypass operations cost about a third of what they do in the U.S.

Even if you are in good health, the probability of needing medical care increases with age. The security of knowing that good health services are available represents an enormous relief. Thus health care should not be a major issue in your decision to live in Costa Rica.

Most Costa Rican doctors are excellent and have been trained in Europe, Canada or the United States. If you don't speak Spanish, you don't have to worry. Many local doctors speak English, but most receptionists and nurses do not. Doctor's fees for office visits vary. A good private specialist usually charges between $30 and $40 for each visit, although some doctors charge a little more and others a little less.

Unlike many other places, doctors in Costa Rica take time with patients to answer questions and listen. Doctors usually give you their office, home and cell phone numbers as well as mobile paging number. It is not unusual for the doctor to call the patient at home to follow-up on care and medications, and they will make house calls.

If you join Costa Rica's national health care system, you do not have to pay for each office visit, only a small monthly membership fee. If you have any questions about medical fees or doctors, you should direct them to the *Colegio de Médicos*, which is the Costa Rican equivalent of the AMA.

To find a good English-speaking physician or specialist, talk to other retirees, look in the Yellow Pages under *Médicos* or look for doctor's ads in the *Tico Times.*

Public medical facilities are so good that you don't usually need private care. Most private specialists are required by law to work part-time in public hospitals. However, private clinics and hospitals do provide quicker services with more privacy, enabling you to avoid long lines and the bureaucracy of the public system.

In Costa Rica the term **Clinica** is used for private institutions that generally include inpatient medical/surgical facilities, doctor's offices, laboratories, radiology, pharmacy, and outpatient services. **Hospital** generally refers to a public inpatient medical/surgical facilities that also provide laboratory, radiology, pharmacy and related services.

You will be happy to know you can receive first-rate care at any of San José's three largest private hospitals. The **Clinica Bíblica** (Tel: 257-5252, 800 911-0800, Fax: 255-4947,E-mail:asoserme@racsa.co.cr, www.clinicabiblica.com), in downtown San José, is now affiliated with the Blue Cross-Blue Shield network. By 2005 they expect to be affiliated with Medicare. It is a first-class private hospital with an excellent coronary unit. This fine hospital is staffed with doctors who are highly trained. Complete hospital services as well as lab work are available.

To find out about benefits for military retirees and their families and for disabled veterns call (506) 522-1500/221-7717 or E-mail: sguros@clinicabiblica.com.

In addition to the main branch in downtown San José the Clínica Bíbilica has smaller satellite branches with a doctor on duty, pharmacies and express delivery of medicines in Heredia (Tel: 260-4959), Cartago (Tel: 551-0511), San Francisco de Dos Ríos (Tel: 218-0035), and in the San Pedro Mall (Tel: 283-6058).

The **Clínica Católica** (Tel: 246-3006, E-mail: info@clinicacatolica.com, www.clinicacatolica.com), in Guadalupe, a suburb of San José, is another fine private hospital with complete hospital and emergency services 24-hours a day, 365 days a year.

Hospital CIMA (Tel: 231- 2781, E-mail cimahsj@racsa.co.cr, wwww.hospitalsanjose.net), in Escazú right off the highway, is the newest private hospital in the San José area and is affiliated with the Baylor University Medical Center in Dallas, Texas and managed by International Hospital Corporation of Dallas, Texas. It is a full service hospital that boasts the latest health care technology, state-of the-art medical equipment and the most sophisticated physical plant in Central America. It offers complete services including X-ray, ultrasound, emergency and intensive care, as well as an advanced coronary unit. The average cost of a room per day is between $130 and $140, very reasonable when compared to the cost of a hospital in the United States. They have an adjacent seven-story medical office building where over 100 specialists have their offices.

Hospital Cima (Tel: 208-1800) recently opened a smaller branch in the eastern suburb of Los Yoses about 100 meters west of the San Pedro Mall. They also plan to open a full-service branch near Flamingo Beach in Guanacaste.

The **Clínica Santa Rita** (Tel: 221-6433), near the court buildings, has an excellent maternity center. The **Hospital Cristano Jerusalem** (Tel: 285-0202), in the Alto de Guadalupe, offers limited services. Although not a hospital, the **Clínica Americana** (Tel: 222-1010), next to the Clínica Bíblica, offers private out-patient service and U.S.-trained doctors on call 24-hours a day. **San Juan de Diós** (Tel: 2 22-0166) is the public social security medical facility in San José.

Hospital Universitario de La Universidad de Iberoaméricana, Tel: (506) 297-2242, Fax: (506) 236-0426, E-mail: admisiones@unibe.ac.cr, located in San José's suburb of Tibás, is the country's newest private hospital. It is a full-service university hospital where specialists treat all patients with students as observers.

C.A.R.E. Tel: (506) 353-7456 or (506) 282-2626 (beeper) or (506) 637-8606 (Los Sueños Resort) or (506) 643-1690 Jaco Beach) is a private emergency medical center located in the Jaco Beach area. They offer Medical consultation, an advanced life support ambulance, minor surgery and special events coverage. The clinic's regular hours are from 8am to 6pm.

If you have to enter a private hospital, costs will generally be well under a hundred dollars a day. This includes a spacious private room and bathroom, cable T.V with English channels. Private and semi-private rooms are often have an extra bed or sofa bed so a relative may spend the night, if necessary.

Our son was just operated on for an appendectomy at the Clínica Bíblica. The total cost including the surgeon's fee was under $1,000. Our INS insurance covered all but $140.

We know an American who spent a couple of days in the private Clínica Católica hospital and said, "The attention was first class, the food was as good as home cooking, and the same care would have cost thousands of dollars in the States." It is important to know that payment can be made at most hospitals and clinics with any major credit card. Foreign medical insurance is not accepted, but you may get a reimbursement from your health insurance company if they cover you abroad.

Health Visions Costa Rica Tel: (506) 265-6394 or 367-3251,836-2328, E-mail: retireeva@racsa.co.cr or see **www.healthvisionscostarica.com**, is a service provider of all retired military, disabled veterans, qualified widows and their families health care in Costa Rica. HVC is structured in such a way that total medical care and medications are provided with no out of pocket cost to qualified members. We know a lot of veterans who are very pleased with this organization's services. HVC is currently located in the Philippines, Panamá, Costa Rica and expanding to all of Latin America.

The following documents are required to be elegible:

(1) A current U.S. military retired ID card

(2) 65 years or over must have Medicare Part B

(3) Current ID cards for all dependents under 21 years of age; up to 23 years of age if in college with proof of enrollment

(4) Copy of DD 214

(5) must be enrolled in DEERS.

(6) Unremarried widows must have the documents above for their husband

Emergencias Médicas Tel: 290-4444 is a private company offering quick ambulance service. For a small yearly fee you can take advantage of their first-rate service.

Emergencias Metro is another company offering emergency medical transportation and care. You may contact them at Tel: 263-2983 or emergenciasmetro@yahoo.com.

Low Cost Medical Insurance

Costa Rica's health care system is available to retirees (*pensionados*) and other foreign residents. Residents may join the **Caja Costarricense de Seguro Social** (Costa Rican Social Security System) and enjoy the same inexpensive medical coverage as most Costa Ricans do. Most foreigners do not enroll in this system because of the long waits for medical appointments, some medications and other delays. However, the emergency care they provide is very good. They also have clinicas all over the country.

Most foreigners and retirees opt for the medical insurance offered by the government's insurance company—the **National Insurance Institute** or **INS**. Everyone is eligible to apply, including permanent residents, *pensionados* and even tourists. Elderly people have to submit to a physical before they can be insured. The medical policy covers expenses due to illness, accidents, hospitalization, office visits, lab work, medicines and medical costs in foreign countries. However, if you do incur medical expenses abroad, the INS will only pay the amount of the same treatment in Costa Rica and you have to pay the difference.

When you purchase a policy, the INS will supply you with an identification card and a booklet that lists the names of affiliated groups such as hospitals, doctors, labs and pharmacies. Most surgical procedures are covered 100%. You only pay a small deductible for office visits, labs, medicines and treatments. If you seek medical services not affiliated with the INS, you have to pay up front. You then submit a claim to the INS and will be reimbursed in a few weeks.

Depending on age and sex, the annual cost of this insurance is around $800 for a man between 50 and 69. For example, rates for a 18-39 year old man run around $250 per year; for a 70-year old man around $1,800; woman of all ages pay an average annual rate of about $1500. Women of childbearing age pay slightly more than men. There is a discount if more than one person is insured on the same policy. It is easy to enroll an entire family for a low monthly rate. If you belong to a group of fifteen or more people—like the Residents Association (ARCR) or American Legion— you can obtain around a 20% discount.

There is a ceiling of around $17,000 per individual. Since medical costs are so low in Costa Rica, this policy is more than enough to take care of your medical needs. Retirees and other residents need not worry about lacking adequate medical coverage in Costa Rica. For information, go to the Residents Association (ARCR) or contact them at: (Tel: 011-(506) 233-8068), Fax: 011-(506) 222-7862) or see www.arcr.net. You can reach the National Insurance Institute at (506) 223-5800.

The INS now offers a new international insurance policy that covers your needs in Costa Rica and the rest of the world. This new medical policy covers medical expenses due to accident or sickness. Here are some of the items covered: Hospitalization and ambulatory expense, maternity, prosthesis, organ transplants, air evacuation, repatriation of remains, funeral costs and a yearly check-up and eye test. The rates are high but the coverage is very complete.

Comparing Costa Rica's Health Care Plans

Here is a brief comparison of the C.C.S.S. (Caja Costarricense de Seguro Social) and the INS (Instituto Nacional de Seguros) medical plans available in Costa Rica.

C.C.S.S. - National socialized system.

1. Covers doctor's visits, medications, examinations and hospitalization.

2. Doctors are assigned to the patient.

3. Covers pre-existing conditions.

4. Covers all medications including dental and eyes.

Some reasons to consider this plan.

1. Have pre-existing health condition and do not qualify for INS insurance.

2. Take medication on a regular basis.

3. Have it as major medical in case of serious illness.

Monthly premiums cover all illnesses for the member and his immediate family for that month. The cost, younger than 55 years old, $55 per month; 55 years or older $37 per month.

INS - The semi-autonomous governmental insurance company.

1. Covers 80% of the cost of doctor's visits, medications, examinations and hospitalization.

2. Individual chooses the doctor.

3. Does not cover any pre-existing medical condition.

4. Does not cover most dental or eye exams, treatments or glasses, preventive medical check-up, illness or disorders related to female reproductive organs during the first 12 months of coverage, or birth of a baby during the first 6 months of coverage.

Some reasons ARCR members have the INS plan.

1. Can choose a doctor.

2. Can make doctor's appointments with less red tape.

Rates of coverage depend on age and sex, 20% deductible for each doctor's visit.

This program generally saves between 20 to 25% of the cost of medical, laboratory and doctor costs. Currently about 400 medical professionals are affiliated with the plan. Members receive a directory that gives the name of a doctor or medical service by specialty, the location, phone number and percentage of discount. Members of Association of Residents of Costa Rica (ARCR) quality for a discount of 35% in this plan, which sells for around $125.00 for a family or $100.00 for a single person. For additional information contact Servicios de Salud de Costa Rica Tel: 256-4747, fax; 256-2141.

Medibroker Tel: 0-191-297-2411/44-191-297-2411, Fax: 0-191-251-6424, www.medibroaker.com, e-mail: medibroker@aol.com. is a company which offers medical coverage for retirees, expats and others living abroad. They have various plans from which to choose.

While checking out Costa Rica, to see if it is the place for you to settle, you can get temporary medical insurance as a tourist through the Costa Rican Social Security office and the **International Organization of Cultural Interchanges (O.I.C.I.).** Contact them at 011-(506) 222-7867.

Medicines and Pharmacies

Pharmacies are numerous in Costa Rica and they stock most standard medicines available in Europe, Canada and the U.S. In general, the cost of most medicines is lower than those in the U.S. Most drugs requiring a prescription in North America are freely available "over the counter" in any Costa Rican *farmacia* . Exceptions are strong pain relievers and narcotics that require a special prescription. In Costa Rica, pharmacists are permitted to prescribe medicines as well as administer on-the-spot injections. They are also available to answer your questions and give free medical advice about less complex conditions.

Some pharmacies open 24-hours a day are in downtown San José at **Clínica Bíblica Hospital**, 223-6422; at the **Clínica Católica Hospital**, 225-9095; and at the **Farmacia del Este** in San Pedro, 253-5121.

The **Farmacia Alvarez** (Tel: 237-5425 , E-mail: farmacia@rxcr.com or see www.farmacia-alvarez.com) in downton Heredia offers the best prices in Costa Rica. You can save up to 80 percent of what you would pay in the U.S. They also have bilingual employees to help you.

The main branch of the **Fischel** pharmacy (223-0909), across from the main post office in San José. It has a doctor on duty to give medical advice. Fichel will deliver medicine and prescriptions in most areas. Many of their employees speak English. They also have smaller pharmacies in other locations around San José and in Heredia, Alajuela, Cartago and Puntarenas.

Full-service pharmacies are found all over the country.

Do not Hesitate to ask
Who's Who in Costa Rica
By Dr. John Williams

When trying to find a competent doctor, lawyer, dentist or other professional in Costa Rica, it's best to make sure you are in the right hands. Just beacuse someone knows how to market their services, doesn't guarantee quality work or customer satisfaction.

When I strarted placing dental implants in my patients way back in 1982 my colleagues thought I was crazy! Very little information about the procedure had been published and dental schools offered no implant courses. Early ideas were exchanged only in whispers within the dental underground. By the early 1980s two pioneer implantologists, Dr. Linkow and Dr. Weiss, had made available insertable blades as a base structure to support prosthetic work. New companies emerged like Oratronics and supplied the new industry. Blades quickly became the method of choice. Dr. Babbush published his first book regarding implants in 1980. The American Academy of Implant Dentistry and The Alabama Implant Study group soon beacme major information sources. Dr. Branemark then published his studies on osseous integrated implants. This important system was slow to catch on due to its start-up costs.

My personal break-through came when visiting Dr. Lazzarra in Palm Beach who took time out of his practice to show this Costa Rican dentist all about his new system. The lights came on and I immediately adopted his superior methodology. Today Dr. Lazzarra heads Implant Inovation Inc.(3i), theworld's leading implant supplier organization. I subscribe to to 3i due to their use of certified high grade titanium and state-of-the-art precision fittings. Their prescribed dental rehabilitation procedures are most reliable, fully functionl, and esthetically beautiful.

Currently our team offers the implant patient highly qualified professional services ranging from oral surgery to an American-board certified periodontist and endodontist. I personally do the treatment planning, team coordination and the final prosthetic work. Starting very young, twenty years ago, in the implant field has given me great experience and sufficient knowledge to treat both the most complicated cases and the routine with great confidence. Our lab work is all done with certified high noble alloys and vita porcelain which are worked by an italian artist of international repute.

For home delivery call them toll-free at 800 Fischel (800-347-2435). Recently, Fischel opened the country's first online pharmacy. They offer the sale of prescriptions and over-the-counter products. In addition, their staff of pharmacists and doctors will answer your questions. Their site also provides general information on topics such as proper use and storage of medicines. You may view their site at **www.fishel.co.cr**. Fishhel doesn't give very good discounts.

Farmacia Sucre and **Farmacia Catedral** are other large pharmacy chains in the Central Valley.

Dental Care

Many tourists come to Costa Rica to have their cosmetic dental work done inexpensively. The quality of dental work in Costa Rica is equal to that found in Europe, Canada or the U.S. On the average, dental work costs about 25 to 30% less than in the U.S. Most dentists charge around $35 for an initial exam. The approximate costs of the most common cosmetic procedures are: wisdom tooth surgery $175, single root canal $150, new crown $250, implants $750, fillings about $30 per tooth, and regular tooth extraction $40. If you have children, orthodontics are very affordable. Check prices with the dentist of your choice since rates vary.

Costa Rican dentists offer the following services: implants, gum treatment, root canals, whitening, oral surgery, crowns, bridges and nitrous oxide sedation.

One word of caution for foreigners, some Costa Rican dentists advertise in English publications and cater almost exclusively to foreigners. Patients will sometimes pay more for the dental services these doctors provide. It's a good idea to shop around and ask for recommendations. **The Costa Rican Surgeons and Dentists Association** (Tel/Fax: 256-3100, E-mail: dentista@racsa.co.cr, www.colegiodentists.co.cr) will give you a list of dentists practicing in Costa Rica. Check with other residents for recommendations. Above all, be sure to find out if the dentist you are considering practicing legally.

You may now combine a dental vacation with one of **Christopher Howard's Relocation / Retirement Tours**. Please see **www.travel.costaricabooks.com** for all of the details or call toll free 800 365-2342.

Cosmetic Surgery

Costa Rica has long been the destination for those in search of the "Fountain of Youth." People from all over the world flock to Costa Rica

Plastic Surgery in Costa Rica
By Arnoldo Fournier M.D.

Within the American Continent, Costa Rican Cosmetic, Plastic and Reconstructive surgeons, has been more and more recognized for their natural post-surgical results.

These surgeons, most likely, are fluent in more than two languages because they have earned the opportunity to study abroad for their post-medical graduate studies in cosmetic procedures.

For the last ten years, cosmetic tourism has increased significantly. One of the pioneers in this field is Arnoldo Fournier, M.D., F.A.C.S., Founder and Board Member of the Society of Plastic Surgeons in Costa Rica, Correspondent Member of the American Society of Plastic Surgeons, and the American Aesthetic of Plastic Surgery. "When I came back to Costa Rica (more than twenty years ago) from St. Luke Hospital in New York, I was told by a former Plastic Surgeon, that cosmetic procedures were not in demand by Costa Ricans."

As a result, this stubborn Surgeon decided that if he was not going to have Costa Rican clientele, he was going to open a market outside the borders of Costa Rica. He placed his first advertisement in the Tico Times (a national English Spoken newspaper) offering his services for Cosmetic, Reconstructive and Plastic Surgery. As time went by, he also placed more advertisements in other well know magazines such as LACSA Magazine, Eastern Magazine, Skyword Magazine, Passages Magazines, etc. "I was the seventh Cosmetic Surgeon in the world who owned a website when the era of the internet began".

The majority of his patients come from overseas, specially from the United States. Cosmetic Surgery Vacations have become more an more attractive, due to the natural beauty of Costa Rica. Most people come to Costa Rica, and tour around for one week, and then have their procedures done. Others, simply come for their procedure, relax during their post surgical recovery, and do day tours to nearby volcanoes, National Parks, etc. Costa Rica's wonderful year round weather (75 F year round!), is an adequate place to recover. Its not to hot, and not to cold, and it has the humidity every skin desires.

One of the most attractive things about the Cosmetic Vacations, are their affordable costs, excellent quality surgery, and safety. "Within the

U.S., you can find rates that vary from $10, 000 to $15,000. In Costa Rica, for the same procedures, I offer rates that are as high as $3,000 and lower", says Dr. Fournier.

The Secretary of Health, yearly supervises several public and private hospitals in Costa Rica. They all need to have the appropriate, and updated equipment for the procedures performed at hospital's operating rooms. A requirement for the patients is to have their pre-surgical medical exams results prior any procedure, and antibiotics. The procedures are done with local anesthesia and sedation to reduce the risk of general anesthesia. "This means, that the patients are given pills for sedation prior and during the procedures, and intravenous medication given by an anesthesiologist". Therefore, the patients will not be aware or awake during the procedures.

His surgery team is lead by Dr. Fournier, and presided by his assistant, anesthesiologist, and two certified nurses. As time goes by, more an more patients call him and write him from around the world for his services. He is known for his personal care with every patient. "I do one to two procedures a day during the morning time. I perform all procedures". Dr. Fournier, says that he likes to work first time in the morning because he feels fresh, clear and energetic for the procedures he performs. "It is better to do one or two procedures a day, than five or twenty supervised or half way done. As a result, I can explain the patient precisely know how the procedure will be or was done at the operating room".

You will notice, that he personally answers all the emails and telephone calls he receives from his patients. He personally visits them at their hospital rooms, and accompanies them throughout their post-operatory period. Patients area asked to stay in San José for a few days at any Recovery Homes after their surgeries. During this time, he sets up appointments at his office several times a week, and revise the recovery in every patient.

Today, his best advertising is the "Word of Mouth". His former patients "spread around" the good things of DR. Fournier whom has "The hands of an Surgeon, the eyes of an Artist, and the heart of a Friend".

For more information you can visit his website at **www.drfounier.com,** E-mail at: **fournier@racsa.co.cr** , or call him at **011-506-223-7314.**

To combine cosmetic surgery, dental work, or a language study vacation with **Christopher Howard's Retirement Tour** see **www.travel.costaricabooks.com** or call toll free **800 365-2342.**

for cosmetic surgery because prices are lower than in the U.S. for comparable procedures. Costa Rica's surgeons are among the world's best. Most of Costa Rica's plastic surgeons are trained in the U.S. or Europe. They keep up-to-date on new trends and methods in their field and attend professional seminars regularly. Rates for different operations vary from doctor to doctor. You can combine several procedures to reduce the price substantially. There are even package prices that combine surgery, hotel and hospitalization.

In general, prices average 25 to 60 percent less than in the U.S., although the final cost is open to negotiation with the surgeon. The low cost of cosmetic surgery should not, however, be interpreted as a sacrifice of quality for affordability. The cost of a full-face lift is between $2000-$3,500 (add a few hundred dollars per day in the hospital to recuperate from the surgery); nose surgery around $2000; liposuction $800-$1,500; with a tummy tuck, $2,000 -$3,000, breast implant $2,500-$3,500 and eyelid surgery between $800-$1,500. Many doctors send their patients to special recovery houses for about $70 a day. Rates will vary from surgeon to surgeon. We suggest you contact **Dr. Arnoldo Fournier** (please see the aritcle in this section). They are the best plastic surgeons in Costa Rica and will be more than happy to send a brochure and answer any of your questions. For information about travel arrangements or cosmetic surgery vacations see: **Unique Costa Rica Tours** at **www.costaricabooks.com/travel**. You may a combine cosmetic surgery, dental work or language study vacation with Christopher Howard's Retirement Tour.

One quick word about cosmetic surgery in Costa Rica. There are a couple of doctors who advertise their services as cosmetic surgeons but have no specialized training in the field. Therefore to get the best results from your surgery, we suggest you do the following:

(1) Ask the U.S. Embassy for a list of certified plastic surgeons; (2) Also check with the *Colegio de Médicos* (the local equivalent of the A.M.A.) to see if a particular doctor is trained as a plastic surgeon. All doctors in Costa Rica must be registered with the **Costa Rica Doctor's Association** or *Colegio de Médicos* (Tel: 232-3433, Fax: 232-2406, E-mail: medicos@racsa.co.cr, www.medicos.sa.cr). Only registered plastic surgeons may advertise their services; (3) Ask a local family doctor for a recommendation of a good plastic surgeon. (4) Find out if they are pleased with the results of their surgery, talk with former patients of the doctor of your choice before you make a decision. Find out if they are pleased with the results of their surgery; (5) Just because some cosmetic surgeons advertise in English publications doesn't mean they offer the best quality

or prices. Contact the Costa Rican Plastic Surgery Asociation (Tel:258-0396, Fax: 257-9413, E-mail: drmacaya@msn.com) for additional informations.

Care for the Elderly

Full service custodial health care is available in Costa Rica for the elderly at a very low cost. Care for less independent senior citizens is around $1000 per month. **Retirement Centers International** offers comprehensive medical care and assistance that includes all medicines, lab work, dental care, physical therapy, rehabilitation and special diets.

Villa Alegría (Tel: (506) 433-8590 or 372-1244, E-mail: info@costaricanursinghomes .com or www.costaricanursinghomes.com) is another full-service facility for the elderly. The staff with more than 15 years of experience, is specialized in elderly illnesses such as Parkinson and Alzheimer. This makes Villa Alegria a unique facility in Costa Rica. Love and dedication are the main ingredients that inspire this group of professional caregivers.

These programs are some of Central America's best and are considerably less expensive than in the United States. However, if these facilities are beyond an elderly person's means, a full-time live-in domestic worker can be hired as a nurse for a couple of hundred dollars monthly. In addition to caring for an eldery person this worker can manage other household chores.

* Once again, to find a good physician or specialist talk to other retirees, look in the yellow pages under *MEDICOS* or look for doctors' ads in the *Tico Times* and *Central America Weekly*. Below are the names of some English speaking physicians.

Dr. Jason Ramke, D.C.—Chiropractor.
Tel: 011-(506) 220-3041 www.quiropracticafamiliar.com

Dr. Claudio Orlich—Urology
Apartado 8040-100, San José, Costa Rica
Tel: 011-(506) 233-1514 Fax: 011-(506) 290-3106

Dr. John Longworth—Family Medicine (fluent English)
Tel: 011-(506) 221-3922 or 011-(506)207-9555 (English)

Dr. Stephen Kogel—Physician/Psychiatrist
A U.S. born doctor who has helped many American clients with alcohol and drug problems. Tel: 011-(506) 224-6176

> **Dr. Manuel Trimiño Vásquez**—Physician/Psychiatrist
> He has many clients from the U.S. and is bilingual.
> He has helped many foreigners adjust to living in Costa Rica.
> Tel: 011-(506) 221-6140 or 011-(506) 233-3333

For the names of more doctors and dentists, see the section in the back of this book titled " More Phone Numbers."

Alternative Healing

Costa Rica has over a hundred chiropractors, homeopathic doctors, massage specialists and natural health practitioners. Check the Tico Times, talk to other foreigners, health-food-stores, the yellow pages.

Taxes

You will have many tax advantages in Costa Rica. Investors pay no capital gains taxes on real estate investments. High interest-bearing bank accounts are also tax -free. The maximum Costa Rican tax rate is around 30% with no city or state taxes and low property taxes.   There is no personal income tax on a salary of less than $800 monthly. Self-employed people can earn up to $3000 a month without paying taxes. The most a corporation has to pay in taxes is 30% on an income of more than $100,000. However, it is easy to form a Costa Rican "offshore" corporation, or *Sociedad Anónima*, to shelter earnings and pay significantly fewer taxes. There are also many write offs to lessen taxes. Tax information is available in Spanish from a government website: **www.hacienda.go.cr.**

Briefly, a *Sociedad Anónima* is an anonymous corporation anyone, even tourists, can set up without their names appearing on any records.   The initials S.A. will appear after a corporation's name instead of Inc.. A Costa Rican corporation is similar to its U.S. counterpart in having a board of directors, shareholders and shares which can be bought and sold freely. You control all the stock in the corporation but your identity remains unknown. This practice is illegal in the U.S. but not in Costa Rica. Thus you are able to maintain some degree of secrecy in financial matters and protect yourself from some tax problems.

Each corporation has a set of six legal books in which changes may be made. Many corporations never even use their books because they never engage in any commercial activity, only to hold vehicles or real estate and other investments

These offshore corporations are used in most business transactions within Costa Rica and abroad. Because they are foreign corporations they are not subject to U.S. taxes. Furthermore, Costa Rican corporations pay only minimal taxes in Costa Rica or none at all.

There are additional benefits to establishing an "offshore" corporation. If you put your property in your corporation's name, it is easier to transfer title. All that one has to do is exchange the company's stocks. This way your assets can be transferred or sold by simply giving your shares to the new owner or visa versa. Owning one of these corporations entitles you to start a business and open a checking account in the company's name, even though you are not a legal resident or citizen. If you have relatives on the board of directors of your company, there will be no probate taxes in case of your death. It is almost impossible to find out whose name appears in the public records since ownership is confidential. Furthermore, if you get involved in any serious litigation, it will be difficult to sue you directly. You will be protected against most judgments and liens. This affords your assets greater protection. If you are a non-resident foreigner you must have one of these corporations to own a business.

Contact your attorney if you are seriously thinking about forming one of these anonymous corporations. Your lawyer can explain how these corporations work and their advantages and disadvantages. The fee for starting one of these corporations is usually between $300 and $1000. It will usually take a few months to finish all of the paperwork depending on how fast your lawyer works.

In order to form a corporation your attorney will have to make sure there are no other corporations with the same name as your company. The name of your company will have to be in Spanish and not English. Your corporation must have a minimum number of shareholders. It also must have a board of directors, consisting of a president, secretary and treasurer—all of whom have the option of being shareholders. The final steps are preparing a set of books, registering your company, establishing a charter and advertising the charter in the local newspaper.

Be forewarned: Costa Rica's bank secrecy is not "foolproof." This is especially true since the September 11th 2001 terrorist incident in the U.S. If you attempt to use your corporation for fraudulent purposes, you are asking for big trouble. Fortunately the IRS usually will not go after you unless you are a "big fish" who has done something obvious to attract their attention. This rarely happens since the country's banks are not very cooperative with the U.S. authorities in such matters. Furthermore, the

U.S. also has to obtain the authorization of a Costa Rican judge in such matters, which is difficult.

If you desire better protection for your assets or business we suggest you form a Panamanian corporation. Many savvy investors put their Costa Rica Corporation in a Panamanian Corporation. This way they are guaranteed maximum protection of their assets. Since we do not know all of the nuances of setting up one of these corporations, we suggest you contact one of the companies listed at the end of the next section.

Foreign income is exempt from taxation in Costa Rica. You will have to pay taxes on income earned in Costa Rica. *La Tributación Directa*, the local eqivalent of the IRS, is in charge of collecting taxes, but is far less efficient. However, if you go into business in Costa Rica and form a tax-sheltered corporation, most of your expenses can be written off. You will pay an income tax on your company's earnings during the prior fiscal year, or *año económico*. If your corporation owns property, there are a couple of property taxes to be paid. Corporations that are inactive pay a small tax.

You must report all income made in Costa Rica. All net income is subject to taxation. Current taxes for salaried employees run from about zero to 15% on a monthly income above $900. Taxes for the self-employed go from zero to $3000 annually to 25% above $15,000 annually. Small companies pay from 10% to 30% depending on their profits.

Due to the need for more revenue, the government has cracked down on individuals and businesses that attempt to evade their fiscal responsibilities. Under the new tax law, evaders are now subject to big fines and possible prison terms. Don't panic! A good accountant or tax lawyer can help you minimize your taxes and avoid problems later on.

Also, unlike some other places, a foreign retiree is not required to pay Costa Rican taxes on his external income (income generated abroad), so you can see why Costa Rica is considered a tax-haven by many people.

There is a yearly municipal property tax of 0.25% on your land or home and sales tax of 13% paid for some goods and service.

U.S. citizens are subject to income tax wherever they are living. You must file your U.S. income tax returns yearly through the American Embassy. You have to declare all income earned abroad but you may claim a tax exemption up to $ 80,000 on overseas-earned gross income. The $80,000 applies to individual, unmarried taxpayers. If you are married, you and your spouse may exclude up to $144,000 of foreign income, but you cannot combine the two exemptions. This exclusion does not apply to passive income such as interest, dividends, capital gains or overseas pensions. It only applies to a foreign earned income. You must reside outside of the U.S. for at least 330 days a year or be a legal resident of a foreign country to qualify for this exemption. Your primary business must also be located abroad to qualify for the foreign-earned income exemption.

Fortunately, if you live outside the U.S. you qualify for a 2-month extension and may wait to file your taxes until June 15th. However, if you mail your return from outside the U.S., it is best to mail your return at least 2 weeks before the due date. You can speed this up by using DHL, FedEx or UPS. You need to use a U.S. tax form 2555 to apply for this extention. Even if you earn no income in Costa Rica, it is imperative to file a standard 1040 tax form to avoid problems. The biggest mistake made by individuals is assuming that since their income is under the exclusionary amount, they do not have to file a return. Payment of taxes, interest and penalties can now be done by credit card by dialing **1-888-2PAY-TAX.**

If you have any tax questions, contact the U.S. Embassy or IRS. Call either the Consular Section of the U.S. Embassy, 220-3939 or the nearest IRS office in Mexico City at 525 211-0042, ext. 3557. You may consult the IRS Web site at www.irs.gov. There is also book titled *The Expats Guide to U.S. Taxes.* It may be purchased through www.amazon.com. Another good resource is found at www.filetax.com/expat.html.

If you need help with your tax forms and returns while living in Costa Rica, contact U.S. Tax and Accounting Tel: 011-(506) 383-7043, E-mail: ustax@lawyer.com and David Houseman at Tel: 011-(506) 257-1655 or 239-2005, Fax: 011-(506) 223-7997 or 293- 2437 for income tax assistance or for help with IRS problems.

If Canadians want to be exempt from income taxes in Canada they need to have severed major residency ties for at least two years. These "residency ties" can include an un-leased house, Canadian health coverage, automobile registration, spouse or child support in Canada, banking or investment ties.

A foreign tax credit is often available for taxpayers who pay tax in another country, i.e. Costa Rica. To find out your tax status, consult form IT221R3 on the Canadian Customs and Revenue Agency Web site: www.ccraedrc.gc.ca. Canadian tax returns should be in by April 30th. Self-employed people have until June 15th.

Canadians will have to contact the local Canadian Embassy at 011-(506) 296-4149 concerning their tax obligations while living abroad.

Panamanian (Offshore) Corporations

Offshore corporations enable you to act as an international citizen with complete confidentiality, privacy and safety. Offshore corporations can legally open offshore bank accounts, brokerage accounts, hold credit cards, own property, stocks etc., and in many cases completely exempt you from any tax reporting requirements and with complete confidentiality.

Why Panama?

For many years Panama has been recognized worldwide as a major international offshore banking center that offers very attractive legal and tax incentives to Panamanian corporations. For example, Panamanian law allows Panamanian corporations to issue "bearer" stock certificates. This means the owners who control the corporation do not have to be named in any public record, since ownership is through physical possession of the "bearer" shares. Panamanian Corporations are not subject to Panamanian tax on income earned outside of Panama. Also, Panama allows you to name your corporation with an English name. This gives you many advantages when using your Panamanian Corporation in English speaking countries. These are just a few of the more important reasons why Panamanian corporations are so popular.

Forming a Panamanian Corporation:

First, we recommend you select a name in English followed by: Corp., Corporation Inc. or Incorporated. You cannot use the words Bank, Trust, Foundation or Insurance in the name of your corporation. You may use any name as long as it is not being currently used in Panama. If you own a U.S. Corporation, you may find some advantages in using the same name for your Panamanian corporation, if available. This would allow you to have identically named offshore and onshore bank accounts as well as other similar advantages.

Panamanian corporations are typically formed with nominee directors, president, secretary and treasurer. These are Panamanian citizens who are modestly paid officer workers. If you wish, you may select your own directors and officers. However, the original directors and officers selected are registered with the Panamanian public registry, and it becomes public information available to anyone who inquires. Therefore, if you wish confidentiality, we recommend that you select the nominee director option. Officers and directors can always be changed later.

Panamanian law allows corporate shares to be issued in "bearer" form. This means that whoever physically possesses the shares, owns the company. This allows for total confidentiality of ownership, since the person who physically possesses the shares is not identified in any public or even private record. Having a Panamanian corporation with "bearer" shares also makes transfer of ownership completely private and not a matter of public record, since transfer of ownership is a simple process of physically transferring the "bearer" shares to a new owner. Very similar to passing a $20 bill to someone else versus writing them a check. This feature makes it very easy to sell or transfer properties confidentially by simply transferring the "bearer" shares and ownership of the Panamanian corporation. Thus you may avoid many forms of taxes and closing costs because title to the property remains in the name of the Panamanian corporation. Essentially you are simply selling the corporation that owns the property.

Your Panamanian Corporation comes with a notarized General Power of Attorney (in English) signed by two officers named in the articles of incorporation. This power of attorney provides a blank space for you to fill in the name of any person you want to act as the legal agent for the corporation with the authority to open and sign on corporate bank accounts, enter into contracts for the corporation, sign and transfer assets for the corporation, etc. Although you fill in your name or another person's name as having Power of Attorney, this is not evidence of ownership. The person named is simply an agent, similar to an employee empowered to act for the corporation. You may order as many additional Power of Attorney forms as you wish.

As you can see there is a world market for Panamanian corporations because they are extremely popular. Older Panamanian corporations with established bank accounts sell for thousands of dollars or more. Selling your Panamanian corporation is a matter of physically transferring the "bearer" stock certificate together with the other corporate records to the new owner.

The one-time cost for setting up a simple Panamanian Corporation is around $1600. You will have to pay an annual Registered Agent and Director's fee of $595 yearly, due one month before the anniversary date of the corporation.

For forming a Panamanian corporation or foundation, we highly recommend **Roberto I. Guardia** . A number of Americans we interviewed speak very well of him. You can contact him at: Tel: (507) 263-3917, Fax: (507) 263-3924 Cel: 612-5429 E-mail:rig@orcag.com, www.orcag.com.

Insurance

The Instituto Nacional de Seguros, or INS as it is called, is a state-run insurance company that controls all insurance in Costa Rica. They will handle all of your insurance needs. INS has a new English section on their website at **www.ins-cr.com** or **www.ins.go.cr.**

All insurance is less expensive in Costa Rica than in the United States. Auto, fire and theft insurance will cost less than half the U.S. premium. All vehicles in Costa Rica have Obligatory Insurance or *Seguro Obligatorio,* which comes automatically with your vehicle registration. It is renewed every December when you pay your car's road tax (*Marchamo*). This insurance gives you a small amount of personal liability coverage, which is the type that protects you if you hurt, kill or maim another person when you are driving your car.

About 65 percent of the cars have only the obligatory insurance which is not really complete coverage. If you want real coverage you must buy a supplementary policy. For an additional cost, supplemental insurance policies provide broader coverage than the basic compulsory policy. Your car's value determines the price of your premium. These supplemental policies are paid in full every six months. They cannot be paid in monthly premiums as in the U.S. Also, as in the States, premiums are increased when you have an accident. However, these increases are not as big as in the U.S. It doesn't matter if it was your fault or not.

When considering coverage remember the general rule of thumb: Insure against everything you would find yourself hard-pressed to overcome financially. The essential coverages are A and C; if you don't get those, INS won't sell you any of the others. For coverage F or H, you must also have D. (By the way, coverages B and G have never existed). Rates are determined by the vehicle's and applicants characteristics.

Here is a breakdown of the basic automobile coverages in Costa Rica:

(A) **PERSONAL LIABILITY** - Covers liability established by the courts as a result of death or injury caused by an accident for which the driver of your vehicle was guilty. The benefits are paid once the Obligatory Insurance is used up and does not cover injury or death of family members or employees of the policyholder or driver.

(C) **PROPERTY DAMAGE** - Covers damage to property (car, house, etc.) belonging to other people if the accident was the fault of the driver of your vehicle. Excludes items being transported by your vehicle.

(D) **COLLISION** - In case of collision with another vehicle, persons, or property belonging to someone else pays for damage sustained by your vehicle: (a) if the accident was not the fault of your driver, or (b) if the accident was not the fault of your driver but the other vehicle has no insurance and the owner cannot pay.

(E) FIRE - Covers damage to your vehicle caused by fire due to either internal factors such as short circuit, or to external factors such as lightning, or if the place where the vehicle is parked burns.

(F) THEFT - Covers total theft of the vehicle or loss derived from the total theft. If it is not recovered, policy pays for damage and/or missing parts. If not recovered within a month, the insured amount is paid or the vehicle is replaced.

(H) ADDITIONAL RISKS - Covers damage resulting from overturning, running off the road, vandalism, floods, hurricanes, quakes, explosions, collisions with birds, falling objects, accidents within parking lots or private property, riots, etc.

OTHER CONSIDERATIONS

Insured values - Cars should be insured at their market value in Costa Rica, and it is up to the policy applicant to determine it. To determine values of vehicles, it is sometimes best to use the newspaper classified ads. Only you can change the value on your policy ; INS will not automatically reduce the insured values on vehicles as they depreciate.

Renewals - Auto insurance is normally for six months, after which you have a grace period of 10 working days to pay for renewal. After that, you would have to apply for new insurance or reinstatement.

Coverage outside of Costa Rica - For cars with Costa Rican registration, coverage extends to all of Central America and Panama.

Deductibles - All coverages except "A" have standard deductibles. "A" has no deductible. Double deductible if the driver is under 22, in cases of vandalism, birds, or accidents on private property.

Alcohol - Policies will not pay for accidents to vehicles being driven by persons under the influence of alcohol or drugs even if the condition did not cause the accident. An alcohol count of 50 mg or more in 100 cc of blood will invalidate insurance coverage, except for liability coverages A and C.

Roadside Assistance - This comes free for vehicles less than 15 years old that have coverage "D". Call 800 800 7000(toll free) if you have a flat tire, dead battery, are out of gas, or need a tow truck.

Special Notes for Tourists: When you bring a car into Costa Rica, you will be given a permit to drive the car into the country. The permit is usually for three months, renewable once. For issuance of the permit you must state who is going to drive the car— they allow the owner and one other person, usually one's spouse. If you don't have Costa Rican plates on your automobile, you can't cover it against collision or theft. All other coverages are available under these circumstances. However, in most cases, after 180 days you can get Costa Rican plates when you pay the corresponding taxes on your vehicle.

(I) HOMEOWNERS INSURANCE - A homeowners insurance policy is called *Hogar Comprensivo* in Spanish. It protects your home against fire and natural disaster. The home fire policy has four sub-coverages: "A" is for fire and lightening; "B" covers damage caused by strikes, vandalism, hurricane, cyclone, explosion, smoke, falling objects and vehicles; "C" pays for damage caused by floods and landslides; "D" covers natural disasters: earthquakes, tremors, volcanoes, etc. You can take coverage A by itself, A+B, A+CD or complete coverage A+B+CD. Rates are based on a percentage of the value of the building and include a 13% tax and an inflationary factory whereby there is a small yearly increase. Depreciation is also factored in at a rate of 1 to 2% yearly.

If you have one of these policies you will have to insure your house's contents as well as the house itself. You will have to submit a complete list of household effects with the value of each item, and the respective brand name, model and serial numbers. If you want to insure the contents of your home, you must put a value on the objects based on depreciated value. The same rate for the house applies to the contents.You should have your house appraised so you can carry enough coverage.

Some people doubt whether the INS would be able to settle claims from a major earthquake or hurricane. The INS is by far the largest insurance company in Central America . In fact, INS is one of the largest insurace compaies in Latin America, is finacially solid, and most importantly, it re-insures worldwide a large percentage of the risk.

We have already mentioned the affordability of medical insurance in Costa Rica in the section titled "Medical Care." Because not everyone's insurance needs are the same and because laws and coverages work differently in Costa Rica, we suggest you consult your attorney or the English-speaking insurance agent, Dave Garrett, we have listed below.

Garrett y Asociados
SJO 450
Miami, FL 33102-5216
Tel: 233-2455 Fax: 222-0007
E-mail: info@segurosgarrett.com www.segurosgarrett.com

MAKING MONEY
IN COSTA RICA

Investing in Costa Rica

A recent study by the *Miami Herald* rated Costa Rica the 27th safest country for investment of 140 countries surveyed. If you are not impressed by Costa Rica's ranking, consider that the U.S. was ranked only 22nd! Another recent study found Costa Rica to be the least corrupt country in Latin America.

In addition, U.S. business magazine, *Fortune,* ranked San José Latin America's fifth best city in which to do business and placed it within the 25 best cities in the world. According to the report, *Fortune* considered the city's ability to create opportunity for its residents, its business climate and how well it can satisfy the business needs of companies that invest here. San José ranked tops in the quality of its labor force, its business environment and the lifestyle it offers resident executives and investors.

Let us review a few of the reasons why Costa Rica has such magnetism for qualified foreign investors. First, and perhaps most important; is the enduring political stability. As you already know, Costa Rica has had a strong, democratic government without interruption since the 1940s and an excellent centralized banking system. The trend towards an open economy and possible trade pacts with such nations as the U.S. and Mexico are conducive to investment in Costa Rica. Privatization of many state-run institutions will undoubtedly help economic growth in the future.

There are also no government expropriations or interference as in many Latin American countries.

Costa Rica is easily accessible from all parts of the world by land, sea or air. Outstanding phone, telex and telegraph systems link Costa Rica internationally to other parts of the world. Also, let's remember that investors in Costa Rica have equal rights and laws to protect them. Regulations for conducting business in Costa Rica are the same for both local and foreign corporations. Both can fully own and control local corporations, as well as real estate without any access limitations or restrictions. Many opportunities await foreigners who start new businesses previously nonexistent in Costa Rica. In addition, the cost of labor is low.

Additional reasons for investing in Costa Rica are: asset protection (creditors, judgments, liens, bankruptcy and divorce), privacy from individuals and governments, and fewer taxes (income tax, inheritance tax, estate taxes and probate fees).

Many attractive incentives are available to foreigners investing in Costa Rica. Investments of $50,000 or more in an approved project qualify the investor for legal residency. However, it is not necessary to become a resident to own or manage a business. Anyone who owns a business can import some items used to operate it and get a tax break on some of the usual duties. Contact the incentive section of the **Costa Rican Tourist Institute (I.C.T.)** for more information about incentive programs.

Tourism is now the leading industry in Costa Rica. Numerous opportunities exist in this field. However, sometimes there can be a lot of red tape and competition. Small hotels and bread-and-breakfasts were good investments a few years ago, but there may be a surplus of them now. We have a good friend who refurbished an old building and turned it into a small hotel in 1990. He has done very well only because he has been in the country for a while, knows all the ropes, and was a pioneer in the field.

Foreigners can invest with Costa Rica's nationalized banking system, private banks or finance companies. Interest rates are higher than in the United States (22 percent or even higher in *colones* and up to 8.75 in dollars) and there are many attractive savings accounts and time deposit programs tfrom which o choose. Presently there is no tax on interest from bank accounts. However, when investing in *colon* accounts you have to figure in yearly inflation to see if you are really getting a good deal. There are some degrees of bank secrecy, liberal money transfer regulations, and favorable tax laws for foreigners (see the section in this chapter titled "Taxes").

Foreigners can also invest in the local Stock Exchange (**Bolsa Nacional de Valores**) to get better returns than from traditional financial systems. The stock market presents a safe investment alternative with great opportunities for the investment to grow through stock appreciation, dividends, stock splits, mergers and acquisitions.

Costa Rica has the largest stock exchange in Central America. Around twenty-nine firms or *Puestos de Bolsa* are registered with the National Stock Exchange. Costa Rican stockbrokers can study economic trends and give you advice on investing in government bonds, real estate, time deposits and other investments. The Costa Rican Stock Exchange is regulated by the National Securities Commission or *Superintendencia Nacional de Valores de Costa Rica* (SUGEVAL), which is the counterpart of the U.S. Securities and Exchange Commission. They can give you information about the reliability of firms and brokers. There exists a strong possibility that the local exchange will be linked with other Latin American trade blocks in the very near future. For more information about the Costa Rican stock market, contact **Grupo Busátil Aldesa** at 1-888-5-ALDESA (U.S. only) or 223-1022, or E-mail: grupo@aldesa.com. Investors can find additional information about the local stock market at www.capitales.com.

You may also invest profitably in blue chip offshore mutual funds. Most people do this to protect their assets from creditors, judgments, liens, bankruptcy, malpractice claims, divorce and separation claims, liability claims not covered by insurance, and seizure by the U.S. government.

AmCham's Guide to Investing and Doing Business in Costa Rica is another source of information for the potential investor. It is available through the **Costa Rican-American Chamber of Commerce** or **AMCHAM**. The Chamber of Commerce also publishes a monthly magazine titled *Business in Costa Rica* that has advice on how to invest in Costa Rica. You may also want to attend a meeting of the **Investors Club of Costa Rica**. For information call 240-2240 or 222 -5601. This is a good way to meet people with common interests.

RELOCATION, INVESTMENT and **RETIREMENT CONSULTANTS** is a firm we highly recommend to any newcomer or potential investor. They have many years of experience, will steer you in the right direction, and will save you a lot of headaches and money. Their expertise, network of reliable contacts, and insider information have already helped hundreds of people find success, prosperity and happiness in Costa Rica. Most important they can show you how to really make money in Costa Rica by hooking you up with time-tested investments. You may contact them at Tel/Fax: 011-(506)-261-8968 or through: E-mail: **centralamericaconsultants@yahoo.com.**

Before investing or starting a business, you should take the time to do your homework. Under no circumstances should you invest right off the plane, that is to say, on your first trip to Costa Rica. Unscrupulous individuals and scamsters will always prey on impulsive buyers anywhere in the world. Be wary of any salesmen who try to pressure you into investing. Remember, it is hard to start a business in your own home country; don't imagine it will be any easier in Costa Rica, where both language and customs are different. The **Better Business Bureau of Costa Rica** will help you find reliable businesses and services. **Global Security Services** will do background checks, criminal history, bankruptcy and lien history if you so desire.

We also suggest you ask a lot of questions and get information and assistance from any of the organizations listed below in order to thoroughly understand the business climate of the country. However, don't solely depend on the help of these organizations. You'll have to garner a lot of information and learn on your own by some trial and error. This way you can find out what works best for your particular situation.

American Chamber of Commerce of Costa Rica: AMCHAM
P.O. Box 4946
San José, Costa Rica
Tel: 011-(506) 220-2200;
Fax:011-(506) 220-233-0969
E-mail; chamber@amcham.co.cr

Coalition for Investment Initiatives-CINDE
P.O. Box 7170
San José, Costa Rica
Tel: 011-(506) 220-0036; Fax: 011-(506) 220-4750
E-mail: aheilbron@cinde.or.cr

Export Promotion Center - CENPRO
P.O. Box 5418
San José, Costa Rica
Tel: 0i1-(506) 220-0066; Fax: 011-(506) 223-5722

Relocation, Retirement and Investment Consultants

Helping newcomers find SUCCESS and HAPPINES in Costa Rica for over 15 years. We offer absolutely the BEST network of contacts and INSIDER information available in Costa Rica.

- Safe real estate investment trusts.
- Real estate (The best brokers and properties in Costa Rica).
- How to really make money in Costa Rica and high-yielding investments up to 25% annually in dollars.
- How to form fool-proof offshore corporations to protect your assents.
- Affordable Cosmetic Surgery.
- Expert legal advice (The best legal minds in Costa Rica).
- Find - a - rental (assistance locating affordable rentals in prime locations)
- Immigration matters and residency.
- TAILOR-MADE BILINGUAL TOURS FOR INDIVIDUALS AND COUPLES.
- Moving household goods.
- Sure-fire safe business ideas, advice and contacts.
- Where to make friends and how to keep busy and happy.
- Opening and bank account and safety deposit box.
- Internet hook-up.
- The quickest and best ways to learn Spanish (secrets time-tested methods).
- Private mail service to the U.S.
- Buying and insuring a car.
- Plus all of the ins and outs and dos and don'ts of living in Costa

Satisfaction Guaranteed!

**Let the experts save you a lot of HEADACHES and MONEY
by contacting us today at:
E-mail: crbooks@racsa.co.cr or
centalamericaconsultants@yahoo.com
PLEASE SEE: www.liveincostarica.com / www.costaricabooks.com
Suite 1 SJO 981 P.O. Box: 025216. Miami, FL 33102-5216**
Be sure to ask about our daily rates, one day free weekly packages, group discounts, informative seminars and special retainers.

Procomer
P.O. Box 1278-1007
San José, Costa Rica
Tel: 011-(506)256-7111; Fax: 011-(506) 233-5755
E-mail: info@procomer.com
www.procomer.com

The Costa Rican Stock Exchange
Bolsa Nacional de Valores
P.O. Box 1756
San José, Costa Rica
Tel: 011-(506) 222-8011; Fax: 011-(506) 255-0531

National Securities Commission
P.O. Box 10058
San José, Costa Rica
Tel: 011-(506) 233-2840; Fax: 011-(506) 233-0969

Canada Costa Rica Chamber of Commerce
Tel: 011-(506) 257-4466

Investment Opportunities According to Risk

(1) Certificates of Deposit in dollars through a state-run bank paying around 3 to 3.6% annually. **Advantage:** Your money is insured by the Costa Rican government and tax-free interest.

(2) Real Estate - **Advantages:** If purchased at the right place and in the right location you are assured your property will double or triple over the next ten years. Areas like the Central Pacific are booming. Real Estate Investment Trusts are also a good bet. **Disadvantages:** Overpaying or purchasing in a bad location. See the section in Chapter 2 and this chapter about investing in Costa Rican real estate.

(3)Certificates of Deposit in *colones* (local currency) from a government bank. **Advantage:** Pay around 20% annually and are insured. **Disadvantage:** Mini-devaluations give you a net annual yield of around 10% at the most. If there is a huge devaluation, you will lose a lot of money. This hasn't happened since 1982. The mini-devaluations exist as a measure to prevent large devaluations.

(4) Personal Loans on Secured Property in dollars or colones. **Advantage:** Can earn up to 3% monthly in *colones* and hold a note on the property. **Disadvantage:** If borrower defaults, you might have to go to court to recover your property.

(5) Certificate of Deposit from a private bank in an offshore account. **Advantage:** You can earn a little more interest than through the state- run banks and investment is tax-free. **Disadvantage:** Your money will not be insured. Several private banks offer these types of investments. It is best to visit several private banks and to shop around for the best interest rate.

(6) Starting a Foreign-Based Business. **Advantages:** You don't have to depend on the small local economy. Dependence on a larger market. You have a low U.S. tax liability if you use a Costa Rican or Panmanian Corporation. An example of this would be an export or internet based business. **Disadvantage:** Not doing your homework and choosing the wrong business.

(7) Starting a Local-Based Business. **Advantages:** There are a lot of opportunities for entrepreneurs here. It is highly advisable to have prior experience in the venture you undertake. You should do a thorough feasibility study. **Disadvantages:** Not understanding the local economy, not doing your homework and thinking that what works abroad will work here. On the average only three of ten foreigners succeed here for a variety of reasons. There is a section in this chapter with details and advice about going into business in Costa Rica including success stories and failures.

(8) Offshore Mutual Funds. Advantages: All the wonderful benefits of investing offshore with the peace of mind knowing your assets are held safe and secure with a major New York Stock Exchange firm. By moving liquid assets offshore, you also achieve substantial protection from illegitimate creditors, financial predators and limit you tax liability.

Costa Rica ..... Right Now !
By Barry Strudwich

You've heard the buzz about Costa Rica at cocktail parties or on the golf course. Who hasn't had a friend rave recently about the friendly people and incredible natural beauty of the "Switzerland of Central America"? When you combine this much positive enthusiasm with the cresting wave of retiring baby boomers, the classic signs of a great investment opportunity are right before us. Remember Florida in the 50's and 60's ? It's like Costa Rica today and it's not too late !

There's absolutely no question Costa Rica is red hot ...right now . But the little known secret is actual investing is lagging behind the popularity of tourism. Why? Because few people understand how easy it is to invest in international real estate venture. Even fewer realize its possible to do this inside your IRA account !

Forget about the bullwhip, you don't have to be Indiana Jones anymore to participate in the coming the Costa Rican land boom! Investing can be almost as easy as purchasing a mutual fund or a stock. Here's why: When you purchase a condo or even a beach front lot, the title for the real estate is usually registered in the name of a private company which actually owns the real estate. By purchasing 100% of the private company shares, you acquire the real estate while avoiding paying real estate transfer taxes twice.

But where can you find the cash ? You might not have to look any further than your IRA account ! When real estate sales are structured as stock transactions, a second very interesting opportunity emerges..... You can purchase the shares inside your IRA account with pre-tax dollars ! This also means, when the time comes to cash out at a profit, you can sell tax free as well ! If you'd like to find out more about this powerful idea visit the website www.omniasset.com.

Even better, several of the higher quality developments have taken the initiative to get "pre-approved" by specialty IRA custodians. Among these is the 350 acre Del Pacifico project on Costa Rica's beautiful Pacific Coast (www.delpacifico.net).

Current IRA approved investment opportunities include 24 new ocean view condominiums units at "pre-construction" prices as well as some spectacular "ocean view" single family lots. The condos will be 2,300 square feet with dual master suites and a third bedroom and are priced at $350,000. William Ramirez of Del Pacifico sees strong rental income potential as well as long term appreciation. Currently comparable condos at the nearby Marriott Los Suenos resort command rental rates of $350 daily, not to mention a resale price of over $650,000. Do the math!

If you want to mix business with pleasure (with a low initial investment as well), a second alternative is "fractional ownership" of a luxury ocean view condo. The best way to do this is to invest in the "preferred stock" of a company which owns and operates several condos units with your stock dividend paid out as either cash or converted into 2 weeks of fun in the sun ! Preferred stock shares in the Villas Del Pacifico luxury condos are currently $25,000 and it's your choice each year to generate income or enjoy the sun and surf! (www.delpacifico.net)

If you simply want to invest in the Costa Rican land boom without the hassles of home or condo ownership , an innovative concept you might want to explore is a "land banking" partnership to acquire beachfront acreage and large farms in the path of current development. Designed as an "entry investment" with a low initial participation of $25,000, Costa Rican land banking partnership will invest approximately 70% in Costa Rica and will also have positions in the emerging markets of Nicaragua, Panama and Belize. (www.delpacifico.net)

It's not too late ! The Costa Rican real estate boom is just starting. Depending on your preference, you can choose between owning "bricks and mortar" in a top quality real estate projects such as Del Pacifico or simply owning an interest in a Costa Rican land banking partnership. Even better, you might also be able to put your pre-tax IRA dollars to work riding this mounting wave. The combination of the mounting buzz about Costa Rica, and the ease and flexibility of investing makes for a very compelling investment, especially when your alternative is just another mutual fund being flogged by a stock broker.

Intrigued? And want to find out more? As a special offer to readers of this article. Mention you saw it in *The New Golden Door to Retirement and Living in Costa Rica* and you can receive a free copy of our latest report on Central American investing *"The Costa Rica Report"* by sending an email to **CostaReport@CostaReit.com**.

Barry Strudwick is an investment advisor and real estate developer serving an international client base from his offices in Maryland and Costa Rica. For more information contact him at **Barry @noload.com** or call **(410) 727-6444**.

Disadvantages: Although mutual funds have more built-in safeguards than regular stocks, they are still subject to fluctuations in the market.

finding Work

Foreigners can only work when they are legal residents depending on the type ogf residency. They don't need a work permit. The only exception to this rule is when you can do a job a Costa Rican is unqualified to do. In this case, you can obtain a work permit (see Chapter 4). However, jobs that will qualify you for a work permit are very scarce. If you do obtain a work permit, it must be renewed annually. *Pensionados*, *Rentistas* and foreigners without permanent residency may only own a company, invest or start a business. If you have questions about work permits, questions may be answered by contacting the Immigration Department at 011-(506) 220-1860.

We have some discouraging news for those living on small pensions and hoping to supplement their income with a part or full-time job or for others who need to work just to keep busy. Finding work can be difficult, but it is not impossible. In the first place, it is not easy for a Costa Rican, not to mention foreigners who do not speak fluent Spanish, to find permanent work.

An American working at a private highschool

If you are one of the few foreigners who have mastered Spanish, you will probably have a fair chance of finding work in tourism or some other related field. However, your best bet may be to find employment with a North American firm doing business in Costa Rica. The best-paying jobs are with multinational corporations.

It is best to contact one of these companies before moving to Costa Rica. Depending on your qualifications, you may be able to find a job as a salesman, an executive or a representative.

When local companies hire foreigners, they are generally looking for a solid educational background and an entrepreneurial spirit that some companies find lacking in Costa Ricans. It helps to have a degree from a well-known U.S. university, preferably an MBA.

Even if you know little or no Spanish, you have a chance of finding work as an English teacher at a language institute in San José. Do not expect to earn more than a survival salary from one of these jobs because the minimum wage in Costa Rica is low. Working as a full-time language instructor will not bring you more than a few hundred dollars monthly.

As supplemental income or busywork, this is fine, but you won't make a living given the kind of life style to which you are probably accustomed. If you can find work at a private bilingual school, you can earn over $1000 a month. The competition for these jobs is very stiff, preference is given to bilingual Costa Ricans and most foreigners hang on to these coveted positions.

There is some work available for English speakers in the sportsbook industry. However, some sportsbooks may be forced to move to other countries because of a change in regulation here.

Try putting one of your skills to use by providing some service to the large expatriate community in Costa Rica. Everyone has a talent or specialty they can offer. For example, if you are a writer, journalist or have experience in advertising, you might look for work at one of Costa Rica's two English language newspapers. Unfortunately, if you are a retired professional such as a doctor or lawyer, you cannot practice in Costa Rica because of certain restrictions, but you can offer your services as a consultant to other foreigners and retirees.

As if finding work were not hard enough in Costa Rica, a work permit or residency is required before foreigners can work legally. Labor laws are very strict and the government does not want foreigners taking jobs away from Costa Ricans. In theory, companies are not allowed to have more than 10 percent foreign labor. It is actually much lower in practice. You are only allowed to work if you can perform specialized work that a

Costa Rican cannot do. However, many foreigners work for under-the-table pay without a work permit.

If you do not seek remuneration, you can always find volunteer work to keep yourself busy. Volunteer work is legal, so you will not need a work permit or run the risk of being deported for working illegally.

Starting a Business

Of a total 115 countries, Costa Rica came in first in Latin America and ninth in the world with respect to nations offering greatest commercial freedom and protection for private business, according to "Freedom and Development," a Chilean research institute.

As a foreigner, you can invest in Costa Rica and even start your own business with only some restrictions.

If you plan to go into business here it is very important to be aware of the local consumer market in order to succeed. Most of the country's purchasing power is located in the Central Valley. A total of 75% of the country's population reside in the central provinces of San José, Alajuela, Heredia and Cartago. Around 60% of the population is less than 30 years old. Intelligent business people will try to meet the needs of this group.

Casey Halloran, pictured with his assistant, founded a successful Internet-based company.

You may also think about targeting tourists and upper-class Costa Ricans. There is a wealth of opportunities available in tourist-related businesses. Upper-class *ticos* have a large disposable income and the greatest purchasing power. They do not mind spending a little more on good quality products. Just look at their expensive designer clothing , their expensive imported automobiles, and many palatial homes. The majority of the country's middle-class consumers values are now more akin to their U.S. counterparts. You can see this starting to take hold with a number of shopping malls being built around the Central Valley and the popularity of stores like Radio Shack and megawarehouses like PriceSmart and Hipermás. Middle and upper lower class Costa Ricans seem to want all of the goodies so much that sales of cellular telephones have temporarily exceeded the availability of available phone lines.

One group to target is the lucrative foreign residents market. There are around 50,000 full-time foreigners living in Costa Rica. All you have to do is look for a product to fill their needs. Most yearn for some hard -to-find-products from home and would rather buy them in Costa Rica than go to the U.S. to shop.

Costa Rica is ripe for innovative foreigners willing to take a risk and start businesses that have not previously existed. Start-up costs for small businesses are less than in the U.S. or Canada. Many of the same types of businesses which have been successful in the U.S. and Canada will work if researched correctly. There is definitely a need for these types of businesses. You just have to do your homework and explore the market. Be aware that not everything that works in the U.S. will work here. Also you may have to adapt your idea due to the vagaries of the local market and different purchasing power. Don't get any grandiose ideas since the country has only around 4 million people. You cannot expect to market products on a large scale as in the North America.

Costa Rica's local artisans make scores of beautiful handcrafted products such as furniture, pottery and cloth. With so many choices a smart person can find something to sell back home.

These are some potential business opportunities worth exploring: building and selling of small homes for middle class Costa Ricans or foreigners an import-export business, desktop publishing, computer services and support, U.S. franchises, importing new foods, specialty bookstores, restaurants and bars, an auto body and paint shop, consulting, or specialty shops catering to North Americans and upper-class Costa Ricans.

Costa Ricans love anything novel from America. There are many stores selling both new and used trendy U.S.-style clothing. Costa Rican

Success Stories in Costa Rica
By Chris Howard

A Coffee Baron

Cafe Britt was founded by American Steve Aronson. Today the company has gone international with their many products available all over the world. They grow, roast and sell some of the best "Mountain Grown" coffeee in the world. They even make a cafe liqueur. Their coffee farm tour is one of the most entertaining half-days you will spend in Costa Rica. It takes place on a beautiful farm nestled in the verdant hills of Heredia. You will learn about the history of coffee, see how it is grown and purchase many interesting products in their gift shop at the conclusion of the tour.

A Service for Expats

About 10 years ago Jim Fendell realized the need for a fast reliable mail service as an alternative to the regular Costa Rican mail system. Thus Aerocasillas was born. Today they offer simiar services in Panama and several other countries in the region. Please see Chgapter 6 for more details about the history of this comapny and the services they offer.

A Company Which Protects Nature

In 1978 Michael Kaye the founded first white water tour company, Costa Rica Expeditions, when tourism was in its infancy. The company was started to help the sophisticated traveller explore Costa Rica - its flora and fauna, its people and culture, its wildlife and beautiful places. Their goal is to create unique travel experiences.

An American-Style School

Country Day School was started by American Woodson Brown around twenty years ago. The present campus is located in the hills of Escazú overlooking San José. You cant't beat the school's beautiful setting. The actual campus evolved from a few buildings into a huge complex which rivals any U.S. private school. The owner is a visionary who recognized the need for a first-rate U.S. type English school to cater to both the local and foreign population.

A Newspaper for Foreigners

Many years ago the late American journalist Richard Dyer founded TheTicoTimes newspaper. It has become Central America's leading independent weekly covering news, business, tourism, culture and developments in Costa Rica and Central America. The classified ad section is very complete and there is now an on-line version of the paper. Fifteen thousand copies are printed weekly with some being shipped overseas.

Bagels Anyone?

David Feingold is from Lexington, Massachusetts. A few years ago with his Costa Rican wife started Boston Bagel. After much experimentation with local ingedients they managed to develop the only authentic bagels in the country. His secrect for success is understanding the local economy. Today his two stores which sell an exotic variety of delicious bagles. His products can also be found in one of the local super market chains.

A Hotel Fit for a King

The dynamic trio of Americans John Emerson, Greg Ruzika and Englishman Tim Hodgsen run San Jose's most successful hotel. The owners spent a couple of years and a lot of money refurbishing the old building. Their hard work and persistence has really paid off.

Today the hotel boasts the highest occupancy rate in the country. It is a haven for fishermen, tourists, expatriates and many local characters. The Blue Marlin Bar on the first floor is the most successful operation in Central American. At night the place really heats up. There is also a casino, travel agency and all-night restaurant on the first floor.

A Place to Learn Languages

American David Kaufman is the founder of Conversa, Costa Rica's oldest and most successful language schools. David had a Masters Degree in linguistics and served in the Peace Corps in the Dominican Republic. At his school's two campuses Spanish is taught to foreigners and English to Costa Ricans. Please see more about Conversa in Chapter 3.

The Local Tax Man

Gordon F. is a former U.S.tax attorney from California. Currently he helps foreigners with business matters, tax returns and other related matters. His services are very high in demand due to his expertise. In addition, he and his wife run Posada Quijote in the Bello Horizonte hills section of Escazú. The view is just spectacular. This small hotel is in a beautiful Spanish colonial home which has been totally renovated and exquisitely decorated.

teenagers dress like their counterparts in the States and even watch MTV. U.S. fast food restaurants like Taco Bell, Burger King, Pizza Hut and McDonald's are extremely popular. Real estate speculation can be lucrative if you have the know-how and capital.

Common Business Sense In Costa Rica

It is important to keep in mind that running a business in Costa Rica is not like managing a business in the United States dur to unusual labor laws, the Costa Rican work ethic, and the Costa Rican way of doing business.

In order for a foreigner to own a business, a Costa Rican corporation or *Sociedad Anónima* must be formed (see the section titled "Taxes" in the last chapter).

If you do choose to establish your own business, keep in mind that you can be limited to managerial or supervisory duties and will have to hire Costa Ricans to do the bulk of everyday work. We also recommend that you do a thorough feasibility study. Spend at least a few months thoroughly analyzing its potential. Do not assume that what works in the U.S. will work in Costa Rica.

Long-time Costa Rican resident, Mark, runs a succesful travel bookstore in downtown San José.

Check out restrictions and the tax situation. And most important, choose a business in which you have a vast prior experience. It's much more difficult to familiarize yourself with a new type of business in a foreign country.

Remember, a trustworthy partner or manager can mean the difference in success and failure. Make sure you choose a partner with local experience. Do not trust anyone until you know him or her and have seen them perform in the work place.

You will be doomed to failure if you intend to be an absentee owner. We know of someone who founded an English book distribution business which initially did very well.

However, they moved back to the States and put a couple of employees in charge and everything eventually fell apart: sales began to lag, money went uncollected, checks began to bounce, expenses were unaccounted for and incompetent salesmen were hired. Their potentially successful business just could not be run from abroad.

You have to stay on top of your business affairs. At times it is hard to find reliable labor and the bureaucracy can be stifling. If you have a business with employees, be aware of your duties and responsibilities as an employer. To avoid problems, know what benefits you need to pay in addition to salary to avoid problems. Remember the more employees you have, the more headaches.

In case things get rough, be sure you have enough money in reserve, in case of an emergency. You should have an ample reserve of capital to fall back on during the initial stage of your business.

Newcomers should not count on obtaining financing in Costa Rica for a new business. If you do become a resident you may be able to obtain some type of financing. Neophytes should learn not just the language but also the rules of the game.

Talk to people, especially the "oldtimers," who have been successful in business and learn from them. Profit from their mistakes, experiences and wisdom. Do not rush into anything that seems too good to be true. Trust your intuition and gut feeling at times. However, the best strategy and rule of thumb is, "Test before you invest."

Newcomers find themselves seduced by the country's beauty and friendly people and are often lured into business and investment opportunities that seem to good to be true, and often are.

When it comes to making money in Costa Rica, it has been said, "The best way to leave Costa Rica with a million dollars is to bring two." In the case of some foreigners this statement is true. During the time we have lived in Costa Rica, we have seen many foreigners succeed and fail in business ventures. About three in ten foreigners succeed in business in Costa Rica. There are few success stories and a lot of failures, in areas as diverse as bars, restaurants, car-painting shops, language schools, real estate, tourism, and bed & breakfasts to name a few. People have impossible dreams about what business will be like in Costa Rica. It is a gigantic mistake to assume that success comes easily in Costa Rica. Initially starting any business usually takes more time and more money. Also, many unforseen problems are surely to arise.

If you decide to purchase an existing business, make sure that it is not over-priced. Try to find out the owner's real motives for selling it. Make sure you are not buying a "pink elephant." Ask to see the books and talk to clients if you can. To ferret out a good deal, look for someone who is desperate to sell their business. Check the newspapers and ask everyone you know if they know of someone selling a business. Finally, make sure there are not law suits, debts, unpaid creditors or liens against the business.

There are some benefits to investing in certain businesses in Costa Rica. As we mention in Chapter 4, you can obtain Costa Rican Residency by investing in tourism or a reforestation project. Also, part of your profits can be sheltered in your corporation.

After reading the above information, if you still have questions or are confused, we advise you to consult a knowledgeable Costa Rican attorney for further information. If you plan to invest or do business in a Spanish-speaking country you should definitely purchase Wiley's *English-Spanish Dictionary*, Barron's *Talking Business in Spanish,* or Passport Books *Just Enough Business Spanish*. All of these guides contain hundreds of useful business terms and phrases.

Beware of the So-called Experts

In Costa Rica the word "expert" is sometimes used very loosely in the expatriate community, on numerous websites, English publications and on business cards. Don't get me wrong there are some highly qualified English speakers here. Nevertheless one should be extremely careful when dealing with foreigners who consider themselves experts in Costa Rica. J ust because a person was a professional in his home country may not qualify him to be an expert here. Some foreigners consider themselves experts just because they have lived here for a few years. Remember anyone can build a website and say anything about themselves.

Many naive newcomers have been taken advantage by other foreigners who call themselves 'experts' who are really incompetent imposters. So, be careful! We know a couple of people who have even lost their life savings because they put their fairs in the hands of an "expert".

What I suggest is that if you happen to come into contact with any foreigner who calls him self an "expert", is to ask do all of the following:

(1) Ask for references from other foreigners who have used the experts services. If your expert won't give you any references you will know immediately you are being duped or sold shoddy second rate services.

(2) Ask how long the person has lived in Costa Rica. If they have been here for under 10 years be careful.

(3) Find out what the person's educational background was when they lived in their home country and if they have any formal training in the Latin American culture, studies or foreign investments. Just because a person was a plumber, an engineer, doctor a policeman in the U.S. or Canada does not qualify him to give professional advice in Costa Rica.

(4) Beware of colorful well-designed web sites which the so-called experts build to attract naive foreigners.

(5)) Most important find out if the person is truly fluent in Spanish. There is no way a person a have expertise unless he/she can communicate with the locals and understand all the nuances of the local culture and language. Beware there are many foreigners who say they speak fluent Spanish with a vocabulary of only a couple of hundred words. I have run into many of them in my 22 years here.

The Best Ways to Make Money in Costa Rica

Until 2003, a large number of Americans and Canadians living in Costa Rica earned "high returns" on their money by investing in private finance companies. In general, these returns in dollars ranged between 13% to 42%, depending on the duration and amount of the investment.

Some foreigners had been in these programs for many years with no complaints and never a single problem. The most successful of these unregulated companies operated for twenty years without missing a single payment to its creditors. Other companies sprung up, but they were basically riding the success and credibility of the company with the longest track record.

Unfortunately this bonanza came to an abrupt halt with a major change in the financial climate of the country. The private banking industry could not compete with these private finance companies. So, with the help of their ally the Costa Rican government they managed to surreptitiously undermine all unregulated investment in the country.

Let me tell you a little about these finance companies and why they were able to pay you more on your dollar accounts than the average bank. This will come as a surprise to most of you, but in fact, the market interest rate for dollar accounts is much, much higher in other countries than what you may be getting from the banks in your country.

The loans these private finance companies made were considerably less risk than the loans made by many banks in countries where the banks are heavily regulated by the government. Government regulated banks rely more on government insurance for their loan security rather than on sound business judgment when making loans. I am sure you have read about the numerous bank frauds in the United States. Who ends up paying the bill? You do, with high income taxes and the low interest rates paid on your savings. Somebody always has to pay.

The high rates the companies were able to receive on making very secure loans in dollars, have more to do with supply and demand for dollars in Central American countries. These countries have very high rates of devaluation in their local currency, and most businesses here need U.S. dollars to buy products from the United States, so there is a big business demand for U.S. dollars. Dollars are scarce here, so the private lending companies can get big returns making loans in U.S. dollars. Why, simple supply and demand. Big demand for U.S. dollars, small supply of U.S. dollars.

Why is it that local banks do not have much money? Would you put your money in a bank paying 7% per year if your local currency lost 20% per year in value against the dollar. Probably not. The result is that the banks do not have enough money to supply the credit demand of a healthy economy, such as Costa Rica. This means the banks here do not have the money to finance various types of short-term business loans. In addition, there is a lot of paper work and endless delays when trying to borrow money from a bank in Costa Rica. So where did some people and companies go to borrow money? They went to private lending companies who had the money and were easy to work with. A couple private lending companies had been operating for decades in Costa Rica and were very, very profitable. Costa Rica is very unique, since it has an extremely stable government, no military, very low wages, one of the highest standards of living in

Central and South America, but very little money in the banks with which to work .

Private lending companies were not government-regulated institutions. They loaned money to large Central American corporations and businesses. In Costa Rica, they paid excellent monthly returns on making short-term loans to businesses that put up more than enough collateral to pay the loan amount several times over.

Most businesses here own their buildings and land free of debt.   So the private lending companies never needed to loan more than 20% to 30% of the liquidation value of the collateral the borrowers put up, which is typically land and buildings. Consequently, the private lending companies were able to very profitably pay their private clients very good rates of return on their deposits.

For example, a large coffee farm had to put up a $10,000,000 coffee farm as collateral to borrow $200,000 at 6% per month for two or three months. Typically, at the end of their harvest season, they would run out of money. So once per year they would borrow to pay their employees and expenses until the coffee beans were sold . Needless to say, they always pay the loan off. Even if something went wrong and they did not get paid for their coffee beans, they would sell off part of the farm to pay off the loan rather than loose the entire farm.

Large department stores here would also borrow dollars from these private lending companies at 6% per month to buy electrical home appliances and other products from the United States.

When a big company negotiates a big loan from a bank here it usually takes 2 to 3 months after the loan approval for the bank to pay out the money. In the meantime, the big company would borrow from a private lending company at 6% per month until the bank paid out the money on their approved loan.

Factories here must give their retail store customers terms of 60 to 90 days to pay for products shipped. Because the stores need 60 to 90 days to sell the products and collect the money from their customers. Most factories were happy to pay 6% per month to get their money sooner so they could manufacture more products. They simply add this cost to the products they ship to the retail stores. Who pays? The consumer does.

However, the days of these unregulated high-yield investments all came to an end due to the Costa Rican government's change of policy.

Fortunately, now there are even more secure investments available in Costa Rica. The hot investment area is real estate on Costa Rica's spectacular Pacific Coast. According to a recent article in the country's, financial daily, *La Republica*, property in the Central Pacific coast has risen 250% in value over the last six years. Furthermore, with the paving of two new sections of the Costal Highway, the driving time between the country's capital, San José and the nearest beach resorts will be reduced in half. The first stage of the new highway will link Ciudad Colón in the Central Valley to the town of Orotina near the Central Pacific Coast. The other section of new highway will link the towns of Quepos and Dominical to the south. Furthermore, there are plans for a major marina in Quepos, a water park with artificial waves between Quepos and Dominical and a new international airport in the town of Palmares. All of this will combine to make result estate values will soar even more.

As an example of this boom, the Marriot Corporation built its crown jewel of Central America "Los Sueños Resort" and pre-sold 50 condominium units of 2,000 square feet each for $250,000. The next year they sold another 50 at $350,000 and this year's upper-end units sold between $450,000 to $850,000. And there is a waiting list!

South of Jaco Beach at the **Del Pacifico** development, the owners say investments will yield at least 25% to 30% in yearly appreciation. Obviousy this area is *the* place to find secure investments with a high rate of return. Liquidity is not a problem since land is in demand.

Let us look at why this real estate boom is happening. The simple fact that almost every bit of coastline worldwide is becoming over- crowded, over-priced and more scare contributes to a high level of interest Costa Rica's beach areas. The U.S. National Association of Realtors says Americans are buying second homes in record numbers, thus driving up the cost of vacation homes everywhere in the country. A recent newspaper article stated one in every seven people in the Untied States now lives in areas bordering the coast. This trend is driving the great migration of Baby Boomer. As a result, land in prime sunbelt areas of the U.S. have become prohibitively expensive and hard to find. This is not the case in Costa Rica.

Savvy people with a thirst for adventure, fun and profitable investments are now taking a closer look at Costa Rica. Actually, an investment in real estate in Costa Rica's Central Pacific is much better than an investment in California real estate 30 years ago.

Along Costa Rica's Central Pacific Coast you will find wide white and dark sand beaches, rocky outcrop and clear water set against a tropical backdrop of primary rain forest. The beaches are reminiscent of those in California and Hawaii, but you can buy here for one-tenth the cost. For a very reasonable price you may purchase a couple of acres of land with an ocean view. You can have a spectacular home perched on a hill, complete with custom tiles, and finished in mahogany, teak and precious woods you never knew existed. The geography looks like California or Hawaii years ago.

Getting in before the crowd has always been the secret to making a lot of money with real estate investments. People who took a chance and invested in real estate in beach property in California, Hawaii and some parts of Florida were ahead of their time. They saw opportunity where others saw nothing. They took well-planned risks and were paid handsomely for their investments and created better lives for themselves and their families. What really gets people excited about Costa Rica is that it offers some of the most undervalued prime beach real estate in the world. As the rest of the world finds out about Costa Rica, prices will only go up.

By the way you can legally use your pre-tax IRA to purchase real estate in Costa Rica. The company listed below can help you with this. Depending on your particular situation, they also have the contacts to help you obtain partial financing in Costa Rica.

To find out about these exciting investment opportunities contact: **Retirement and Vacation Properties** at E-mail: **robert@costaricaretirementvacationproperties.com** or **costaricaretirementproperties@yahoo.com** or call toll free from the U.S. or Canada **1-888-581-1786**. You may view some of these incredible properties at: **www.primecostaricaproperty.com**.

Common Business Lingo

A pagos	Paymemts, buy on time
Abogado, Licenciado	Lawyer
Acciones	Stocks
Accionista	Stockholder, Shareholder
Activo	Asset
Agrimensor	Surveyor
Al contado	For cash
Anualidad	Annuity
Año Fiscal	Fiscal year
Anticipo, prima, depósito	Down payment
Arrendamiento	Lease
Autenticar	Notarize
Avalúo	Appraisal
Certificado de depósito	C.D.s.
Cheque	Check
Cláusula	Clause
Comprador	Buyer
Contrato	Contract
Corredor	Stockbroker, real estate broker
Costo	Cost
Cuenta	Bank account
Cuenta Corriente	Checking account
Déficit	In the red, deficit
Depreciación	Depreciation
Deuda	Debt
Divisas	Foreign exchange (hard currency)
El Justo Valor del Mercado	Fair market value
Embargar, Enganchar	Attach assets
En efectivo	Pay in cash
Escritura	Deed
Estado de Cuenta	Bank statment, statement
Facilidades de Pago	Payment plan
Fideicomiso	Trust

Financiamiento	Financing
Gastos	Costs, expenses
Giro	Money order
Hipoteca	Mortgage
Impuestos	Taxes
Intereses	Interest
Impuestos Prediales	Property taxes
Inversiones	Investments
Lote	Lot
Montar, Poner Un Negocio	Start a business
Negocios	Business
Notario	Notary
Pagaré	Promisory note
Parcela	Parcel of land
Plazo	Term, period of time
Precio	Price
Préstamo	Loan
Principal	Principal
Propiedad	Property
Registro	Record of ownership
Renta	Income
Rentabilidad	Profitability
Saldo	Balance of an account
Seguros	Insurance
Socio	Partner
Sociedad	Corporation
Subcontratar	To subcontract, farm out
Superávit	In the black, surplus of capital
Tasa de interés	Interest
Testaferro	Person who lends a name to a business
Terreno	Land
Traspaso	Transfer
Timbres Fiscales	Tax stamps
Valor	Value
Vendedor	Seller

RED TAPE

Dealing With Bureaucracy

Just as in the rest of Latin America, Costa Rica is plagued by a more inefficient bureaucratic system than is the U. S. This situation is exaggerated by the Latin American temperament, the seemingly lackadaisical attitude of most bureaucrats, and the slower pace of life. The concept of time is much different from that in the U. S. or Canada. When someone says they'll do something *"ahorita"* (which literally means right now), it will take from a few minutes to a week, or maybe forever. It is not unusual to wait in lines for hours in banks and government offices and experience unnecessary delays.

This situation is very frustrating for foreigners who are used to fast, efficient service. It can be especially irritating if you don't speak Spanish well. Since very few people working in offices speak English, and most North Americans speak little else, it is advisable to study basic Spanish. However, if language is an insurmountable obstacle at first, use a competent bilingual lawyer or ask the **Association of Residents of Costa Rica** (ARCR) to help you deal with Costa Rica's bureaucracy or "red tape jungle" as it is known. Above all, learn to be patient and remember that you can get the best results if you do not push or pressure people. Try having a good sense of humor and using a smile. You will be surprised at the results.

You shouldn't despair if Costa Rica's "bureaucrazy" gets you down. For a small fee you can get a person (*gavilán)* to wait in line for you while you run errands or make better use of your valuable time.

A few words of caution—there are some individuals, (*choriceros* in popular jargon), who pass themselves off as lawyers or who befriend you and offer to help you with red tape, claiming they can short-cut the bureaucratic system because of their contacts. As a general rule, avoid such individuals or you will lose valuable time, run the risk of acquiring forged documents, most certainly lose money, and experience indescribable grief.

Since bribery and pay offs are common in most Latin American countries and government employees are underpaid, some people advise paying them extra money to speed up paper work or circumvent normal channels. This bribery is illegal and not recommended for foreigners; they can be deported for breaking the law. However, in some instances it may be necessary to pay extra money to get things done. Use your own discretion in such matters. A tip here and there for a small favor can accelerate bureaucratic delays. We have a friend who was in the process of getting all of the required paper work to marry a Costa Rican. He was in a hurry and did not have time to waste. He went to the National Registry to get his future wife's birth certificate and was told he would have to wait a week. So, he passed out a little extra money and had it the next morning.

United States
Embassy Services

Everyone planning to live, retire or do business in Costa Rica should know that the American Embassy (in the San José suburb of Pavas) can help with Social Security and Veterans benefits, notarizing documents, obtaining new U. S. passports, reporting lost or stolen passports, obtaining a marriage license, registering births of your children, registering to vote, complying with Selective Service registration requirements, private mail service, reporting deaths of U.S. citizens abroad, and getting a U.S. visa for your spouse (if you choose to marry a Costa Rican). They also assist in obtaining absentee ballots for U.S. elections and getting U.S. income tax forms and information. However, if you get into any legal trouble in Costa Rica, do not expect help from the U.S. Embassy.

Social Security - in the past there were two ways of receiving your Social Security check if you lived abroad. You could have it sent directly to your P.O. box in Costa Rica through the U.S. Embassy. The only problem with this method was that it the checks did not arrive until almost the third week of the month. The other way was to have your check directly deposited

A Trip Through Costa Rica's Bureaucratic Maze
by Loyd Newton

It's always an adventure in paradise when you have to deal with the bureaucracy in any of it's many forms. Fortunately, it's not something I have to do very often. I've been in Costa Rica for a little over two years now and things are starting to expire and renewal times coming near. My drivers license was due to expire at the end of this week so Monday I went down to the offices in San Jose on Calle 7 to renew it.

I parked my car in one of the public parking lots and they conveniently had a sign posted with the requirements for new and renewed licenses. Besides money, I needed to get a doctors exam for my renewal. I didn't even make it halfway from the parking lot to the drivers license office when I was waved into a doctors office. The exam took about 5 minutes which consisted of answering a few questions and reading the eye-chart above the green line. The doctor also mentioned he had a private practice near my home town and handed me a few business cards to take with me.

At the office I discovered a line that went out the door. Luckily for me, the line that stretched out the door was for new licenses. The one for renewals was doubled around the inside of the offices. I noticed a lot of people armed with newspapers for the long wait. My helper (interpreter, guide, etc.) went to get us a newspaper while I started my hour long wait in line. The people in line near me were very friendly and immediately started up conversations. The man ahead of me spoke English pretty well and was a fountain of information about the process. So instead of reading a newspaper, I spent my hour in line conversing with the ticos and the time went by quickly.

Once I got to the head of the line, I showed my doctors certificate and old license to the man at the first stop. He was very concerned about the fact that my residency card was expiring in June but said I could renew my license. Just use my passport he said and don't show them the residency card. Well, to be honest, I figured out what he was saying at the time but didn't understand what he meant until I hit the last stop.

I took my papers, got back in another line for the bank. There I paid 10,000 colones for my 5 year license. I told them the sign said it was only 4000 colones but they explained that was for the 2 year license. Sounded good to me, so I took my receipt and got into another line for the cameras. After about 15 minutes, I made it to the head of the line and went up to have my photo taken for the new license. When I got there, I handed over my papers and receipts and the man asked for my *cedula*.....mistake, because I gave it to him. He took one look at it and said he would not take my photo. He took me back to the start, "do not pass go, do not collect license". There the man asked me why I should him my cédula and I explained because he asked me for it. He told me, that the man would not take my photo or give me the license because my cédula was expiring in two months. This didn't make any sense to me, since I don't even need a residency to get a license here....perhaps it

When people get a little excited here, they talk very fast so I was having a hard time understanding what they were telling me. My helper had gotten separated between the last stop and the return to go. Fortunately, a *tica* came over and translated for me. There are some wonderfully helpful people here! While they were explaining the man's reason for not taking my photo, another photographer stepped up and said he would do it. So they took me around to another camera station, and within 5 minutes I had my new drivers license.

A low level bureaucrat that likes to have little power or just doesn't like gringos decided that a *cédula* that expires in 2 months was a big problem. Fortunately for me, kinder hearted people stepped in and took care of things. "I have always depended upon the kindness of strangers." So I left the place with mixed feelings....distaste for the petty bureaucrat and the hitch after over an hour of waiting and happiness that the good *ticos* and *ticas* won out and I could finish business that day.

I felt so good at not having anything else to do this week, that I went out and played 18 holes of golf today at Valle del Sol. First time I've played golf in a year so I gave up keeping score on the first hole. A great day to be outside and enjoy the weather though so I thoroughly enjoyed it though my golf game needs a lot of work. Guess I'll just have to get out once a week and practice on it.

Pura vida,
Loyd Newton

into your account. Now things are much simpler. After August 2003, your Social Security payments may be deposited electronically to your account in a Costa Rican bank by the 3rd of each month. Banco Nacional, Banco de Costa Rica, Banco Interfin and Citibank offer direct deposit of Social Security checks. All you have to do is complete a form and make sure it gets sent to the Federal Benefits Unit of the US Embassy. Call the embassy at 220-3050 if you have any questions. Your bank will charge $6.00 for this convenient monthly service.

Passports - Effective in 2002, American citizens residing or traveling abroad who need a U.S. passport are issued the latest, state-of-the-art passport incorporating a digitalized photo image and other innovative security features. U.S. Embassies and Consulates will send the applications to domestic U.S. passport facilities. This increases processing time at some Embassies and Consulates, but it ensures that American citizens receive secure documents in a timely manner. Therefore, American citizens are encouraged to apply early for renewal of expiring passports.

U.S. embassies and Consulates issue passports in emergency situations. Such passports have limited validity and cannot be extended. Bearers are required to exchange their limited validity passports for full-validity digitalized photo passports upon completion of their emergency travel, either through passport facilities in the U.S. or U.S. embassies abroad.

First-Time Passport Applicants - To apply for a U.S. passport, a native-born, U.S. citizen must present a certified copy of his or her birth certificate, two passport photos measuring 2 inches by two inches, (color or black and white with a light background), photo ID and the applicable fee. You will need to present the certificate of naturalization together with the photos, a photo ID, and the fees.

Passport Renewal - You will need your current passport as evidence of citizenship and two passport photos measuring two inches by two inches (color or black and white with a light background). To be eligible you must have been issued a U.S. passport in your name within the past 12 years. There are different fees for adults and for those under the age of 16.

Lost or Stolen Passport - You will need to report the loss of your passport to the police and obtain a copy of the police report. In addition to the two passport photos, you will need to present proof of identity and proof of U.S. citizenship. The proof of identity could be any photo ID like a U.S. driver's license. Proof of citizenship could be a certified, sealed copy of your U.S. birth certificate and/or old cancelled U.S. passport.

Report of a Birth Abroad - Children being registered as U.S. citizenss must be brought to the Embassy or Consulate by the U.S. citizen parent along with the following documents:

(1) Child's Costa Rican birth certificate may be obtained from the Civil Registry or *Registro Civil*.

(2) Evidence of parent's U.S. citizenship. This may be in the form of original U.S. birth certificates, U.S. passports, Certificates of Citizenship, or Naturalization Certificates. Military IDs are not proof of U.S. citizenship.

(3) Parents' marriage certificate.

(4) Evidence of dissolutions of previous marriages. If either parent has been previously married, submit original divorce decrees or death certificates.

(5) If only one parent is a U.S. citizen there are additional requirements. Please check with the embassy.

How to Become a Legal Resident of Costa Rica

People find Costa Rica attractive and want to live in the country for a myriad of reasons: good year-round weather, tired of the rat race and hustle-bustle, a new start in life, inexpensive living and retirement, tax benefits, the country's low-cost health care system, start a business or invest, learn Spanish, separation or divorce, enjoy the country's large expatriate community and even to find companionship. Whatever your motives may be for wanting to move to Costa Rica, there are a number of ways to remain in the country on a long-term basis.

Tourists from North America and many countries in Europe may remain legally in the country for three months without having to apply for legal residency. You may own property, start a business or make investments with no more than a tourist visa.

We know many Americans, Canadians and other foreigners who started businesses as tourists. If you plan to reside in Costa Rica full-time, however, one of Costa Rica's residency programs will appeal to you.

Several residency categories permit you to retain your current citizenship and obtain long-term legal status in Costa Rica. They are *pensionado*, *rentista*, and *inversionista* (resident investor). Which program you choose depends on your needs and financial position. Becoming a legal resident will by no means affect your U.S. or Canadian citizenship.

In March of 1992, a change in the *pensionado* law eliminated many tax privileges retirees had enjoyed since the program started in 1964.

Under the old system foreigners with official *pensionado* or *rentista* (permanent retiree) status, were required to live in the country four months a year. They were entitled to the following perks: residency without immigration hassles, all the privileges of Costa Rican citizens except the right to vote and work for hire, the right to import one of each of the major appliances such as refrigerator, stove, microwave, television, washer and dryer, and many unlimited personal household goods free of taxes.

Pensionados could import a new car every five years duty-free, provided it was worth less than $16,000.00. In 1992, low taxes on imported cars and duty-free household goods were eliminated. Since then, all *pensionados* have to pay taxes on their automobiles and household goods the same as ordinary Costa Rican citizens do.

Said benefits were really taken away because everyone saw that they were unconstitutionally giving something to foreigners that Costa Ricans could not have themselves. Incentives will always be used to attract people to less attractive countries, but Costa Rica does not have that problem.

Despite this law, Costa Rica is still an attractive retirement haven. People continue to flock to Costa Rica because of its high quality of life, peaceful atmosphere, political stability, excellent climate, friendly people who like foreigners, excellent business environment and natural beauty. In fact, Costa Rica has more American residents per capita than any other country in the world. They can't all be wrong!

The Costa Rican government has reduced taxes on some cars and other imported goods, making them affordable for most Costa Ricans as well as foreign residents. Consequently the need for a tax- exoneration program has been eliminated.

If it is absolutely necessary to have an automobile, you can bring a car from the States. You can also go to Golfito, the free port in southern Costa Rica, and buy a stove, refrigerator or other appliance without paying high import duties.

Now let's look at the requirements and specific documents that you will need to present to the Costa Rican government if you choose to apply for the *pensionado* or *rentista* categories.

A **Pensionado** is someone who lives on a pension (a U.S. Social Security check or permanent retirement program). A husband and wife cannot combine their pensions, but the wife can live under the husband's *pensionado* status or visa versa. The individual applying can combine pensions to achieve the total required. If the recipient of the pension dies, the spouse can retain *pensionado* status if the pension is inherited. Some paper work, naturally, is involved.

Here are the requirements for this category:

Pensionado

1. A lifetime income of at least $600 a month generated outside of Costa Rica. Social Security recipients need a certification that can be done at the U.S. Embassy in Costa Rica.
2. A signed letter confirming that you will receive this money in Costa Rica. This is not needed if issued by the U.S. Embassy.
3. A letter from a C.P.A. stating that you will receive at least $600 for life if the pension comes from a company's pension plan.
4. If the money comes from a private company, two letters from bank officials showing that your company is financially sound and that the pension plan has been in existence for at least 20 years.
5. A detailed account of your company's pension plan or a yearly corporate report..

As a *pensionado* you are obligated to exchange $7,200 ($600 per month) a year for *colones* at a government bank. You need proof of this to update your file. If you cannot prove that you converted enough money during the year, you can lose your status. You also have to renew your *pensionado* I.D. card every two years ($100) and reside in the country for at least four months yearly (not necessarily consecutively). As a *pensionado* you can own and operate your own business but not work. As a *pensionado* you do not have to pay taxes on your income from outside Costa Rica. After two years you may change to permanent residency status.

Rentista is a category designed for those who are not retired or receive no government pension. To qualify for *rentista* status, you must have an income of $12,000 a year ($1,000 per month) coming from an investment or annuity outside of the country. As a *rentista*, a good way to do this is to buy a certificate of deposit for $60,000 from a Costa Rican bank that yields a monthly income of at least $1000 (from the capital).

As a *rentista* you must prove that this investment will be stable for at least five years. At the end of five years, you have to prove your source of income again or change to permanent residency after two years. Furthermore, every year as a *rentista* you have to prove that you changed $12,000 into *colones* and show your passport to prove you were in the country at least four months (not necessarily consecutively).

Why Belong to ARCR Administration and Association of Residents of Costa Rica?

By Ryan Piercy

- Assistance within Costa Rica before you arrive—advice, contacts and information.
- Recommendation of professional people you can trust, including lawyers, accountants and other specialists.
- Assistance with language.
- Service to establish residency, starting before you arrive.
- Assistance in getting acquainted with the country when you arrive.
- Recommendation of trustworthy real estate firms.
- Assistance with importation of cars, furniture and personal effects through our office.
- Assistance in locating various firms you may require who speak your language.
- Assistance with government agencies and departments, and an explanation of local rules and regulations.
- Assistance in establishing banking contacts.
- Advice about how various investments work in Costa Rica.
- Processing of resident government file updates and I.D. card renewals.
- Full insurance service through our office, including group plans for health, home and vehicles.
- Discount rates for Costa Rica social service medical insurance.
- Safe, inexpensive international mail and courier service.
- ARCR computers are on line with the computers at the Central Registry for property and vehicle title search and company name searches.
- Personal or company credit studies. ARCR computers are on line with the largest checking agencies.
- ARCR is on the Internet; ARCR receives and transmits E-mail for members.
- In the ARCR office, photocopy, fax, postal and document translation services are available to members.
- Hundreds of merchants and professional services provide discounts to members simply by showing the ARCR membership card.
- ARCR can arrange work permits for domestic help in Costa Rica.

- For provisional members who have overstayed their time as tourists, ARCR can arrange for their passport to be brought back to legal status.
- Membership includes subscription to the bimonthly ARCR magazine, "El Residente".
- Participation in the Residents Association's social and cultural events and the opportunity to meet other foreign residents.
- Travel and tourism assistance.
- Gold Key Plan—medical discount program with over 400 medical professionals and hospitals.
- Access to ACCR (Automobile Club of Costa Rica)—"AAA-USA". At special prices.
- Publications about Costa Rica are available from the ARCR office.
- Importing of pets.
- Funeral services.
- Newcomers Seminar   .

Who are we?
The ARCR Administration is an organization serving all types of foreign residents in Costa Rica, as well as people living abroad wishing to become residents of Costa Rica.

What do we do?
- Advocate for members before the Costa Rican government in matters of legal and human rights.
- Inform interested persons about procedures for becoming legal residents and to assist and advise them during the process.
- Organize social activities for members.
- Promote member participation in Costa Rican society and culture.

In Costa Rica:
ARCR Administration
Address: Apdo. 1191-1007
Centro Colón
San José, Costa Rica
Tel: (506) 233-8068
Fax: (506) 255-0061

WebSite:
http://www.casacanada.net/arcr
e-mail: arcr@casacanada.net
Street address:
Casa Canada, corner of Calle 40 and Avenida 4, San José.
Tico style address:
200 meters sur de Iberia, Paseo Colón .

As a *rentista* you can own and operate a business but not labour. The disadvantage to being a *rentista* is tying up your funds for over two years. Like *pensionado*, dependants are allowed.

We just heard of a new method for obtaining *rentista* status from one of our readers. He said, "If anyone has to get residency under the *rentista* category, they can do it by setting up a business in the States if they already do not have one. The business has to hold $60,000 which is to be dispersed over 5 years."

In brief, to qualify for *rentista* status you need:

1. An income of $1,000 per month for the next five years in Costa Rica.
2. Documentation that attests to the company or bank's solvency, if the income is from a foreign source.

Inversionista is another resident status for people who are not retired and want to invest in Costa Rica. If you have a lot of money to invest, this might be the best route to go. The government will grant residency under this category if you invest at least $50,000 in high priority projects like tourism, $100,000 in reforestation or $200,000 in any other business. No dependents can be included under this category.

The paperwork and requirements are similar to the other residency programs, but there are a few basic differences. Under this program you must reside in Costa Rica at least six months of every year (do not have to be consecutive) and live as a temporary resident for two years. After the initial two-year period you are eligible to become a permanent resident.

If you plan to start a project, additional paperwork such as a feasibility study and bank references may be needed. If you are going to get involved in tourism, you will need permission from the Costa Rican Tourism Institute (I.T.C.). When investing in an established company, you will have to show the company's books.

Since every circumstance is different and requirements change often, contact the Association of Residents of Costa Rica (ARCR) for a good lawyer to answer your questions.

The following documents are also required for *pensionado*, *rentista*, *inversionista* (resident investor), and all other types of residency in Costa Rica:

1. **Police Certificate** - from your local area stating that you have no record. (This document is good for only six months, so make sure it is current.) Required for applicant, spouse, and any children age 18 to 25.

2. **Birth Certificate** - Required for applicant, spouse and all dependent children (up to 18 years old or up to 25 if a university student - proof of enrollment is required).

3. **Marriage Certificate** - if applicable. Proof of divorce is not needed.

4. **Income Certificate** - for *Pensionados* and *Rentistas* (required only for the applicant). Please see the previous sections for specific details.

Note: all the above documents usually must be authenticated by a Costa Rican consulate or embassy located closest to the origin of the document (see the list for the nearest one in this chapter). The charge is $40 per document. The people at the consulate must affix stamps worth the amount to collect the money. If the documents do not have the required stamps, you cannot buy them in Costa Rica. Talk to the ARCR before processing documents.

Translation of Documents: Don't forget that all of these required documents must be translated from English into Spanish by an official translator. Translations from other languages to Spanish have to be either done by the Costa Rican consulate (no one else) in the country where the document was issued or in Costa Rica by an official translator for the specific language to Spanish. The Costa Rican government does not accept translation of the original language to English.

The formal application should have the following information: your mother's maiden name, full name, nationality, passport number, dependent's names, date of entry into Costa Rica, origin and amount of income, address in country of origin or Costa Rica, authentication by a notary public and corresponding stamps.

5. **Certified copy** of your entire passport. (Not stamped by consulate),

6. **Photos** : Twelve passport size photos—6 front views and 6 profiles.

If you meet the prerequisites for any of the residency categories and have gathered all the required documents, you are ready to apply for your chosen status.

Next, have the ARCR Administration or an attorney present your papers to the proper agency, which will process them in four months or so.

Renewing *cédulas*/Residency - In order to renew, you must change a total of $7,200 per year as a *pensionado* or $12,000 as a *rentista*. If you spend only part of the year here, you must still exchange this total amount. You can exchange it in as many increments as you like, be it once or 60 times a year. You must keep all exchange receipts for the total required. The *only* receipts accepted are those you get at a bank every time you change dollars to *colones*. You can use any Costa Rican state or private bank to change your money. The receipt *must* show your name, amount of dollars exchanged, rate of exchange, and amount of *colones* received. You can then change it all back into dollars if you wish.

You must renew before your *cédula* expires (*vencimiento*). We also recommend you show your exchange each year since it means less paperwork. This keep you correctly up to date at immigration.

If you want to avoid the many inconveniences of Costa Rica's giant "bureaucrazy" and save time and money in the long run, we suggest you join the **ARCR.**

The 1500-member ARCR association has been reorganized and revitalized. They now offers services to all legal residents in Costa Rica, not just the *pensionados*.

A provisional membership, which entitles you to all information and services, costs $100 yearly. Members with legal Costa Rica residency pay dues of $50 per year. Spouses and dependents of members may join for $10 per year as Associate members. ARCR offices are located at Casa Canada, two blocks south of Centro Colón on the corner of Avenida 4 and Calle 40. They will assist you when you need help applying for *pensionado* or *rentista* status for $735 for the primary applicant, *inversionista* or *representante* status for $1000 for the primary applicant. These prices are a good deal since many lawyers charge up to $2,000 and take much longer. Dependents documents cost $365 for a spouse and $155 per child.

The ARCR can also help in buying and selling cars, obtaining a Costa Rican driver's license (see chapter 8 for details), assisting with English to Spanish translations of any required documents or papers, and making sure your annual papers are up-to-date. The association can also notarize all your important documents, help with the renewal of your I.D. card or *cédula,* and help you obtain medical coverage with the Costa Rican Social Security System and the new supplemental coverage they now offer (see the section on medical care for details). Should you desire additional information, contact:

ARCR Administration
Apartado 1191-1007 Centro Colón
San José, Costa Rica
Call: 011-(506) 233-8068 or 221-2053 inside Costa Rica and
011-(506) 233-8068   outside the country. Fax 011-(506) 255-0061.
E-Mail: arcr@casacanada.net
Website: www.arca.net

Address in the U.S. for your convenience:

ARCR

SJO 170, P.O. Box 025723

Miami, Florida 33132

Note: Some of the requirements for Costa Rican Residency may be subject to change. It is highly avisable to check with the ARCR before applying.

Additional Methods of Obtaining Costa Rican Residency

As we mentioned in the last section, most of the *pensionado* program's privileges were revoked in 1992, so the only real advantage for becoming a *pensionado* is to be able to stay in the country legally. Now more and more people are looking at other ways of obtaining Costa Rican residency.

The residency program is for people who wish to reside in Costa Rica full-time but who cannot qualify for *pensionado* or *rentista* status. It is also for those who can qualify, but choose not to because some of the advantages were taken away. In the latter case, a $600 per month pension from an approved source is required.

(1) Residente Inversionista - There are several other ways for foreigners to obtain legal residency. As we mentioned in the last section, they can become *inversionistas* (resident investors) by investing $50,000 in an approved organization such as tourism, export businesses, $100,000 in a reforestation project or $200,000 in another type of business.

(2) First Degree Relative - Foreigners can also claim permanent residency if they have an immediate or **first-degree relative** in Costa Rica, i.e. a child, siblings, spouse or parent (mother or father) who is a citizen. They must also prove they have financial means to support themselves while living in Costa Rica (about $600 per month). Relatives of foreigners who have become Costa Rican citizens are also eligible for residency. In all cases you will be asked to prove your relationship. You can usually work under this category. All the documents required for other residency applications must be provided.

(3) Marriage - Marrying a Costa Rican also entitles you to residency. This is the fastest way to become a resident. Most foreigners who marry Costa Ricans choose this means of acquiring residency. We personally know of many expatriates who have married Costa Ricans for this very reason.

In addition, anyone who has lived for at least two years under another residency category, such as *pensionado* or *rentista*, may apply for Costa Rican residency. Many *ex-pensionados* do this because they can generally qualify for this status easily. With this type of residency you have to live in the country six months a year.

As in the case of the other residency categories you need an application, birth certificate, marital status certificate, police report, several passport photos and in some cases documents proving your relationship to your Costa Rican relatives.

(4) Working Costa Rican Corporation - There is a newly added residency status for those who have a working company or *Sociedad Anónima*. You must have a minimum number of local employees and provide financial statements. Just having a Costa Rican corporation will not qualify a person for this status.

Summary of Residency Requirements

Retired Residents PENSIONADO	Earning Residents RENTISTA	Investor Resident INVERSIONISTA	Company Visa REPRESENTANTE	Permanent Residency
Requires proof of US$600 per month income (equivalent) from permanent pension source or retirement fund. (combined pensions from one individual qualifies)	Proof of US$1,000 monthly income for at least 5 years, guaranteed by a banking institution. (A sample letter with the required wordings is available at the ARCR offices) or a $60,000 deposit in a approved Costa Rican bank.	Investment of US$50,000 in approved sectors such as tourism or export, $100,000 in reforestation, or $200,000 in any other business.	Applicant must be director of a company meeting certain requirements, such as employing a minimum number of local workers as established by the labour law, with financial statements certified by a Public Accountant.	First degree relative status with a Costa Rican Citizen (or marriage, or chiuld that is Costa Rican) or citizen of Spain or after 2 years in any other residency status.
Must remain in the country for at least 4 months per years.	Must remain in the country for at least 4 month per year.	Must remain in the country for at least 6 month per year.	Must remain in the country for at least 6 month per year.	Must visit Costa Rica at least once per year.
Dependants*	Dependants*			
Cannot work as an employee.	Cannot work as an employee.	Can receive income from the project.	Can earn a salary in the company.	Can work.
Can own a company and receive income.	Can own a company and receive income.	Can own a company and receive income.	Can own a company and receive income.	Can own a company and receive income.
Must exchange income within the National Banking system.	Must exchange income within the National Banking system.	No exchange requirement.	No exchange requirement.	No exchange requirement.
Renewable every 2 years.	Renewable every 2 years.	Annual renewal.	Annual renewal.	Variable renewal.
US$100 *Entero*	US$100 *Entero*	US$300 guarantee	US$300 guarantee	US$300 guarantee

* *Pensionados* and *Rentistas* can claim their spouses and children under 18 as dependants (or a child between 18 and 25 enrolled in University). No further income is required.

- *Entero* is the fee charged by the government for identity cards each time residency is granted / renewed (aech person)

Courtesy of the Residents Association and Tico Times.

(5) Residency Under Special Circumstances - Residency is sometimes granted in cases to some people who does not fall into any of the previous categories. Not all people who apply under this category will obtain residency. If there are two people with the exact circumstances, one may be granted residency and the other may have it denied. Since each case is different we suggest you talk to Roger Petersen. He is listed in the section about attorneys in this chapter and has helped a few of his clients obtain this type of residency.

(6) Temporary Residency - *Residencia temporal* is for students enrolled in a university or language school, Peace Corps volunteers and members of affiliated church service groups, employees of foreign firms, employees of many national companies and other categories. Language teachers at any language institute in San José may obtain temporary residency. Others doing jobs that Costa Ricans cannot do are also eligible for this status.

Temporary residency permits are valid for three months to a year and can be renewed. Temporary residents may enter and leave the country as often as they wish, paying the tourist's rate of exit tax. Once all documents are correctly presented, temporary permits are approved as quickly as possible.

Because each person's situation is different, the procedure is complicated. All residency programs require mounds of paper work, so we advise you to consult a lawyer to facilitate this process. To find a competent, trustworthy attorney, go to the ARCR office after reading the section in this chapter titled, "How to Find a Lawyer."

Immigration and Other Matters
Work Permits

Applicants for work permits must submit the following documents:

1) Letter on certified paper to the Immigration's Temporary Permits Department outlining the reason for the request, with all necessary stamps affixed.

2) Temporary work permit application, available along with the list of requirements at the Immigration information desk in La Uruca district.

3) Four recent passport photographs.

4) A full set of fingerprints, taken at Puerta (door) 4 of the Immigration office in La Uruca.

5) Proof of guaranteed income while in the country. This could be provided via a letter from the applicant's employer here.

6) Applicants who will be working for a government or international institution in Costa Rica must provide a confirmation letter from the institution.

7) Photocopy of the photo page and last entry stamp of the applicant's passport.

8) Guarantee deposit of $100 at Immigration's temporary permit department once the permit is approved. If the applicant is also applying for a permit under a residency category, this deposit may be waived. The deposit is refunded when the applicant returns home.

Immigration will approve work permits only for Costa Rican companies authorized by Immigration's Executive Council. Businesses that have a long history of operating in the country are generally considered eligible to receive foreign workers.

Student Permits

For a student permit, an applicant must submit the following:

1) A letter, on certified paper affixed with all necessary stamps, to Immigration's temporary permit department explaining the reason for the permit request as well as the name of local "sponsor" – a legal resident of Costa Rica, Tico or foreign, who will accept responsibility for the applicant's actions while he/she is in the country. Letter must be certified by a local attorney or Costa Rica Consul.

2) Application form available at the La Uruca Immigration office's information desk.

3) Four recent passport photographs.

4) A guarantee of $100, which must be deposited with the Temporary permit department after the permit is approved. Deposit is refunded when applicant returns home.

5) Proof of the sponsor's income here — a certified letter from the sponsor's employer, financial statements, etc.

6) Photocopy of sponsor's identification card (*cédula*) or residency card (*carnet*).

7) A full set of the applicant's fingerprints, taken at the Immigration office in La Uruca, Puerta (door) 4.

8) Photocopies of the photo page and final entry of the applicant's passport.

9) Registration letter or card from the school where the applicant will study.

10) Minors must present a certified authorization from their parents.

Perpetual Tourist

If you don't want to invest the time and money to become a *pensionado* or resident, you can live as a perpetual tourist in Costa Rica. No paper work or lawyers need to be involved. Just leave the country leave the country for at least 72 hours every three months to renew your tourist visa.

You can repeat this process over-and-over again to stay in the country indefinitely. The only disadvantage is that as a tourist you may not work in Costa Rica and it is almost impossible to become a legal resident unless you marry a Costa Rican or have immediate Costa Rican relatives.

If you don't want to bother leaving the country every few months to renew your papers, you can stay in the country illegally. You no longer have to pay the $0.90 fine for each overstayed month. "Perpetual tourists," foreigners who repeatedly overstay their tourist visas, now only pay the country's exit tax. We have personally met many people who have lived as tourists for years without problems, some even started businesses.

Bear in mind that it is always better to have your papers up-to-date because you may be deported almost instantly at the whim of a Immigration official or if you get into any kind of trouble and are in the country illegally. Costa Rica's Immigration Law gives airport or border officers the right to deport any illegal tourist. We know of a Canadian woman who is now fighting deportation after 7 years of being here illegally.

Extending Your Stay

Every tourist with a valid passport (U.S. citizens, Canadians and most Europeans) has permission to remain in Costa Rica without a visa for up to 90 days.

U.S. citizens and Canadian citizens may enter the country with just a 30-day tourist card or another piece of identification such as a driver's license, passport or birth certificate.

You can get tourist cards from any Costa Rican consulate or embassy prior to your trip or at the airline ticket counter on the day you leave for Costa Rica. Tourist cards can be renewed monthly by applying for an extension called a *prórroga de turismo*. To obtain this extension you will need your passport, a ticket out of the country (see the section titled Bus Travel to and from Costa Rica in Chapter 8), three passport-size photos, and at least $200 in cash or travelers checks for each additional month you're staying. Many people opt to pay the fine instead, since this process is such a hassle.

This process takes a couple of days and is a bureaucratic nightmare. To save yourself many headaches, long lines and time, you should go to any local travel agency. Most of the agencies in San José will help extend your tourist card or obtain an exit visa for about $5, even if you didn't purchase your ticket there. This service is worthwhile and usually takes two working days.

The immigration offices are in the suburb of La Uruca, about a half mile west of the Irazú Hotel. Information may be found online at: **www.migracion.go.cr.**

Leaving The Country

Any tourist who has stayed in Costa Rica more than 30 days with just a tourist card will need an exit visa or *visa de salida* to leave the country. Likewise, foreigners who entered Costa Rica using just a passport and overstayed the maximum permitted time of 90 days, will also have to get an exit visa.

To obtain this document you first need *pensión alimenticia* stamps to prove you have not left dependent children behind. Go to the court buildings or *Tribunales de Justicia* (Calle 17, Aves. 6-8) for these stamps. Then

Long-term residents will have to make many a trip to Costa Rica's Department of Immigration in La Uruca.

take your passport, the stamps, and your return ticket to the Immigration Office to get an exit visa. The whole process takes two working days. As we just mentioned above, most tourist agencies will do all of the running around for a small fee.

One good thing about an exit visa is that it is valid for 10 days from date it was issued. You can stay in the country another thirty days using this extension, so you can remain in Costa Rica for a total of 100 days.

Costa Rican citizens, retirees and permanent residents must also get an exit visa and *pension alimenticia* stamps. A foreigner living under any of the three residency categories will pay about $50 for an exit visa.

Everyone has to pay an immigration tax according to their status. You can avoid a lot of hassles and lines at the airport if you pay in San José before going. This tax may be paid in the rear of the basement level of the Bancrédito across from the southwest corner of the Central Park. Take your documents with you, passport or *cédula*, and the cashier will tell you the amount.

(hildren's Exit Visas

Children under 18, including infants, who remain in Costa Rica for more than 30 days are subject to the country's child welfare laws and will not be permitted to leave the country unless both parents request permission from the National Child Welfare Agency or *Patronato Nacional de Infancia* (Calle 19 and Ave. 6). This can pose a real problem for a single parent traveling with children who overstays the permitted 90 days. One parent or guardian cannot get exit papers without written permission from the non-accompanying other parent. A Costa Rican consul in the child's home country must be notarized this document.

If you don't adhere to this procedure, your child <u>cannot leave</u> the country. A travel agent or lawyer may be able to get permission from the *Patronato* if given the child's passport and two extra Costa Rican-sized passport photos.

Costa Rica's child protection laws can be a real pain-in-the-neck. However, in some cases they can work to your advantage and enable you to stay in the country.

If you support minor children, you cannot be deported from the country under most circumstances. Although we don't recommend using this method, some foreigners remain in the country indefinitely this way. Your attorney can explain how to use this law to protract your stay in the country.

By the way, the *Patronato Nacional de Infancia* handles adoptions in Costa Rica. This process can take a couple of years even for a newborn or child if you satisfy all of the requirements. It is easier and faster if you adopt a child rather than a newborn.

Costa Rican Citizenship

After living in Costa Rica for a number of years many foreigners decide that they want to acquire Costa Rican citizenship (Dual citizenship is permitted.) If you qualify, this is another way to stay in the country legally. As a naturalized citizen you will have the same rights as a Costa Rican citizen, including the privilege to vote and a Costa Rican passport.

There are some U.S. citizens who give up their citizenship voluntarily to take care of tax benefits for those living abroad. This is an extreme measure and we recommend thinking about the advantages and disadvantages. We heard of one case where the founder of Tupperware moved to Costa Rica about twenty years ago and became a Costa Rican citizen for tax reasons. In this case, millions of dollars were involved. The average person would not benefit from such a move.

We have been told that after living in Costa Rica for more than 7 years under the category of "Permanent Resident Status," you may apply for citizenship. Applicants will need to prove they have the financial means to live in Costa Rica. They'll also need a certificate from the computer section of the Department of Immigration showing their exits and entries into Costa Rica from the time they entered Costa Rica to the day they apply for citizenship. Permanent residents and resident investors will need a certificate from the National Immigration Council showing the names of their parents, your date of birth and your current immigration status.

Applicants will also need to take a written test through the Department of Public Education in geography and the Spanish language. These exams are usually given four times a year.

Foreign men and women married to Costa Ricans for a minimum of 2 years and who have lived in the country for at least 2 years, may also become citizens. The Costa Rican spouse can either be through birth or naturalization. You may also be able to become a naturalized citizen if you have been divorced from a Costa Rica citizen. However, you must comply with both the minimum time requirement for marriage and residence in the country.

As far as we know, the United States does not favor dual nationality for its citizens but does recognize its existence. We just checked with the embassy here and U. S. citizens may obtain Costa Rican citizenship without renouncing U.S. citizenship.

A birth certificate issued by the Civil Registry for your Costa Rican spouse is also required. Applicants will need a certificate from the computer section of the Immigration Department showing your exits and entries into Costa Rica up to the day you file for Costa Rican citizenship. You will need to have your birth certificate notarized by the Costa Rican consul (You may use the same one you used to obtained for Costa Rican residency). In lieu of this last requirement you may obtain either a certificate from the Immigration Department or from the Tourist Institute showing your date and place of birth, parents' names and a sworn statement of your birth.

The naturalization process is slow and can take over a year. Once approved, you'll be sworn in at a special ceremony.

Check with the U.S. Embassy in San José for the latest regulations. We know of a number of North Americans who have both U.S. and Costa Rican citizenship. One expatriate friend uses his Costa Rican passport for travel because he claims there are fewer problems than with his U.S. passport.

We suggest consulting a Costa Rican attorney for all the details and specific requirements if you are really interested in this subject. Attorneys charge from $700 to $1000 for this service. However if you speak fluent Spanish you can do it yourself. There are several people who work outside of the immigration office who will assist you for a nominal fee.

Getting Married and Fiancée Visas

Getting married in Costa Rica is really quite simple. All you have to do is complete the required paperwork and have the appropriate documents like a passport, divorce papers (if you were previously married), birth certificate and any other pertinent information. We suggest consulting your lawyer if you are marrying in Costa Rica to find out exactly what documents are needed and what procedures to follow.

Lawyers can marry people in Costa Rica much like a justice of the peace in the States. This type of marriage is called *por civil* and is usually quicker than a traditional church wedding or *por la iglesia*. In Costa Rica, people get married either way.

If you do choose to have a lawyer marry you, you will need to have two witnesses for the ceremony. Your lawyer will be able to round up a couple of people if you can't find anyone. For additional information about getting married in Costa Rica go to: **www.costarica.com/embassy/marriage**.

If you are interested in obtaining a finaceé visa you should be aware of the following process. Marrying a foreign national is a completely different experience than marrying a resident of the United States. In this country, you go down to the license bureau, apply for a marriage license, and then tie the knot. When joining your life with an alien spouse, marriage alone does not necessarily allow the married couple to be together in the country. The United States government must be petitioned to permit your spouse to live with you in the United States.

When a foreign marriage occurs, the American spouse must file a Petition for Alien Relative and endure many months or even years of separation from his new spouse while the petition is approved and finally processed at the foreign consulate abroad.

A citizen of the United States has an additional option available to him: the fiancée visa. The US citizen can petition for a visa for his alien fiancée to allow her admission the United States for a period of ninety days to allow for them to prepare for their marriage and life together. The fiancée process can be completed in a much shorter time period than a spousal petition.

Upon entry into the United States, the fiancée is only permitted to remain for a period of ninety days. There are no extensions allowed. During the admission to the United States, the fiancée will receive employment authorization from the INS.

The petitioner and beneficiary must marry with the ninety-day window or the beneficiary must leave the United States. If marriage to the petitioner occurs, the married couple will then apply for adjustment of status to lawful permanent resident at the INS district office in their area. If the marriage does not occur and the fianceé returns to her home country within the ninety-day period, then the gentleman retains his eligibility to pursue his options with other potential spouses in the future.

This is intended to provide general information on the visa process. There are many other factors in this complex and ever changing area of the law.

Purchasing an Automobile

High taxes make the purchase of a new vehicle in CostaRica more expensive than in the majority of other countries. In the past, people chose to buy new cars in the U.S., where prices are much lower. Now prices of new cars in Costa Rica are more affordable than before, and more people are choosing to purchase locally rather than deal with the paperwork of importing a vehicle and high taxes.

One more reason to buy locally is to ensure your vehicle will be under warranty in case anything goes wrong. Most local dealers offer two to three-year warranties on new cars.

Due to the high price of new cars , used cars are plentiful in Costa Rica. Most of these second hand cars are priced higher than they would be in the U.S. or Canada, so Costa Ricans tend to keep them longer and take better care of them. This makes resale value high.

The majority of automobiles in Costa Rica are made in Japan, so most replacement parts are for Japanese automobiles. Spare parts for U.S. cars must be imported, are expensive, and sometimes hard to come by. Therefore, you should think twice about bringing an American car to Costa Rica. If you do decide to bring a car from the U.S. or Canada, it is best to bring a Toyota, Nissan, Honda or some other Japanese import for the reasons just mentioned.

If you plan to drive mostly in the country's larger cities, smaller new or used cars will help reduce fuel consumption and are easier to maneuver on crowded streets. Prices for new small cars are extremely affordable and range between $9,000 and $14,000,while new mid-sized cost between $13,000 and $20,000. Those of you who plan to drive outside of the city and off-road should consider a Sport Utility Vehicle (SUV), pick-up or jeep. Many of the country's roads are unpaved and filled with potholes, and a solidly built vehicle is absolutely necessary especially during the rainy season. Prices of new SUV's run between $20,000-$75,000 depending on the model and size of the vehicle. Used cars are priced substantially lower.

Since new cars are so expensive in Costa Rica, buyers have the option to lease or finance. The dealer can usually arrange financing. If not, many Costa Rican banks offer financing for cars. Interest rates are generally in dollars instead of *colones* and vary according to market rates.

If you decide to bring a car to Costa Rica there are two ways to do it; by sea or by land. If you ship your car to Costa Rica by boat, contact a shipping company near to where you have your car in the U.S. or one of the companies mentioned in the next section. This method of transportation is relatively safe since your car can be insured against all possible types of damage.

If you have all of your paperwork in order, your vehicle should not take more than a month at the most to reach Costa Rica depending on your port of departure. If you send your car from Miami, it only takes one week to reach Puerto Limón on the East coast of Costa Rica and costs about $800 plus taxes. From the West coast or New York, you can expect to pay over $1300 plus taxes and some other fees to process your paperwork.

To import a new or used vehicle you will have to make sure your shipping company sends the following documents : a driver's licenses for all potential drivers, the original clear title or pink slip (*título de propiedad*), originaal registration, copy of passport, original bill of lading (*conocimiento de embarque*) if the vehicle has been shipped and the name of the shipping company. Also make sure your car has Canadian or U.S. plates or the whole process may be delayed.

Note: **ALL VEHICLES**, since June 7, 2001, now require an Emissions Control Certificate certified by the Department of Motor Vehicles from your country of origin or by the vehicles manufacturer if new, dated no later than 30 days prior to the shipping date. The certificate must also be translated into Spanish by an official translator and authenticated by the Consulate of Costa Rica nearest to the Emissions Inspection Station that issued your certificate. This even applies to used vehicles, and any car without it will not be able to be registered in the country. This change in fact caused many vehicles to be stuck in customs for a time, as the law passed in December 1999, but was never enforced until the middle of 2001.

To be safe call the nearest consulate to check out what documents are actually required. In many cases they will ask for a notary public to authenticate the gas emission test and then have the Department of State certify that the notary is registered.

If your name does not appear on the original title of the vehicle, you must provide a document from an attorney certifying that the owners allow you to drive their car. Said document must be notarized and approved by the nearest Costa Rican Consulate in your country of origin. Cars that are being financed in the U.S. and are not fully paid off fall into this category.

If you do not provide all of documents above including the gas emission certificate, you cannot import the vehicle to Costa Rica.

Make sure that the VIN (vehicle identification number) number and all details of the car are correctly typed on all documents. Any errors will void the documents and you cannot import the car.

Calculating Taxes on a Vehicle

Long-term imported vehicle duties are calculated by multiplying the Vehicle's Appraised Value (VCAV) by the Customs Duty Percentage (CDP).

The VCAV is the sum of the vehicle's market value, freight and freight insurance. The Black Book Guide, a consumer Research magazine, based on the model and date of manufacture, determines market values. Freight is the cost of transporting your vehicle to Costa Rica.

If there is no bill of lading or you drove your vehicle, freight will equal seven percent of the market value of your vehicle, which could equal thousands of dollars more than actual freight charges. Freight insurance is the amount of money you pay to insure your vehicle. If you did not pay insurance, customs will multiply the sum of the market value and freight first by 110 percent, then by 1.5 percent.

Duties are calculated by taking the higher value between the Black Book average retail value and the value at the *Ministerio de Hacienda*. You can check these on line at: **www.hacienda.go.co/autovalor/**.

These duties are determined by the age of your vehicle. If your vehicle is a 2004, 2003 or 2002, you pay 52.28 percent of the retail value. If your car is a 2001 or 2000, you pay 63 percent of its value. For any vehicle older than 1999, a tax of 79.02 percent will be charged.

As you can see, taxes are now higher for used cars. In order to establish the value of a used vehicle, you present the commercial invoice with the purchase value of the vehicle. In case you do not have an invoice you have to declare the value.

Customs will compare this value to the Black Book and to their own Costa Rica market value. These values are extremely high and are based on the selling price of used vehicles in Costa Rica. They will multiply the sales price times 0.502, 0.469 or 0.432 depending on the model year to establish the import value of the vehicle. They will accept your declared value as long as it is within 3% of their established value. If not they will apply their value.

For example, let us assume that you import a vehicle model year 1993 and with the black book value of $10,000. Let us also assume the shipping cost from the USA is $600, so the value is $10,600. Finally let us assume the local market value times 0.502 is within 3% of the $10,600. The duties would be: $10,600 times 59.33% = $6239.00 .

Do not think you can fool the customs inspectors by putting an arbitrary value on your vehicle. They have a list showing the manufacturer's suggested retail price of every vehicle manufactured when it was new, including extra equipment.

In order to calculate depreciation, customs agents refer to the market value based on their "Black Book," a manual published in the U.S. with a listing of new and used car wholesale auction prices. The book is a bible for U.S. car dealers, loan officers and Costa Rican customs agents. For additional information about the Black Book, contact **National Auto Research** at 2620 Barrett Road, PO Box 758, Gainsville, GA 30503. Tel: (800) 554-1026, Fax: (770) 532-4792, www.blackbookguides.com. Another good resource is **www.crautos.com**.

To obtain an estimate of the duties to be paid, send a fax or e-mail to The Association of Residents or Charles Zeller at **movers@racsa.co.cr**, Fax:011(506)-228-3073. Be sure to include the make of the car, model, serial number (VIN), automatic or stick shift, extras like air conditioning, power windows or other non-standard equipment. Be sure to specify the country from where you plan to ship the car.

After reading the above, if you still decide to import a used vehicle, we recommend using a customs broker to run around, obtain all the necessary documents and massive paperwork, and help with the taxes. After going through this process a friend of ours told us, "A good customs agent can save you money." A bilingual attorney is also important and will save you days running around from one office to another. He can take you step-by-step through this whole ordeal."

However, if you do decide to do this yourself, you will need to follow the procedure below. First, you have to go to either the East or West Coast to pick up your vehicle at the port of entry. This can be a real pain in the neck, requiring a lot of paperwork and patience. It is best to have a customs agent do all of this for you or go with you in person to pick up the vehicle. A good customs agent will have all the paper work done and your car out of the *aduana* when you arrive at the port of entry.

When we picked up our 1990 Montero in Limón we arranged everything beforehand. We took an early morning bus from San José and arrived in Limón with our agent three hours later. Our car was waiting for us in a private parking lot. We just signed one paper, got in the car and returned to San José. The process would not have gone as smoothly had we not planned carefully and coordinated everything with our customs agent.

Next, you need to register your car, which usually takes a few working days. First, get your paperwork from customs. Then have your vehicle checked at the nearest **Retieve SyC Inspection Center**. At present there are 11 inspection centers scattered around the country. Call 800-788-0000 to make an appointment and to locate the nearest station to your home. Cars also have to be taken to these stations yearly for general inspections to assure they are roadworthy. Then take the papers they give you to the *Registro Público* or Public Registry vehicle section (*Registro de Vehículos*) in the suburb of Zapote. Call 011-(506) 224-0628 if you need information. The cost of your registration depends on the value of your car. Finally, take the documents from the registry to the Ministry of Public Works (*Ministerio* *de Obras Públicas y Transportes*) at Plaza Víquez, south of downtown San José. Your temporary paper license plates will be issued a few months later at the *Registro* in Zapote.

Due to the huge backlog you will have to wait a year or more for your permanent metal plates. When you find out your metal plates are ready, you'll need to take the following documents to the National Registry (*Registro Nacional*)in Zapote: the temporary paper plate (*placa provisional*), title of ownership (*título de propiedad*), yellow registration card (tarjeta de circulación) and resident ID card (*cédula*) or passport.

You can find information about vehicles and property by viewing the National registry's website at: **www.registronacional.com.**

Every year you have to pay your *marchamo* or sticker which indicates you have paid your obligatory liability insurance. You have to do this between November 1 and December 31. You also have to pay $10 for an *echo marchamo*. This is a certificate that shows your vehicles emissions are within the legal limit. It is like a smog certificate in the U.S.

Driving an Automobile to Costa Rica

If you have sufficient time and enjoy adventure, drive your automobile to Costa Rica. The journey from the U.S. to Costa Rica (depending on where you cross the Mexican border), takes about three weeks if driving at a moderate speed. The shortest land distance from the U.S. to Costa Rica is 2250 miles through Brownsville, Texas.

Take your time to stop and see some of the sights. We recommend driving only during the day since most roads are poorly lit if at all. At night, large animals—cows, donkeys and horses— can stray onto the road and cause serious accidents.

Your car must be in good mechanical condition before your trip. Carry spare tires and necessary parts. Take a can of gas and try to keep your gas tank as full as possible because service stations are few and far between.

Have your required visas, passports and other necessary papers in order to avoid problems at border crossings. Remember, passports are required for all U.S. citizens driving through Central America. You also need complete car insurance, a valid driver's license and a vehicle registration.

You can purchase insurance from AAA in the U.S., or contacting **Sanborn's Insurance** in the U.S. Tel: 800-222-0158, Fax: (956)-686-0732 or **www.samborns.com**. They offer both Mexican and Central American policies.

Instant Auto Insurance offers a 24-hour 800 number and fax service so you can have your policy ready. In the U.S. and Canada, call 1-800-345-47-01 or fax 619-690-65-33.

The web site **www.drivemeloco.com** has information about border crossings and people's experiences while making the trip.

You can also buy insurance at the border before entering Mexico. Having an accident in Mexico is a felony not a misdemeanor. So do not forget to be fully insured.

If you are missing a driver's license, a vehicle registration or insurance, border guards can make your life miserable. Also, remember some border crossings close at night, so plan to arrive at all borders between 8 a.m. and 5 p.m., just to be safe.

When you finally arrive at the Costa Rica-Nicaragua border, expect to be delayed clearing customs.

If you bring many personal possessions to live in Costa Rica permanently, some or all of them may be inventoried and taken to the custom's warehouse in San José. You may pick them up at a later date after you have paid the necessary taxes. However, if you come in as a tourist you usually will not hassled by customs at the border.

As a foreigner in Costa Rica (a non-resident) you are allowed to drive a car with a tourist permit for 3 months without paying taxes. Your initial three-month permit to drive your car in Costa Rica may be obtained at the

A four-lane stretch of the Pan-American Highway.

customs office at the port of entry. The documents required are the title, registration of the car and proof of having paid the local minimum insurance (It is important to understand that this insurance does not cover any vehicle or any damage. You cannot obtain additional insurance locally while driving with this permit.) Mandatory liability insurance from the **Instituto Nacional de Seguros** is $10 for three months.

Another three-month extension is usually granted, but after six months the vehicle must leave the country or the duties paid. To get the one-time three-month extension you will have to leave the country prior to the three-month limit for 48 hours. Upon re-entry your passport will be restamped, allowing you to drive the vehicle for three more months. **Warning:** Do not drive the car if the permit has expired—it will be considered an abandoned vehicle and can be confiscated.

When your second 3-month extension expires, you have to either leave the country or store the vehicle in a customs storage facility until you pay the customs duties and purchase your Costa Rican license plates.

Any person who brings a car to Costa Rica and pays all of the taxes, may keep the car in the country indefinitely as soon as all paperwork is completed. One advantage to bringing your vehicle yourself by land, is that you don't have to pay taxes immediately as you do when you have your vehicle shipped by sea. **Warning:** if you have permanent residency status and bring a car by sea you will have to pay all of the taxes almost immediately before you can get your car out of customs.

If you do keep your vehicle in Costa Rica, you will have to apply the corresponding tax formula we listed above.

For additional information about driving from the U.S. to Costa Rica, you can purchase a useful guidebook, ***Driving the Pan-American Highway to Mexico and Central America***, by Raymond and Audrey Pritchard with help from Christopher Howard. You can now order this one-of-a-kind book through **Amazon.com**, **www.drivetocentralamerica.com** or **www.costaricabooks.com**.

Bringing Your Boat or Plane to Costa Rica

Those of you who own yachts and sailboats will be pleased to know that there are two marinas where you may dock your boats in Costa Rica and plans call for a couple more to be built in the future. The country's marinas are the **Flamigo Marina** in the Northwest and the **Los Sueños Resort** in the Central Pacific. The latter has 75 slips and is the only marina where you can keep your boat in the country legally for over 6 months. Slips rent for about $13-$15 per month per foot. The marina offers membership in the Los Sueños Yacht Club, a full range of sport fishing charters, day cruises as well as other water sports activities.

In the past the longest you could keep a boat in the country was 6 months without having to pay taxes on it. Duties can be as high as 57 percent of the boat's real value for brand name boats. This is still the case at the Flamingo Marina in Guanacaste. Most people get around this by taking the boat out every 6 months and then returning. With all types vehicles you cannot keep doing this. However, the Los Sueños Marina is the only licensed marina in the country and has a special agreement whereby a boat may be kept in the country under the cover of the marina for up to two years without taking it out of Costa Rica. We understand that you can then renew your permit for another two years. This exemption is only for non-commercial boats and does not apply to those who use their boats for sport fishing. For additional information we urge you to call the Los Sueños Marina at 011-(506 -643-3941/2.

We understand that a new law will be passed soon which will enable owners of small aircraft to keep the planes in the country like boat owners do at present. The government figures anyone who owns a boat or plane will possibly make sizeable investments in the country.

Shipping Your Household Goods to Costa Rica

As previously stated, the old *pensionado* program allowed retirees to import household items including an automobile virtually duty-free. Since most of these privileges have been rescinded, you may well have second thoughts about importing anything.

Keep in mind that most imported used items are also taxed. Taxes range from 40 to 90 percent or more of the value of the article plus your shipping costs. Taxes can be raised on a whim of the Costa Rican government. You can, however, save money by purchasing many imported items at the duty-free zone or *depósito libre* in the southern city of Golfito.

The duty-free zone was designed in 1990 for Costa Ricans and residents. Most popular goods sold there are domestic electrical appliances ranging from refrigerators, freezers, and stoves to sound systems and television sets. Many brand names are available in a variety of models. Although you may find many of them cheaper in the U.S., they are big bargains compared to San José's prices—up to 50% on some large appliances. When you add shipping costs from the U.S., taxes and possible headaches, it is more practical to buy your appliances at the free port.

Some restrictions and paper work may irk you, but this will be easier for you than importing things from the U.S. You can only purchase $500.00 worth of items every six months. The first period of the year ends on June 30th and the second begins on July first. You are limited to $500.00 during the first six months. You cannot carry it over to the second period of the year and buy $1000.00 worth of merchandise. You can, however, combine your card with a family member and buy $1000.00 per period. You must furnish proof that the person you do this with is really a family member.

You may pick up your Purchase Authorization Card or "TAC" (*Tarjeta de Autorización de Compra*), as it more commonly called, at the booth in the duty free zone in Golfito. You must be over 18 years old and have a Costa Rican ID or passport to do so.

To find out information about shopping, contact ACODELCO in San José at Tel: 232-1198, Fax: 232-2692 and in Golfito at 775-0717, Fax: 775-1940.

For small items, many foreign residents go to the town of David, Panama, near the Panamanian border. Prices on everything including household goods are nearly as low as in the U.S. However, because of taxes you will have to pay on large electronic goods and appliances, it is better to shop at the duty-free *depósito* across the border in Golfito. Nevertheless, foreign residents living in Costa Rica on a 90- day visa can go to David for 72 hours to renew their papers for another three months.

After taking high shipping costs into consideration, you may be reluctant to ship any household items from the U.S. This is a matter of personal choice. Most foreign residents and even Costa Ricans prefer U.S. products because of their higher quality. However, many retirees live comfortably and happily without luxuries and expensive appliances.

You can rent a furnished apartment. If you choose, you can furnish an apartment, excluding stove and refrigerator, for a few hundred dollars. Wooden furniture is inexpensive in Costa Rica. You can also purchase good used furniture and appliances from expatriate and others who are moving out of the country. Check the local English newspapers. What you need to import depends on your personal preference and budget.

Make an effort to get rid of "clutter" and bulky items, and do not ship what can be easily or cheaply replaced in Costa Rica. Try to leave large appliances and furniture at home. You pay more for these items in Costa Rica, but in the long run they turn out to be less expensive when you take shipping costs and taxes into consideration. Talk to other foreign residents and retirees to see what they think is absolutely necessary to bring to Costa Rica.

Shopping in Golfito
By Martha Bennett

Appliances are very expensive in Costa Rica because of the import tax. Large appliances are half the price in Golfito, comparable to U.S. costs. After pricing an American washer in San José at $600, I went to Golfito and bought a washer and dryer for $600. Golfito is near Panamá and used to thrive with the United Fruit Company. When this outfit left, the Costa Rican government allowed the residents to set up a free-zone to maintain their economy.

The procedure for buying appliances is not too difficult but there are steps to follow.

1. There are many excursions which take you there and set up your hotel arrangements. The cost is about $15 round trip plus hotel. You can drive there in about 8 hours. You may also fly, but this uses up your savings. You must stay overnight. This is one of the economy boosting rules. It is hot, but the area away from the freeport complex is quite beautiful.

2. At the shopping complex, get your boleto. This form is your permit to buy about $500 on each passport every six months. If you want to buy more, residents of Golfito will sell you their boleto for around $25.

3. Procede in an orderly fashion while shopping. The stores are numbered but they all look alike and you won't want to hit the same one twice. Each shop will give you a paper with their price and store number. Discounts do happen but only for cash. It's worth trying to bargain. Prices vary for the same brand of appliance so throw away papers with higher prices immediately. This saves confusion. If you can decide what you want on the first day, pay for it at once. You can pay the next morning, but lines are long and there are other things to do.

4. Go to your hotel and relax.

5. Return to the stores early, 7:30 a.m., to retrieve your stuff and pay if you haven't. They inspect everything. For big items, there are boys with trolleys to gather everything in a waiting area. Then these boys will take your purchases through the gate where you need to show your passport, boleto and sales slip one more time. Do not lose any papers. Your life will be a nightmare. Tips are expected for trolleying your stuff around.

6. Outside, are trucking firms that will deliver your purchases the next day to a warehouse or directly to your house for less than $20. Everything is guaranteed and inspected again. Smaller items can go with you on the bus. If this sounds exhausting, it is. But remember, you can sell these appliances for more than you paid five years down the line. I don't want to do it again, but I'm glad I did it once.

If you still want to import your U.S. belongings and household goods and want to save time and money, purchase and ship them from Los Angeles, Houston, New Orleans or, preferably, Miami. The latter is the U.S. port nearest to Costa Rica and shipping costs are lower. Look in the yellow pages of the Miami phone book for a shipping company or call the company listed at the end of this section.

Ways to Bring Your Belongings to Costa Rica

Here are some money saving tips for bringing small items to Costa Rica. First, when entering the country as a tourist by plane, you can bring in a lot of personal effects and small appliances. A tourist is sometimes waved through customs without ever having to open any luggage. Costa Rica has become a popular tourist destination.

(1) The government understands that tourists come here to enjoy the country and have many different hobbies and reasons for visiting. They know that tourists need such items as surfboards, bicycles, kayaks, musical instruments, photographic equipment, small stereos and more. The government permits items for personal use and that are not intended for resale. The number of these personal items has to be reasonable in relation to the length of the stay or needed for the exercise of one's profession during his or her trip. Finally, all items have to be portable and considered luggage.

The amount of luggage allowed on the plane by airlines is limited in most cases to 2 pieces which must not exceed 66 pounds. Sometimes they allow excess luggage for an additional fee. If they do allow you to take more, do so because it is the cheapest way of bringing items into Costa Rica.

While in the plane you have to fill out a customs declaration form. If you are bringing anything that is not considered luggage under the law, declare it at a very low price. Once you have picked up your luggage from the carousel you will have to go to customs. If they red light you, you must go through an inspection, otherwise you'll walk through unstopped.

There is a duty-free exemption of up to $500. If you exceed the $500 limit, the back of your passport will be stamped, *"bonificado"*, which once again means you will be restricted from bringing more imported items into the country for a period of six months. If you bring in more items within six months, you will have to pay the corresponding taxes. Do not think you can get away with bringing more items before then if you rip out the last page of your passport. They keep all records on computer.

You have two options if your duty free $500 exemption is not enough. You can pay the duties right then and there or you can ask for a receipt and return the following day to pay.

Tourists and residents have the right to bring in $500 in merchandise purchased abroad every six months tax-free, in addition to personal items considered part of a traveler's luggage. There is a long list of personal items you may bring in such as: clothing, toys, sports equipment, such as surf boards or fishing equipment, a personal computer, photographic equipment; radios, tapes and musical instruments. Personal items are not limited to this list. Almost any article that will be used by the resident or traveler while in the country, whether to work or play, may be considered a "personal item." The $500 tax does not apply to personal items, but is additional to them. Any merchandise that exceeds the $500 limit and cannot be considered a personal article will be retained in customs until the import duties are paid. Be forewarned that customs officials will usually stamp the passports of people who bring in obviously new merchandise.

Used clothing and books are not subject to taxes. Do not pack them with taxable articles or you may have to pay taxes on them anyway

Have friends bring a few things when they come to visit you in Costa Rica. Always try to take as much as possible with you on the plane rather than shipping items by boat because most used personal things are not taxed at the airport. Even used appliances have a good chance of clearing airport customs if you can fit them on the plane.

(2) If you have a small amount of items (less than 500 pounds) that you cannot take with you as luggage, you should consider sending it as air cargo. One slightly crazy friend of ours, who has moved back and forth between Costa Rica and the U.S. four times, highly recommends American Airlines Cargo. He always uses them to ship his belongings to Costa Rica.

If you choose to ship your belongings by air, try American Airlines. Call their 800 toll-free number. They will ask you your intended destination. You will then have to give them the number of boxes you are planning to ship, and the respective weight and dimensions of each box.

The operator will then figure the approximate cost. All items will officially 2be weighed at the airport cargo facility. The cost is based on either the total weight or the combined dimensions of all your boxes, whichever is greater.

You will then be given the choice of sending your things by express or standard freight. The latter is your best bet if you are not in a hurry. It only takes two to five days to reach Costa Rica from the U.S. The only drawback to shipping standard rate is that it will be on a space-available basis, your merchandise may be slightly delayed. The cost works out to be about a dollar per pound.

It is highly advisable to make your travel plans so as to arrive in Costa Rica before your shipment arrives. This way you can go directly to the customs house and remove your things after paying the corresponding taxes.

We recommend packing your belongings in unmarked plain boxe, especially if you are shipping computers, stereos or other electronic equipment. Number each box and put the name and address of the person who will be receiving them in Costa Rica. Make a list of the contents of each box for yourself, the airlines and customs. This will help ensure your boxes get there intact. All of your boxes should be made of thick cardboard and have plenty of packing materials to protect any fragile items. Airline employees often heap heavy boxes on top of other cargo. Be sure to write on any paperwork and air bills "Not for resale." This will save you a lot of money when the customs people figure out how much you will pay in taxes.

If you decide to get your things out of customs yourself, the process goes like this. First, you will have to go to American Airlines Cargo, located near the airport, pay a small fee and take the paperwork to the customs house. When you arrive there, you go to a couple of windows. Next, you will sit and wait until they call your name. While you wait you can peek inside of a large glass window and watch the workers load and unload boxes of all sizes and shapes from the twenty-foot high storage shelves .

When your name is finally called you go inside and the inspector opens all of your sealed boxes and determines what the contents are worth. Due to a lack of knowledge or because the custom inspector will want to they you, they sometimes apply the same rules as luggage and you will pay nothing or very little. Most of the time you do not need a customs broker to help you with a small shipment.

Finally, you go to a window, which also serves as a branch of one of the national banks, and pay the taxes on the items you have imported.

There are small trucks or *taxis de carga* available outside the customs building that you can hire to take your belongings to your house or apartment. Prices are quite reasonable. We took a full load to San José and the driver only charged us around $30. He even helped us load and unload.

(3) If you have over 500 pounds and large items like refrigerators it is too expensive to ship by air. Your best option is to send your things by boat in a cargo container. It is more cost effective to use a large container and the transit time will be shorter. As a rule of thumb shipping a quarter of a container will cost as much as a half and a half will cost as much as a whole container. So it is best to use a whole container. Your customs agent can get all of your household items and belongings out of customs.

(4) Driving through Mexico and Central America is another way to bring your household goods and personal belongings to Costa Rica. However, because of the length of the journey, delays at border crossings and other hassles this method is not recommended. We understand that some trucking companies will ship your belongings overland.

Whether you chose to send some of your possessions by ship or plane as unaccompanied luggage, you will learn to exercise extreme patience. Be prepared to face some unnecessary delays and frustrations when dealing with the Costa Rican customs house, or *aduana*. Since the new modern customs warehouse opened near the airport this process has been somewhat streamlined.

However, it is more usual than not to make several trips to the customs warehouse to get your belongings. At worst you may spend all day dealing with mountains of paperwork only to hear at the end of the day that you must come back tomorrow. Furthermore, fickle customs officials sometimes decide the value of the shipped goods and two identical shipments, can be taxed differently depending on who examines them at the *aduana*.

The documentation required to import personal effects and used household goods are: An original bill of lading, a copy of your passport including the pages with the last entry to Costa Rica, and a list of the value of each item. This list should include brand name, model and serial number of all appliances large and small. All items have to be used for at least 6 months before shipping.

Because of this lengthy process and hassles, many people pay a local customs broker, *Agencia Aduanera*, or hire some other person or their lawyer to do this unpleasant task for them. It may cost a little more this way, but it will save valuable time and hassles.

We recommend the following company (Please see their ad in the classified ads section of this guide.)

aBc Mudanzas
P.O. Box 147-1009
San José, Costa Rica

Tel: 011-(506) 289-3716 Fax: 011-(506) 228-3073
Toll Free from the U.S. or Canada 1-877-750-0237
Toll Free within Costa Rica 800-MUDANZA (800-683-2612)
E-mail: movers@sol.racsa.co.cr

Be sure to do the following when choosing a customs agency: Does the agency have English-speaking employees? Talk to them to see if they are customer-service oriented. Find out if they have the resources to access computerized customs information. Talk to long-time residents who have dealt with reputable agencies and get referrals.

Carlos Bravo of **Sexvex International** is another good customs broker. You may contact him at Tel: (506) 253-1152, Cell: (506) 383-2904 or e-mail: servex@racsa.co.cr.

You may also choose to consult the yellow pages for listing of *Agencias Aduaneras* (Custom's brokers). The **Association of Residents of Costa Rica** (ARCR) can give you the names of several customs agencies.

How to Find a Lawyer

If you plan to go into business, work, buy or sell property or seek long-term residency status in Costa Rica, you will definitely need the services of a trustworthy and professional attorney.

Your attorney can help you understand the complexities of the Costa Rican legal system, which is based on Napoleanic law. You are guilty until proven innocent, just the opposite of the system in the U.S.A. A lawyer is one of the best investments you can make because he can assist you with bureaucratic procedures and handle other legal matters that arise.

If you are not fully bilingual, be sure to choose a lawyer who is bilingual. The secretary should be bilingual too (Spanish/English). This helps avoid communication problems, misunderstandings and enables you to stay on top of your legal affairs.

It is very important to watch your lawyer closely since most Costa Rican lawyers tend to drag their feet as bureaucrats do.

Never take anything for granted. Refuse to believe that things are getting done, even if you are assured they are. Check with your lawyer on a regular basis and ask to see your file to make sure he has taken care of business. As you might imagine, paper work moves slowly in Costa Rica, so you do not want a procrastinating lawyer to prolong the process.

When you first contact a lawyer, make sure he is accessible at all hours. Make sure you have your lawyer's office and home telephone number in case you need him in an emergency. If you are told your lawyer is always "in meetings" or "out of the office", this is a clear sign your work is being neglected and you have chosen the wrong lawyer.

Know your lawyer's speciality. Although most attorneys are required to have a general knowledge of Costa Rican law, you may need a specialist to deal with your specific case. Some people find it is a good idea to have several lawyers for precisely this reason.

Take your time and look around when you are trying to find a lawyer. This should be fairly easy since there are over 7,000 lawyers from whom to choose. You should ask friends, other people, retirees and other knowledgeable people for the names of their lawyers. Above all, make sure your attorney is recommended from a reliable source. Then try to inquire about your potential lawyer's reputation, his work methods and integrity.

If you find yourself in a jam before finding a lawyer, contact the Asociation of Resident of Costa Rica (ARCR) for assistance, or you can ask a friend for a recommendation.

All over the world, there are always a few incompetent, unscrupulous attorneys, so be careful with whom you are dealing before you make your final choice. Remember, one of the most important people in your life in Costa Rica is your lawyer, so it is imperative that you develop a good working relationship.

A reliable hard-working Costa Rican lawyer is indispensable.

Most attorneys charge from $25 to $50 an hour depending on your problem and their expertise. It is inadvisable to select your lawyer solely on the basis of legal fees. Lawyer's fees, or *honorarios*, vary. Just because a lawyer is expensive does not mean he is good. Likewise, you should not select an attorney because his fees are low.

Check with the Costa Rican version of the Bar Association (*El Colegio de Abogados*) if you have any questions about legal fees. They establish minimum legal fees, however some fees are determined by the amount of the transaction.

In Costa Rica it is not uncommon to hire a lawyer on a full-time basis by paying what amounts to a small retainer. If you find a lawyer who will handle your *pensionado* or residency paperwork for under $ 500, you have found a bargain.

However, if you speak fluent Spanish and have a lot of patience, you can do your residency or *pensionado* paperwork yourself. Just pick up a list of the requirements from the immigration office. Outside the immigration office there are men who will help push your papers through or make sure they are at the "top of the pile." They charge about $10.00 for this service. There is even a lawyer who works with them on the premises.

Do not pay them all the money up front. If you choose this route you can save yourself hundreds of dollars in attorneys' fees. All a lawyer does is just sign a couple of papers, turn them in at the immigration office and take your money.

There is a small amount of paperwork involved in giving your lawyer power of attorney *(poder)* so he can take care of your personal business and legal affairs.

This is not a bad idea when you may have to leave the country for a period of time or in the event of an emergency. However, first make sure your lawyer is completely trustworthy and competent. You may either choose to give your attorney *poder general* (General Power of Attorney) or *poder especial* (Special Power of Attorney). You may revoke both of these types of power of attorney at any time.

If you want answers to most of your questions about the complex Costa Rican legal system, purchase *The Legal Guide To Costa Rica* by Roger Petersen. Although this book is no substitute for a good lawyer, it is still very useful for the layman. This excellent guide may be purchased from Costa Rica Books. (See Chapter 10 for the details.) If you have any questions and want to contact Mr. Peterson, his address, telephone and fax are listed below.

Costa Rica Business and Legal Summary
By Roger A. Petersen
Attorney at Law

Introduction: With the proper guidance and preparation, Costa Rica can be a profitable place to establish a business enterprise while enjoying the tranquility and diversity of the countryside. The business practices, customs and organization that you may be accustumed to in your country of origin may not be applicable to those in Costa Rica.

Be patient, learn the procedures and the local way of doing things before you embark. If you arrive trying to change the country, attitudes and practices you will be in for a surprise. The summary that follows will hopefully assist you in understanding the basic structure of Costa Rican business.

The Costa Rican Political System: Costa Rica is recognized world wide for its stable and democratic political system. All changes of government have occurred by way of free elections which are held every four years. The core of Costa Rica's democratic political system is its Constitution. Originally adopted on November 7, 1949, it remains in effect today establishing a clear system of checks and balances between the three branches of government: the Executive, Judicial and Legislative.

The Legal System: The Costa Rican legal system is based upon the French civil law system as opposed to English common law used in England and the United States. The common law system relies more on case law which is generated by the judicial system and binding on lower courts. In the civil law system the laws passed by the legislature are codified into codes which are then applied by the courts. Only the decisions of the Supreme Court of Costa Rica are binding on the lower courts. The court system is made up of: Lower Courts, trial Level Courts, Appellate Courts and the Supreme Court.

At the present time, delays in processing claims through the legal system are a serious problem. There is a backlog of cases and the government does not have the financial resources to adequately staff and modernize the judicial system to handle those cases.

The country has recently passed legislation which allows for private mediation and arbitration services in the hope that more cases will be resolved by way of alternative dispute resolution methods.

Foreign Investment: The Constitution of Costa Rica provides entrenched protection of fundamental human rights and freedom to nationals and foreigners alike. Since the Constitution of Costa Rica grants foreigners the same rights to conduct business, buy own and sell property as it does to Costa Rican nationals, foreign investment has traditionally been welcome and encouraged.

Foreign investors may also participate or invest in Costa Rica using any of the legal entities recognized by Costa Rican law.

Costa Rican Corporate Law: The most common corporate entity used in Costa Rica is the Sociedad Anónima (S.A.) mainly because the liability of the shareholders is limited to their capital contributions and the shares of the corporation may be freely transferred. The corporation must maintain the following three books: (1) Shareholder's minutes book, (2) Board of Directors minutes books, and (3) a Shareholder's log book.

Taxes in Costa Rica: Yes, we have them also. The Costa Rican tax laws were completely overhauled in 1995 with the passage of the new Tax Code. Taxation is based upon source income, in other words, Costa Rica only taxes revenue that is generated within Costa Rica and not worldwide as other countries do.

Personal income taxes range from 10% to 25% depending on the amount earned. Corporate taxation ranges from 10% to 30% depending on the amount. Costa Rica applies a sales tax of 13% and a special consumption tax on selected items which range from 8% to 10%.

The government also collects a property transfer tax of 1.5% which is triggered whenever a property deed is presented at the Costa Rican National Public Registry to record the transfer of ownership of property from one person to another. The same applies to the transfer of ownership of a motor vehicle which triggers a 2.5% transfer tax.

Property taxes are levied and collected by the municipal government where the property is located. The property values on the books of municipalities is far below the actual market value of the property and each municipality is implementing its own property tax program to update its property tax data base.

Mr. Petersen is a partner in the law firm of Vargas, Petersen & Odio in San José, Costa Rica where he specializes in commercial and real estate law and litigation. He is a member of both the Florida Bar and the Costa Rican Bar. Mr. Petersen is the author of the well respected and best-selling book, The Legal Guide to Costa Rica. He was born in Costa Rica, speaks fluent Spanish and English and attended college and law school in both the United States and Costa Rica.

This comprehensive guide contains sample forms and documents. It covers the most common situations you will encounter in Costa Rica; real estate transactions, corporations, commercial transactions, immigration, labor laws, taxation, wills, marriage and much more. To get a copy write to the address we list in the back of this book. For additional legal information on the World Wide Web contact **www.costaricalaw.com**.

We also recommend purchasing a copy of *Diccionario de Términos Jurídicos* by Enrique Alcaraz. It is a complete English/Spanish dictionary of legal terms.

Here is a partial list of bilingual attorneys who have many North American clients:

Roger Peterson (Costa Rican born American lawyer)
Interlink 553
P.O. Box 02-5635
Miami, FL 33102
Tel: 011-(506) 233-5219; Fax: 011-(506)233-2507
E-mail: crlaws@racsa.co.cr

Ruhal Barrientos Saborio (our lawyer)
Apdo. 5576-1000
San José, Costa Rica
Tel: 011-(506) 290-4948; Fax: 011-(506) 290-5864 Cell: 381-5580

Lic. José Fernando Carter Vargas
P.O. Box 5482-1000,
San José, Costa Rica
Tel: 011-(506) 257-6646, Fax: 011- (506) 258-4101,
E-mail: jfcarter@racsa.co.cr
www.carterlaw.co.cr

Sergio Leiva Urcuyo
Apartado 3379-1000
San José, Costa Rica
Tel: 011-(506) 225-1318 or 253-5856 Fax: 011-(506) 225-6592

Costa Rican Consulates and Embassies Abroad

Costa Rican Consulates provide information about visas, work permits, marriage and residency. They can issue tourist visas, authenticate documents and assist Costa Rican Citizens living abroad.

Anyone seeking permanent residency in Costa Rica needs to have certain documents notarized by a Costa Rican consulate or embassy in their country of origin. Documents that must be notarized are a birth certificate, police certificate (stating you have no criminal record), and a proof of income statement. All this paper work should be taken care of before coming to Costa Rica.

If you apply for permanent residency in Costa Rica, it may take months to get notarized documents from your home country, if it's possible at all. If worse comes to worst, you may have to make a trip home to take care of these matters. While you are waiting for papers from abroad, other documents may expire and you will have to start all over again. Bureaucracy is slow enough as it is in Costa Rica, and it is foolish to delay this process any more than necessary.

Each Costa Rican Consulate has its own business hours and its area of coverage. Please locate your nearest consulate for personal attention. If there is no consulate in your state, please locate the state or city nearest to your residence in the list below.

Consulates in the United States:

Atlanta: 1870 The Exchange Southeast N.W. Suite 100, Atlanta, GA. 30339 Tel: (770) 951-7025 Fax: (770)-951-7073 E-mail: consulate_ga@costarica-embassy.org

Boston: 175 McClennan Highway, East Boston. Ma 02146 or 175 McClennan Highway, East Boston, MA 02128-9114 Tel: (617) 561-2444 Fax: (617) 561-2461, E-mail: consulate_bos@costarica-embassy.org

Chicago: (Includes Illinois, Indiana, Michigan, Ohio, Iowa, Minnesota, Missouri, North Dakota, South Dakota, Indiana, and Wisconsin) 203 North Wabash Avenue., Suite 1312, Chicago, IL 60601 Tel: (312) 263-2772 Fax: (312) 263-5807 E-mail: crcchi@aol.com

Dallas (Coverage: Dallas): 7777 Forrest Ln., Suite B445, Dallas, TX 75231 Tel: (972) 566-7020 Fax: (972) 566-7943

Denver: 3356 South Xenia Street, Denver, CO 80231-4542; Tel: (303) 696-8211 Fax: (303) 696-1110 E-mail: crconsul@ecentral.com

Houston: 3000 Wilcrest, Suite 112, Houston, TX 77042 Tel: (713) 266-0484 Fax: (713) 266-1527 E-mail: consulatccr@juno.com

Los Angeles: (Includes Southern California, Arizona, Nevada, Utah, and Hawaii): 1605 West Olympic., Suite 400, Los Angeles, CA 90015 Tel: (213) 380-6031 Fax: (213) 380-5639 E-mail: kieffer@inetworld.net

Miami (Covers Florida): Consulate General, 1600 Northwest 42nd Avenue, Miami, FL 33126 Tel: (305)- 871-7487, 871 7485 Fax: (305) 871-0860 E-mail: consulate_fla@costarica-embassy.org

New Orleans: (Includes Alabama, Arkansas, Kentucky, Louisiana, Mississippi, New Mexico, Oklahoma and Tennesse)World Trade Center Bldg., 2 Canal St., Suite 2334, New Orleans, LA 70130 Tel: (504) 581-6800 Fax: (504) 581-6850, E-mail: consulno@aol.com

New York (Includes Connecticut, Maine, Massachusetts, New England, New Hampshire, New Jersey, Pennsylvania, Rhode Island andVermont) : 80 Wall Street, Suite 718, New York, NY 10005Tel: (212) 509-3066 Fax: 212 509-3068 E-mail: consulnewyork@hotmail.com

Phoenix (Area of coverage Arizona):1426 W, Key Largo Court,Gilbert, Arizona, 85034 Tel: (561) 5620-8307 Fax: (561) 620-5821

Puerto Rico: Avenida Ponce de Leon, Edificio 1510, Oficina P1, Esquina Calle Pelaval, San Juan, Puerto Rico 00909 Tel: (787) 723-6227 Fax: (787) 723-6226, E-mail: consuladopr@yunque.net

San Antonio: Continental Building , 6836 San Pedro, Suite 116, San Antonio, TX 78216 Tel: (210) 824-8474 Fax: (210) 824-8489

San Francisco (Includes, Alaska, Idaho, Montana, Northern California, Oregon and Washington): P.O. Box 7643, Freemont, Ca 94536, Tel: (510) 790-0785 Fax: (510) 792-5249 E-mail: consulsfo@hotmail.com

St. Paul: 2424 Territorial Road, St. Paul, MN 55114, Tel: (651) 645-410 3Fax: (651) 645-4684 E-mail: lupita.barahona@2424group.com

Tampa: 2204 Barker Road, Tampa, FL 33605, Tel: (813) 248-6741 Fax: 813) 248-6857 E-mail: crica@integracom.net

Washington (Covers all of U.S. territory): 2114 "S" Street, NW, Washington, D.C. 20008; Tel: (202) 3286628 Fax: (202) 265-4795 E-mail: consulate@costarica-embassy.org Web-site: www.costarica-embassy.org.

Consulates Abroad:

England
14 Lancaster Gate
London, England
K2P 1B7
Tel: 071-723-1772

Canada
325 Dalhouse St, Suite 407
Ottawa, Ontario   K1N 7G2
Tel: (613)562-0842
Fax: (613) **562-2582**
    E-mail: rolomadrigal@
hotmail.com

Canada
614 Centre A. Street N.W.
Calgary, Alberta

Canada
164 Avenue Road
Toronto, Ontario M5R 2H9
Tel: (416) 961-6773

Canada
145 Chadwik Court
Suite 320
North Vancouver, B.C.
V6C 1H2
Tel: (604) 983-2152
Fax: (604) 983-2178
E-mail: consulado@sprint.ca

Canada
1425 René Levexque-West
 Suite 602
Montreal, H3G 1T7
Tel: (514) 393-1057
Fax: (514) 393-1624

*To obtain a complete list of embassies and consulates visit the Costa Rican Foreign Ministry web site at: www.rree.go.cr or www.costarica.com/travel/missions-worldwide.

Embassies and Consulates in Costa Rica

If you are planning to travel and explore Latin America and other parts of the world, when you are settled in Costa Rica, you will need the addresses of the embassies and consulates listed below in order to get visas and other necessary travel documents.

Most embassies and consulates are located in downtown San José.

The rest are found in upscale neighborhoods like Rohrmoser, Los Yoses and San Pedro, about 10 minutes from the center of the city. Before visiting any of the consulates or embassies below, we suggest you find out their hours.

Argentina — Ave. 6 Calle 21-25		221-6869
Austria (consulate) — Ave.4 Calle		363-8255-0767
Belize — Guadalupe		253-9626
Bolivia — Ave. Central, Calle 9-12		255-1805
Brazil — Ave. 2, Calle 20-22		233-1544
Canada — Ave. ct. 1 Calle 3		255-3522
Chile — Barrio Dent		225-0413
China — San Pedro		224-8180
Columbia — Ave. 1, Calle 29		221-0725
Ecuador— (consulate) Paseo Colón, Calle 38-40		232-1503
El Salvador — Los Yoses		257-7855
France — Curridabat		234-4167
Germany — Ave. 5, Calle 40-42		232-5533
Great Britain — Paseo Colón		221-5566
Guatemala —(consulate) Barrio California		283-2555
Honduras — Los Yoses		234-9502
Italy — Los Yoses Ave. 10, Calle		224-9415
Israel — Ave., 2-4, Calle 2		221-6011
Japan		232-1255
Mexico — Barrio Amon		257-0633
Nicaragua — Barrio California		233-3479
Panamá — San Pedro		281-2442
Perú – Los Yoses		225-9145
Puerto Rico — Ave. 2, Calle 11-13		257-1769
Spain — Ave. 2 Paseo Colón, Calle 32		222-1933
Switzerland — Paseo Colón Calles 38-40		221-4829
Taiwan — Guadalupe		224-4992

United States of America — Pavas, Rohrmoser...............220-3050
Venezuela — Los Yoses 225-5813

The U.S. Embassy in the suburb of Pavas just outside San José.

STAYING BUSY AND HAPPY IN COSTA RICA

Some Sound Advice

Retirement or just living in another country often presents new challenges for people. For the first time they are confronted with having a plethora of leisure time and the problem of what to do to with it. As you will see throughout this chapter, Costa Rica is wonderful place to live. In addition to being relatively inexpensive, there are many interesting activities from which to choose. As one of our American friends stated when referring to his busy life in Costa Rica, "My days are so fulfilling that each day in Costa Rica seems like a whole lifetime."

In Costa Rica you have no excuse for being bored or inactive, unless you are just plain lazy. There is some hobby or pastime for everyone regardless of age or interests. Even if you cannot pursue your favorite hobbies, you can get involved in something new and exciting. Best of all, by participating in some of the activities in this chapter, you will meet other people with common interests and cultivate new friendships in the process. You can even spend your time continuing your education or studying Spanish. Most people you meet will also be expatriates, so you probably will not need that much Spanish to enjoy yourself. However, the happiest expats seem to be those who speak Spanish. They are able to enjoy the culture more fully, mix with the locals and make new friends in the process.

Whatever you do, don't make the mistake of being idle. The worst thing you can do is spend all your time drinking in one of the many *gringo* hangouts in downtown San José. Over the years, we have seen many fellow Americans fail to use their time constructively, and they destroy their lives by becoming alcoholics while living in Costa Rica—a few even died prematurely. So, use the information we provide in this chapter and take advantage of the many activities Costa Rica offers.

English Books, Magazines and Newspapers

Books, newspapers, magazines and other printed materials in English are available at most leading bookstores, in souvenir shops of larger hotels, and at some newsstands.

Many bookstores carry a large selection of books in English. **7th Street Books**, in downtown San José, is one of the city's best bookstores (Calle 7, between Ave. 1 and Central, Tel: 256-8251 e-mail: marroca@sol.racsa.co.cr). The North American owners, John and Mark, stock a wide range of new and used books in English with an excellent selection of travel, Spanish, nature books and U.S. magazines. They will even special order books for you.

Librería Internacional is a European-style bookstore. This bookstore is not global in name only since it sells books in English, Spanish and German. Locations: Barrrio Dent San Pedro 300 meters west of Taco Bell Tel: 253-9553, Centro Comercial Multiplaza second floor Tel: 201-8320, Rohrmoser 200 meters east of El Fogoncito restaurant Tel 290-3331, Mall Internacional Alajuela Tel 442-3800, Plaza Cemaco, second floor 100 mts. north of Garantias Sociales traffic circle Tel: 257-8065, Central Ave. 75 meters west of la Plaza de la Cultura Tel: 257-2563, Paseo de las Flores Mall Heredia.

LibroMax is a discount bookstore chain offering up to 50 percent off on some titles. Locations: Real Cariari second floor Real Cariari Mall, Heredia across from the parking lot of the former Ferretería Las 3 Américas, Cartago across from the Banco Nacional de Costa Rica, Multiplaza Escazú first floor across from Banco Nacional de Costa Rica, Outlet Mall diagonal to the church of San Pedro, Mall San Pedro, Main floor of the San Pedro Mall, Telephone for all stores : 800 Libromax (800-5427662)

You can also find a good selection of English books in the book section of any of the three **Librería Universal** department stores (Ave. Central, Tel: 222-2222), and **Librería Lehmann** (Ave. Central, Calles 1 and 3, Tel: 223-1212). **Papyrus**, (next to Más por Menos supermarket in Sabana Este, Tel:

Why Did You Come Here? What Do You Do?

By Martha Bennett

There are several species of estranjeros living in Costa Rica for a variety of reasons and doing different things. They come to retire, for adventure, to invest or open a business, or to study with one thing in common: changing their life style.

There are tourists. Some come to appreciate the flora and the fauna, volcanoes, beaches and mountains, and observe the Costa Rica culture. Others flock for sports: deep sea fishing, diving, surfing, white water rafting, hiking and hanging out. Everything is available except snow sports. Cultural events may be added on to either group's activities. A third group comes entirely for the bars, casinos and massage parlors. No one comes for the great food which has not inspired restaurants in other parts of the world. No matter, the ingredients are available to create your own cusine.

The people who park here for six months to life do these things and more. Missionaries come for Latin language and culture. Old men come looking for young Ticas. They get them too. This unlikely alliance builds the men's egos and the girls like the upgraded standard of living. Others of all ages earn or supplement their income teaching languages, writing, renting rooms or acting as tour guides. There is a group, usually college educated, who can't find, satisfactory jobs in North America. They are found in the tourist industry or working for international companies. A foreigner can work here if the task is something a Tico can not do. There are regulations, but in Latin countries, these are worked around. A slower pace of life and close family ties appeal to people in high stress jobs who have children. They come for a change of atmosphere. There is crime and substance abuse here, but the tightly knit community provides a healthier climate for raising children.

Retirees participate in many things. Some renovate a dream house. Some persue the World Wide Web. There is a Theater Group, a Canadian Club, Women's club, Scrabble, bridge and T'ai Chi clubs and even a society for refrigeration engineers. The country club set plays golf, graces swimming pools, and dines elegantly. One can study yoga, painting, writing, language, pottery, gardening, holistic medicine and dance.

Remember, living takes longer here. Time is spent finding things, fixing things, cutting red tape and avoiding long lines. But this pace allows more time for reading, observing, listening to music and just being. In Costa Rica, we are more human beings than human doings. *Pura vida*! Pure life!

221-4664) has an excellent selection of magazines, newspapers and paperbacks in English and Spanish. They have another branch in downtown San José.

Mora Books (Tel: 255-4136/383-8385) is located in downtown San José in the Omni Building on Avenida 1 between streets 3 and 5. They have over 25,000 volumes on display and specialize in used books.

Some ex-pats order books on line though www.amazon.com and have one of the local private mail services like Aerocasillas bring them to Costa Rica.

Major libraries in the San José area have large collections of English language books and magazines. The place to go for the best selection of books is the **Mark Twain Library** at the **North American–Central American Culture Institute**, commonly known as the Centro Cultural. You can browse all day or check out books. They also have nearly one hundred English magazines from which to choose. Call 253-5783 for more information.

The **National Library**, near downtown San José, is not a browsing library but has a large selection of novels and magazines in English. You have to use the card catalog to select your book and then request it at the front desk. Also, the University of Costa Rica Library has some materials in English.

There are public libraries in the San José area and suburbs that have mainly Spanish language books. They can be found in the cities of Desamparados (Tel: 250-0426), Hatillo (254-1028), Montes de Oca (272-0809), Ciudad Colón (249-3516), Santa Ana (282-9106), Puriscal (416-8300) and Tibás (236-3087).

There is no problem obtaining copies of New York Times, Time or Newsweek in Costa Rica. The Miami Herald international satellite edition is now also available in Costa Rica. You can pick up most English newspapers and magazines at local newsstands, hotels and some bookstores. You can also arrange to have many of the newspapers we mention in this section delivered to your home or office the same day they are published by calling **Agencia de Publicaciones** at 259-5555, 259-5656, or 259-0812.

Other English Language Publications:

- *Barron's*
- *International Herald Tribune*
- *Sporting News*
- *Sports Illustrated*

Opening an English Language Bookstore in Costa Rica
By Mike Jones

My business partner and I are often asked how we decided to start a bookstore in Costa Rica. We began by listing all the businesses we thought might be interesting to operate and/or potentially profitable. The list we came up with included a pool hall, music store, bar, pharmacy, bagel shop, bookstore and laundromat. As we were mulling over the possibilities, we heard about a bar that was for sale. After talking to the owners of the bar and consulting with our lawyer, we decided to make an offer, contingent upon our being able to discuss with the building's landlord the changes we wanted to make to the bar. When the owners of the bar told us that it wouldn't be possible to talk to their landlord prior to purchase, we balked at the deal, sensing bad faith. A few weeks later, some friends contacted us about an excellent retail location that was becoming available in downtown San José. Because the location is near to the Plaza de la Cultura, a point visited by nearly every tourist, we decided that an English language bookstore, whose main market would be tourists, might work. And so, within the space of two weeks we went from being bar ownwers to bookstore owners.

Our bookstore has now been opened nearly four years, and each year sales have nudged upward. There have been moments of despair, frustration and crisis, but the business appears to have finally left the crawling stage behind and is walking. I never owned a business before in the U.S. and do not think that only four years of business ownership prepares me to give general business advice. What I could instead offer is a handful of tips that relate specifically to expatriate business ownership.

The first relates to your decision about opening a business in Costa Rica. You must decide if you like the country! This is an obvious point, but I have seen many tourists arrive and decide to move here mainly on the basis of having enjoyed their vacation. The rythm of day-to-day existence versus that of tourist life is entirely distinct. If you can pull it off financially, I would recommend first arriving for a six month visit to really test the idea that this is where you would like to live. Even then, you must keep in mind that there is a big difference between living here while not working and living here while running a business; all the things you enjoyed doing when you were free of work obligations, you will find little time for when you are starting up a business.

When you do decide to start a business, be prepared for a dual challenge, you will be facing all the standard problems of business ownership (managing cash, monitoring competition, attempting to increase sales, etc.) at the same time that you are learning a new culture and language.

As you go through the process of trying to decide what kind of business to open, it is common to make a list of kinds of businesses that exist in the home country but do not exist in Costa Rica. For several years we expatriates were clamoring for a bagelry and a micro brewery, and when they did finally arrive they met with considerable success. Nevertheless, it is important to keep in mind the significant cultural differences that exist between the home country and here, and that what works there won't always work here. The expatriate community is not so large that you can succeed simply by targeting that group. You need tico customers too, and disposable income is not too high here. Also, whatever business you choose, it is obviously important as an expatriate to respect the customs and moral standards of this country. One gentleman from Canada entered the store and told me he was planning on opening a topless car wash. I said, "I would suggest doing that in another country."

Expatriate business people need to resist the occasional pull toward paranoia, toward the notion that "they", the locals are all trying to take advantage of me. A more reasonable stance, I think, is to asume that in business everyone is trying to take advantage of everyone, regardless of national origin. So far, our only slightly significant encounters with less than honorable people have been two unfortunate business deals with other expatriate business people, who , because they had no strong family or financial ties to this country, were able to flee the country.

Despite a strong tendency on the part of U.S. media to represent Latin American governments as bureaucratic, inefficient mazes, we have found the opposite to be true in Costa Rica. Nearly all the legal and regulatory issues that we have been required to comply with have generally been handled swiftly and fairly inexpensively by our lawyer. Get a good lawyer whose practice focuses on expatriate clients. A related stereotype about Latin America is that it is rife with corruption. While there are great differences between countries, we have never had anyone approach us and insist that we pay a bribe as a condition for conducting business. True, we have had people offer us the option of a bribe in order to receive faster or better service. I've seen similar things happen in New York. A last word of advice...don't expect to get rich.

- *USA Today*
- *Wall Street Journal*
- *Washington Post*

Originally founded in 1992, ***Costa Rica Today*** is Central America's largest bilingul newspaper (English/Spanish) with more than 100,000 readers. The paper has good information about tourism, retirement and business tips. It is distributed in all of the Central American countries, airports, embassies and consulates abroad and is free. For additional information or to advertise see: *Costa Rica Today*, SJO -117, P.O. Box 0025216, Miami, FL 33102.Tel: (506) 520-0303 Fax:(506)520-1234 E-mail: crt@506tv.com.

The ***Tico Times***, the largest English newspaper published in Central America, is available almost everywhere in Costa Rica. Reading it is an excellent way to keep up with local Costa Rican and Central American news in general. Car sales, cultural activities and other useful information can also be found in this newspaper. The newspaper costs about one dollar and it comes out every Friday.

To subscribe to the *Tico Times* (if you live in the U.S.), write Dept. 717, P.O. Box 025216, Miami, FL 33102. If you live in Costa Rica: Apdo. 4362, San José, Costa Rica. You can read this newspaper on line at: www.ticotimes.net.

A.M. Costa Rica is an online newspaper published Monday through Friday. In additional to the usual daily news events and features there is an excellent classified ads section. You may access this online newspaper at www.amcostarica.com. For additional information contact them at A.M. Costa Rica, Apartado 6318-1000, San José, Costa Rica, Tel/Fax: (506)-231-7528 E-mail: editor@amcostarica.com.

Inside Costa Rica is another good online publication. It is published daily and has both local and international news articles. *Inside Costa Rica* may be accessed at: www.insidecostarica.com.

La Nación, Costa Rica's best Spanish newspaper, has a new online version in English at: www.nacion.com/In_ee/english.

Television and Radio

As in the United States, Costa Rica has satellite cable television. A variety of American television channels provide viewing and entertainment at a low cost from **Amnet** (231-38380, 231-2811 or 231-3939), **Cable Tica** (254-8858), or **Cable America** (238-1756). You will not miss much TV while living in Costa Rica since these companies offer local channels in

Spanish as well as 38 English channels including CBS, NBC, ABC, FOX, HBO, CNN, ESPN, TNT,the Discovery Channel and more. There is an initial sign up fee of around $25 and a monthly charge of $23. If you want to hook up additional TV in your house or apartment you will pay only $2.50 extra per month.

Since 1997, **DirectTV** (Tel: 296-7681, Fax: 296-7684, E-mail: galaxia@racsa.co.cr) has been available in Costa Rica. With this system you can receive up to 100 channels. The cost has dropped considerably. The basic cost is an $89 installation fee and $23 monthly for the basic package. For the complete movie package including movie and sports channels the cost is around $45 monthly.

DirectTV systems purchased in the U.S. will not work with the satellite systems in Costa Rica or the rest of Latin America. NFL and NBA sports packages are now available. Members with Direct TV pay-per-view can now order over 30 first-run movies per month for about $3 each. Call 201-7171 for more information.

Even better than DirectTV is **Dr. Dish** Satellite TV, offering digital alternative programming. For a one-time installation fee of around $1,700 and a reasonable monthly rate, you get hooked up to digital TV viewing, a slice of home so to speak. Some of the many programs they offer include Fox, Fox Sports, HBO (10 channels), Show Time (10 channels), NBC, CBS, ABC, TNT, and over a hundred more channels. We have several friends who have this system and rave about it. Also feel free to contact Dr. Dish about any interest or questions you may have concerning internet and the latest technology available in Costa Rica. To find out more call 011-506-8DR-DISH.

Most radio stations play Latin music. However, there are four English language radio stations that play pop, oldies and modern rock. Both foreigners and younger locals listen to these stations since they play a lot of past and present hits. Many of the bus drivers play rock music that the English stations play. **Radio Dos 99.5 FM** plays Top -40 music from the 1960s, '70s, '80s and '90s. **Radio 107.5 FM**, the country's only all-English radio stations offers, 100 percent rock from all decades. **Super Radio 102.3** specializes in the oldies.

Radio 95.5 plays a great selection of tasty jazz and fusion.

Video Rentals

Video buffs will be happy that many video rental shops do business all over the country. For a small initial fee you can acquire a membership at one of these stores and enjoy many privileges. Most movies you rent are in English with Spanish subtitles.

Video de las Américas (two locations) 253-6545, 257-0303
Video Movies (Curridabat) 272-5494
Hollywood Video Club (many locations) 225-0630, 225-0630
Video Centro Escazú (several locations)...........228-8382,239-4285
Video Happy (Rohrmoser) 231-7295

See the phone book for additional listings.

Shopping

One way to keep active is to go shopping. Although Costa Rica is not as good for shopping as the U.S., you can still spend your free time doing some serious shopping, browsing or just window-shopping.

Due to the large number of U.S. and Canadian citizens living in Costa Rica, and a growing number of Costa Ricans exposed to U.S. culture by cable TV and visiting the States, there has been an influx of American products. The only problem is that many of these goods are more expensive in Costa Rica because of import duties.

Everyday more and more imported goods from the U.S. are available in Costa Rica. Imported brand name cosmetics, stylish clothing, appliances and some foods can now be found in many stores in San José and other areas catering to foreigners. A number of new stores and shopping centers in or near San José now sell imported items.

In downtown San José a few specialty shops and a couple of department stores sell American-style clothing and other imported goods. San José's Central Avenue or *Avenida Central* has virtually been turned into a pedestrian outdoor mall and walking street.   This section begins a block beyond the Central market and ends at the east end of the Plaza de La Cultura. La Gloria department store, Lehman bookstore and the Universal department store are all found along this promenade.

There are a variety of shops around the Central Market which offer products at low prices.   Prices in this section of town tend to be much more reasonable than in the local mega-malls. Boutiques, a multitude of shoe stores, a record shop, a pharmacy, an outdoor sidewalk café and fast food restaurants like MacDonald's, Burger King and Taco Bell dot both sides of the street. For you mall-rats or mall-crawlers, there are also a number of local shopping centers that closely resemble U.S. style malls. **Plaza del Sol,** Costa Rica's first U.S.-style mall, is about five minutes east of San José in Curridabat. A mall is also found at the **Plaza Mayor Shopping Center** in Rohrmoser. It has 21 businesses including a movie theater, supermarket, bank, pet store, pharmacy and food court. In the suburb of Escazú, home of many foreigners and well-to-do Costa Ricans, a number of U.S.-style mini-malls have sprung up. Most of these newer stores have products that foreigners seek. The **Multiplaza** mega-mall west of Escazú houses a large mall and shopping center. There are the usual chain stores plus a host of specialty shops. **Multiplaza Este,** in the San José eastern suburb of Curridabat, belongs to the same company. **Terramall,** east of San José on the way to the city of Cartago is the country's newest mall complex.

Within a year there will be two new malls in the city of Heredia. Both **Paseo de Las Flores** and the **Heredia Centro** malls will have stores, food courts, multiple screen movie theaters, ample parking and a more.

The **San Pedro** nine-story Mall is one of Central America's largest shopping centers. This mega-mall will eventually have over 260 stores, 35 restaurants, a hotel, a couple of discos, video arcades and parking for 1,200 cars.

A few blocks east of the San Pedro Mall is the new **American Outlet Mall.** It has over 150 shops including a movie theater, a food court, and outlet stores. The latter operates like the factory outlets in the U.S. by selling clothes and other items at discounted prices. **Plaza Real Cariari**, the San José areas newest shopping center, has around 110 stores, a food court, and theaters.

The **Mall Internacional,** on the main road just before the city of Alajuela, is smaller than the other giant shopping complexes but offers shoppers an ample variety of shops.

Other smaller mini-malls include **Plaza Colonial** in San Rafael de Escazú, **Santa Ana 2000** in Santa Ana, **San José 2000** near the Hotel Irazú, **Plaza Heredia,** in the neighboring city of Heredia, **Centro Colón** on Paseo Colón **Centro Comercial Guadalupe** in Guadalupe, the new **Nova Centro** in Moravia, **Plaza America** near Hatillo, **Metrocentro** in the city of Cartago and **Gran Centro Comercial del Sur** south of San José.

There are also music stores, supermarkets, and natural food stores located in the San José area. There are even arts and crafts stores and gift shops. Check out **La Casona**, the **National Artisan Street Market** or the new **International Market of Arts and Crafts** in the suburb of Curridabat to the east of San José.

The newest shopping craze is the U.S. warehouse-style mega-stores like Wall-Mart and Target. It promises to change local shopping habits and pricing. The new **HiperMás** stores have groceries, furniture, toys, a deli, clothing, appliances and more all under one roof. Best of all, the stores stock a huge amount of U.S. products. Costa Rica's first wholesale shopping club, **PriceSmart**, opened in San José's Zapote district in mid-1999. This store is similar to the Costco chain in the U.S. The company is pioneering the "club" concept in Costa Rica. The store purchases large amounts of imported products, and in turn passes its volume-buying savings on to its club members. They also have stores in Heredia and Escazú.

In addition, **GNC** (288-1049) opened several vitamin stores in the San José area. Now all types of vitamins and nutritional products are available.

The **Cemaco** department store chain operates stores in Pavas, Curridabat, Multiplaza, Alajuela and Zapote. The new store in Zapote's Plaza Cemaco has 37 departments and over 60,000 items.

The mammoth U.S.-style San Pedro Mall.

In general, despite the availability of many new imported products and the growing number of malls, mini-malls and specialty shops, shopping in Costa Rica still leaves a lot to be desired if you are used to the U.S. or Canada. Do not expect to find every product you may need in Costa Rica.

As we mention in Chapter 9, if you live in Costa Rica, you have to substitute many local products for items you ordinarily use and do without some things. This is easy due to the variety of similar products available in Costa Rica.

If you absolutely must have products from the States, you can go to the U.S. every few months—as many foreigners and wealthy Costa Ricans do—to stock up on canned goods and other non-perishable foods, clothing, sundries and cosmetics. We know of one American retiree who goes to Miami every three or four months to buy all the goodies he cannot find in Costa Rica. These frequent trips to the States are unnecessary if you learn to make do with the local products.

One thing you may need some time to get accustomed to is the way purchases are handled in some stores. One clerk will wait on you, another will ring up the purchase, and finally you will pick up your merchandise at another window. You find this system in most department stores, pharmacies and older businesses. This system seems to create a lot of extra work for employees and delays for customers. The good news is that every day more and more stores are adopting the American style one-step self-service system.

Costa Rican Pastimes

Costa Rica has a wealth of indoor and outdoor activities designed for everyone regardless of sex, age, personal taste or budget. All of us, Costa Ricans, tourists and foreign residents, can participate in river rafting (some of the world's best), camping, walking groups, dancing, raquetball, weight lifting, tennis, baseball, soccer, swimming and surfing, jogging, bicycling, horseback riding, and sailing. There are also plays, ceramic classes, movies, bridge clubs, art galleries, social clubs, museums, parks, zoos and more. Dedicated couch potatoes can even stretch out and admire the lovely landscape or work on improving their suntans.

Metro Bowl near the Multiplaza Mall is a new entertainment center with 20 bowling lanes, restaurants and a pool hall.

There is something for everyone, so enjoy. Check the activities section of the *Costa Rica Today* or *Tico Times*. If you speak Spanish there is a listing in the weekend section of *La Nación* called *Buscando Diversión*. You can find activities, cultural events and all sorts of entertainment listed there.

Gyms and health clubs are a good place to socialize and make new friends while working out. Some gyms even have spas, tennis courts and swimming pools. There are over 32 gyms in the metropolitan area. Call around and visit those in your area to find out which is right for you.

If you wish to join a private athletic club, country club or gym we suggest:

The Indoor Club Curridabat 225-9344
Costa Rican Tennis Club 232-1266
The Spa Corobicí Gym 232-5533
Spa Cariari Hotel Gym.. 239-0022
Club Olímpico Gym... 224-3560
Fitzsimons Gym.. 296-0264
Hi-Line Gym 232-1464
Grupo MultiSpa Gym (Escazú).................................... 289-5051
Grupo MultiSpa (Hotel Radisson)............................... 257-8224
Grupo MultiSpa (Curridabat) 253-0303
Sports Connection.. 234-9668
Ironman Gym... 233-3025
Troyanos Gym (Downtown)... 222-1641

* Check the phone book for more listings of gyms and private athletic clubs.

Golf in Costa Rica

Costa Rica's beautiful scenery and spring-like weather provide a perfect setting for playing golf. It is no surprise the sport has really taken-off over the last couple of years and is on the verge of a boom.

The country promises to become a premier golf travel destination in the future with the opening of public courses. **Golf La Ribera**, the country's first public driving range, recently opened (Tel: 381-4433). It is located in La Ribera de Belén near a famous water park called Ojo de Agua, about 15-20 minutes from downtown. It is a good place to begin your golf experience in Costa Rica. The **Marriot Hotel** has its own range but it's reserved for the guests of the hotel for now. **Parque Valle de Sol** (Tel: 282-9222) is a nine-hole public course near San José. It is very popular with local expatriates.

Most of Costa Rica's golf courses have rental clubs and provide caddies. There is sometimes a staggering difference in green fees if you are with a member as opposed to showing up at the course as a walk-on. Below is a description of some of the country's courses.

In the Central Valley the **Cariari Country Club** is one of Costa Rica's two 18-hole course. The Cariari has hosted such world-famous golfers as Tom Weiskoff, Ray Floyd and many more. The Cariari is significantly more expensive than Valle de Sol or Los Reyes.

Costa Rica Country Club is a nine-hole course and boasts Central America's most lush clubhouse. You have to be with a member to play but a personal chat with the pro might get you through the gate and on the course. Incidentally, almost all the Costa Rican pros speak English, so a hint at perhaps taking some lessons could help open some doors.

Los Reyes Country Club is just nine-holes for now but designed to be a full eighteen eventually. It is about 45 minutes from downtown San José.

Currently there are several places to play golf on Costa Rica's west coast. Over the next few years more will open. A word of advice: schedule your tee-off for early in the morning or wait for a leisurely, twilight round because the sun and humidity can be brutal during the day.

Tango Mar Resort and Country Club is a ten-hole course located at Playa Tambor on the bottom of the Nicoya Peninsula. You do not have to be accompanied by a member and chances are you will have the course all to yourself.

Rancho Las Colinas Golf and Country Club, near Flamingo, overlooking Playa Grande in mid-Guanacaste, is the newest course in Costa Rica. This course will become the jewel of a quickly developing community.

Las Colinas is about a five-hour drive from San José, or better a 30-40 minute flight. Flamingo is the center of the Guanacaste sport fishing fleet with the largest marina in the country. If your golf game is off, maybe the fish are biting.

The **Four Seasons Hotel** at the Papagayo Peninsula opened its new 18-hole golf course in February of 2004. Friends who have played are raving about it.

Please see the golf chart in this section for a complete update on all course openings.

A Golfer's Dream
By Landy Blank

My wife Susan and I have lived in Costa Rica for two years. We vacationed here many times before deciding to make our big move. It often feels as though we arrived here just yesterday, at other times I don't remember living anywhere else. However, I will always remember the reaction of family and friends upon being told that we were packing our bags, three large dogs and heading to Costa Rica. I thought everybody would be excited and offer lots of encouragement, but read on to get an idea.

"What will you do on that island?" "We'll bring people to Costa Rica on golf vacations, and actually it's not an island. Oh, I didn't know it was a golf destination, they must have some great courses." "Well, not exactly...They do have one great course, the Cariari, and more are being built." "Landy, they only have one course and you're going to sell golf vacations?" "We're looking ahead and new courses are being built!" "When will they be finished?" "That's a tough question, nobody sems to know, but it will happen! The only way I can find out is to move there, get ourselves settled, and be ready when they do open."

Inevitably at this point in the conversation there was a rolling of the eyes and a small smile would pass across the face of my friend, family member, or golfing buddy.

"Why in the world would you want to leave Charleston? You get to play golf as part of your job at the country club, and then go downtown and eat and drink for free at your restaurant. You must be crazy, I just don't understand."

How do you explain that Costa Rica has gotten into your blood, the people, the beauty, the climate, and despite the bureaucratic hassles, you're determined to live there. It didn't take long for these conversations to become tiresome, and as quickly as possible we made our move to our new home. With dogs, computers, golf clubs, and anything that would fit into a suitcase, we were off to Costa Rica in search of our destiny.

Many of the people we met in Costa Rica expresssed the same incredulity when we told them we were planning to bring groups of golfers here on vacation. The look we got was, "Well, you're not the first crazy *gringo* to hit Costa Rica, and I wish you all the best luck in the world. Let me buy you a drink!"

(Author's note: In the past two years, two world class championship golf courses have been completed. Costa Rica is quickly becoming known around the world as a golf destination and we are very happy that we made the move!)

Golfers may now keep up to date on Costa Rica's growing golf scene by subscribing to *Central America's Golf Magazine*, Tel: 011-(506) 231-6931, Fax: 011-(506) 232-1930, E-mail: golftennis@hotmail.com, www.golfmagazine.net.

For golf tours to Costa Rica see **Costa Rica Unique Tours**: www.costaricabooks.com/travel or **Costa Rica Golf Adventures** at www.golfcr.com.

Museums and Art Galleries

There are more than 30 museums scattered around Costa Rica displaying everything from pre-Columbian artifacts to the history of railways. Many are conveniently located in downtown San José. Most guidebooks have maps showing their locations.

Although not as impressive as museums in the States or Europe, there is still a lot to see. In general, Costa Rica's museums provide a good perspective on the history and culture of the country. Here is a list of some of the best museums:

Museums:
Dr. Calderón Guardia Museum, Barrio Escalante 255-1218
Costa Rican Scientific and Cultural Center, (for children) .223-7003
Costa Rican Art Museum, Sabana Park 222-7155
Entomological Museum 225-5555
Museum of Criminology 221-1340
Museum of Contemporary Art 257-7202
Gold Museum 223-0528
Jade Museum 223-5800
National Museum 257-1433
Maritime Museum 661-3666
Juan Santamaría Museum, Alajuela 441-4775

Galleries:
Alterna, Pavas 232-8500
Arte 99, Rohrmoser..232-4035
Andrómedia, Barrio Amón...223-3529
Café de Artistas, Escazú...228-6045

Contemporary National Art Gallery.................................257-5524
Jacob Karpio, San José..257-7963
José Joaquín García Monge 221-1329
Kadinsky, San Pedro..234-0478
National Gallery, Children's Museum............................258-4929
For more listings see the yellow Pages under *Galerías*.

Excellent Fishing

Costa Rica has some of the world's best sport fishing. Take your choice. Fish either the Caribbean or the Pacific, but do not forget those gentle miles of meandering rivers or the fresh water lakes. Lake Arenal is famous for its *guapote* bass. More importantly, most fishing areas are only a few hours driving time from anywhere in Costa Rica.

Costa Rica is considered to be one of the best year-round fishing areas in the world. The fishing is outstanding almost all of the time and almost everywhere in Costa Rica. Even when it rains your chances of catching some excellent sport fish are very good. When it comes to sailfish, tarpon or snook, no place is better than Costa Rica.

If you are really hooked on fishing and want to keep up with the local fishing scene, pick up a copy of the *Tico Times*. It has an excellent weekly fishing column written by legendary local fishing expert, Jerry Ruhlow.

Listed below are some of the better fishing camps all of which have great accommodations and experienced English-speaking fishing guides.

Carribbean Fishing:
Lucky One...221-0096
Tortuga Lodge...223-0333
Parismina Tarpon Rancho...235-7766
Casamar 381-1380
Río Colorado..232-4063 or 232-8610

Pacific Fishing:
Flamingo Bay Pacific Charters......................680-0444 or 680-0620
Papagayo Excursions 680-0859
Oasis del Pacífico (Nicoya).. 661-1555
Sports Fishing Quepos 233-9135

A Fisherman Finds a Home in Costa Rica
By Todd Staley

A writing assignment first brought me to Costa Rica in 1987. Being an outdoor journalist, I was very excited to test some of the country's "world famous sportsfishing". This trip brought me in contact with the late Archie Fields and we became immediate friends. While sitting on the veranda of his famous Rio Colorado Lodge, I asked Archie if he ever needed someone to run his lodge I would like to be considered. He chuckled and said I was about number 1000 on the list.

I returned to the States and told all that would listen that I didn't know how, but one day I would be living in Costa Rica. In the meantime I sought out other Costa Rican writing assignments and began bringing groups of fishermen down to Costa Rica.

In June of 1991 Archie called my house in the US and asked me to "think" about coming down and managing his fishing lodge. I took less than three seconds to think it over. In the next three months I condensed my life belongings to 7 suitcases and 35 fishing poles and headed for Costa Rica.

In Barra del Colorado where I lived there are no cars. The river, creeks and canals are the streets and avenues. I worked long hours often going as many as three months without a day off and loved every second of it. I used Norman Paperman, the character in Herman Wouk's "Don't Stop the Carnival" as my relief when problems arose concerning employees or guests.

I was awestruck by the culture of the Caribbean side of Costa Rica, especially the stories told to me by the older generations. I met people with zero education but with more wisdom than anyone I had met in my life. The people are a mix of Spanish, African, several types of Indian and Chinese. For the first time in my life, through this experience, I came to believe in "magic" both black and white.

For nearly five years I lived in the jungle. Today I'm in the concrete jungle, but you would have to drag me back kicking and screaming the whole way for me to give up the lifestyle I have grown accustomed to in Costa Rica.

What worked for me is that the first thing I did was throw any American attitude I may have had down the river that flowed in front of the lodge and immersed myself in the culture, language and people. *Tuanis*!

```
Costa Rican Dreams  (Quepos) .........................................777-0593
Tango Mar  (Tambor).......................................................661-2798
Golfito Sports Fishing.....................................................775-0353
Reel'n Release Sportfishing  (Dominical).........................771-1903
Blue Marlin Fishing  (Flamingo Beach) ...........................654-4043
Freshwater Trout Fishing:
Adventuras Tilarán  (Arenal) .........................................695-5008
Finca Zacatecales...........................................................771-1732
```

Some of these fishing companies, camps and lodges provide overnight accommodations that include meals. Fishing equipment and boats are also available.

For a listing of other fishing camps and tours, read the *Tico Times*, contact **Costa Rica Unique Tours** at www.costaricabooks.com/travel, or consult **Tico Travel** at www.ticotravel.com.

Pristine Beaches

Unlike many resort areas in Mexico and Latin America, Costa Rica's beautiful tropical beaches and 767 miles of coastline stretching along two oceans are virtually unspoiled. Water temperatures are very warm so you can stay in the water all day.

There are many white and dark sand beaches and numerous resorts along the west coast.

In the northwest Guanacaste area the best beaches include: Playa Naranjo, Playa Panama, Playa Hermosa, Playa del Coco (a favorite *gringo* hangout) Ocotal, Bahía Pez Vela, Playa Potrero, Playa Flamingo, Playa Brasilito, Conchal, Playa Grande, Playa Tamarindo, Playa Avellana, and Playa Junquillal.

As we move south these beaches are scattered along the coast of the Nicoya Peninsula: Playa Azul, Playa Nosara, Playa Sámara, Playa Carrillo, Playa Coyote. Playa Montezuma, near the eastern tip of Nicoya, is a nice beach.

Moving even further south along the Central and Southern Pacific Coast are Puntarenas (Costa Rica's main port), Boca Barranca (good surfing beach), Mata Limón, Playa Tivives, Playa Tarcoles, Playa Escondido, Playa Herradura, Playa Jacó, Playa Hermosa, Esterillos, Quepos, Manuel Antonio (considered by many to be the most beautiful beach in Costa Rica), Playa Dominical and the beaches around the towns of Uvita and Ojochal.

On the Atlantic side some beautiful beaches are: Playa Bonita (Portete), Punta Cahuita (beautiful beach), Puerto Viejo, Playa Uva and Playa Manzanillo.

Surf's Up!

Surfers of all ages will be pleased to know that Costa Rica is quickly gaining popularity on the worldwide surf circuit due to its warm weather and great waves. The country boasts close to forty prime areas for surfing on both the east and west coasts. In Guanacaste, many prime surfing locations line the peninsula from tip to tip. **Roca Bruja** (Witches Rock) inside Santa Rosa National Park, is famous for its tubular waves. Other recommended places to surf in Guanacaste are **Playa Grande**, **Nosara**, **Playa Coyote** and **Manzanillo**.

In the Central Pacific region **Playa Jacó** and the surrounding area is also worth checking out. Nearby **Playa Hermosa** has been host to some surfing tournaments and is steadily gaining popularity. **Esterillos** and **Bejuco** are other options in the Central Pacific area. Further south is **Dominica**l, which is considered a top spot for surfers.

Pavones in the South Pacific area is a legendary surf spot famous for its endless waves and touted as having the world's longest rideable left break. Try **Matapalo** and **Punta**, located near the Panamanian border. **"Salsa"** at Pureto Viejo on the east coast has good surfing. There are numerous a surfing schools in Costa Rica and **Tico Travel** offers surfing tours to the country.

Parks for Nature Lovers

Costa Ricans take pride in their extensive national park system. Since Costa Rica is rich not only in natural beauty but in all varieties of wild life, Costa Ricans have set aside 20% of their territory and established 36 national parks and preserves to protect the flora and fauna of their country. This is reportedly the largest percentage of any country in the world. Five percent of the world's biodiversity can be found in Costa Rica. The country has 850 species of mammals, 218 species of reptiles, 160 species of amphibians and about 360,000 species of insects. The country also has 10,353 species of plants.

Costa Rica's parks are in every region of the country, with some parks more accessible than others. The variety of birds, butterflies, amphibians, mammals, trees and flowers has to be seen to be believed.

Additional information and a list of parks may be obtained by calling 233-5673, 233-5284 or 233-4160. Most hotels and tourist information centers can be helpful to nature lovers. Foreigners pay about $6 admission and Costa Ricans and residents $1 to enter Costa Rica's parks. After an international uproar over hikes in park fees, the "Green Pass" was instituted to offer the most affordable way to visit Costa Rica's world famous parks. For $29, you receive a coupon booklet with four tickets to any national park and one ticket to one of 10 parks.

Costa Ricans take the same pride in their urban parks. Every neighborhood in Costa Rica, from the biggest cities to the tiniest villages, always has a park usually adjacent to the Catholic Church. San José's **Sabana Park** is the country's largest city park. The park is crisscrossed by miles of jogging, biking and walking trails. *Ticos* flock by the hundreds to this park to indulge their loves of family, children, sports and the outdoors. Go to the park any Sunday and you will see people walking, jogging, picnicking, cycling or playing soccer on one of the many playing fields.

There are also free tennis and basketball courts. The park is located on the sight of the old national airport and the terminal building now houses the National Art Museum. La Sabana is also the home of the National Stadium and National Gymnasium, where events of all types are held. There is an Olympic-size swimming pool just west of the gymnasium. In the center of the park a large lake and fountain attracts many people. It is a favorite gathering spot for families.

Your whole family can have fun at WaterLand water park.

Another popular weekend destination in San José is **Parque de La Paz**. It does not have the peaceful seclusion of La Sabana, but it still has all the activity. The park is set around three artificial lakes. **Waterland** is the country's first U.S.-style water park. There are several pools, water slides, miniature golf and a soon-to-be-completed pool with artificial waves. An even more spectacular water park is being built a few miles off the costal highway between Quepos and Dominical. When completed, it will have artificial waves and a whole lot more.

Where to Make New Friends

You should have no problem making new friends of either sex in Costa Rica, but you might have some difficulty meeting Costa Ricans if you speak little or no Spanish. You will be surprised how many *ticos* speak some English and are dying for the chance to perfect their English language skills while you work on your Spanish. Perhaps you can find someone with whom to exchange language lessons. This is a good way to make new acquaintances and learn how Spanish is really spoken.

You most certainly will find it easier to meet fellow Americans in Costa Rica than in the U.S. because Americans living abroad tend to gravitate toward one another. Newcomers only have to find an enclave of fellow countrymen to make new friends.

A group of expats having coffee at a local hangout.

You cannot help bumping into other Americans since Costa Rica is such a small country (there are over 30,000 *gringos* living there permanently). This is especially true if you live in one of the areas where many North Americans reside, such as Escazú, Heredia, Rohrmoser or along the Pacific Beaches. Another good way of contacting other foreign residents is by participating in some of the activities listed in the weekend editions of the *Tico Times*. These newspapers serve as a vital link within the foreign community, or "*Gringo* Grapevine"and help to put you in touch with a whole network of expatriates and the services they offer.

At any of the local *gringo* watering holes in downtown San José, such as Nashville South, the New York Bar or the Casino Colonial, you can watch live sporting events from the U.S. on cable T.V. or simply shoot the breeze with your compatriots. Many Americans also congregate at the Plaza de La Cultura and at McDonald's across the street, where they linger over coffee every morning and watch the beautiful women pass by.

You have no reason to be lonely unless you want to be. Just be yourself and you will find Costa Rica is just the place for you. Oh yes, we might add that there are poetry readings, art and sculpture exhibitions as well as other activities where people can easily socialize. The American Costa Rican Cultural Center has many events where you can also make new acquaintances. Here is a sample of the many organizations.

CLUBS AND ORGANIZATIONS

Aikido Club	289-7479
American Legion Post 11	233-7233
American Legion Post 12	775-0567
Canadian Club	282-5858
Chess Club	384-0936
Democrats Abroad	290-5798
Disabled American Veterans	443-2508
English-Spanish Conversation Club	260-4869
Internet Club	220-0714
Investment Club of Costa Rica	256-5075
Lions Club	670-0447
Mac User Group	257-2160
Mountain Bike Club	290-7870
National Bridge Association	253-2762
Newcomers' Club	232-3999
PC Club	224-9926

Readers Club 228-9167
Republicans Abroad 239-2262
Rotary Club..222-0993
Spanish/English Conversation Club 390-9759
Singles Club 289-8433
Women's Club of Costa Rica..282-6801

* For a complete listing of clubs and related activities, look under the weekly "What's Doing" section in the *Tico Times* or see *Costa Rica Today*. You mayalso check out the Association of Residents of Costa Rica's community calendar. Call 233-8068 for more information.

Love and Permanent Companionship

If you are looking for someone for romance, Costa Rica might just be the right place for you. Ladies will find gentleman admirers if they so desire. Due to *machismo,* Costa Rican men are more flirtatious and aggressive than North American men. Most Costa Rican men think foreign women have looser morals and are easier conquests than *ticas* (Costa Rican women). Be careful to take time to develop a long-term, meaningful relationship and do not rush things.

Men of any age will have no problem meeting Costa Rican women. The women in Costa Rica seem to like older, more experienced men. It is not unusual to see a wife who is ten to twenty years younger than her spouse. This practice may be frowned on in some countries but is accepted in Costa Rica. Many retirees we know claim to feel rejuvenated and to have a new lease on life after becoming involved with younger women. Costa Rican women have an unparalleled reputation as being the most beautiful, flirtatious, and accessible women in Latin America, including Brazil. The ladies of Costa Rica are more warm-hearted and devoted than their North American counterparts. They consider you a joy. One retiree we know boasts, "The women here really know how to treat you like a king!"

A man doesn't even have to be rich to meet women; a $1,500 to $2,000 Social Security check translates to a millionaire's pay in Costa Rica.

No wonder Costa Rican women are highly sought by foreign men. However, before becoming involved with a Costa Rican woman, you should realize many cultural differences can lead to all kinds of problems, especially if you do not speak Spanish fluently.

Generally, Latin women are more jealous and possessive than American women, and tend not to understand our ways unless they have lived in the North America. Also, be aware that because of their comparative wealth, most Americans, especially the elderly, are considered prime targets for some unscrupulous Latin females.

As we alluded to at the end of the first chapter, in some cases there is another bad side of marrying a Costa Rican woman. You can end up supporting her whole family either directly or indirectly as many foreigners complain. There is an out-of-print book, *"Happy Aging With Costa Rican Women - The Other Costa Rica"* by James Y. Kennedy. It tells all about the trials and tribulations and experiences many *gringos* have with Costa Rican women. You may be able to find a used copy in a second-hand bookstore in San José or borrow it from a local expatriate.

We advise you to give any relationship time and make sure a woman is sincerely interested in you and not just your money. You will save yourself a lot of grief and heartaches in the long run. Since prostitution is legal and available to men of all ages, be careful of the ladies of ill repute. Many foreigners, after inviting one of these females to spend the night, wake up the next day without the woman and minus wallets and other valuables.

One of Costa Rica's beutiful women.

One scam we recently heard of involves a well-dressed woman with a brief case who approaches strangers. She claims to be from another Latin American country and wanting to celebrate her birthday. She says she is alone and has nobody to celebrate it with her. She then invites the unsuspecting victim to accompany her to a bar for a drink. Once in the bar she slips a drug into the glass of the foreigner. Within minutes he is unconscious. The woman then relieves him of his cash and credit cards. She then takes the credit cards to an accomplice who quickly charges large amounts of money to the cards.

Most single men can avoid getting involved with gold diggers, prostitutes, or other troublesome women if they know where to look for good women. The personals section of the *Tico Times* is an excellent place to advertise for companionship. It is relatively inexpensive and many Costa Rican women read this section each week. Check out the current or past issues of the *Tico Times* for ideas on how to write one of these ads.

One American we know ran an ad in the *Tico Times* and the local Spanish newspapers and ended up screening hundreds of women before finding his ideal mate. As far as we know he is still happily married. Taking classes at the university is another way to meet quality women. The University of Costa Rica in San Pedro is full of beautiful well-educated females. Cafés, restaurants, bars and other places around the university are good places to meet women. If you have Costa Rican friends, they will usually be able introduce you to someone worthwhile.

The key is finding a nice, traditional Costa Rican woman and avoid getting involved with "bad" Costa Rican women. Costa Rica has plenty of working girls and hustlers. They hang out at the popular bars and discos specifically to pick up guys. They also go shopping in the malls, ride buses and go to grocery stores. So just because you have met a nice girl in a typical working girl hang out doesnot mean you have met a quality person. If you know what to look for, they are easy to spot.

Many men have knowingly and unknowingly married bad women. Some girls are honest and will directly ask you for money. The hustlers are more dangerous because their agenda is to really take you to the cleaners, and they do not rule out marrying you to achieve this objective. Some men say that have lost everything from airline tickets that are cashed instead of used, large sums of money the girls claim they need to get visas, houses and more. These are the women who contribute to the bad stories you may hear about some Costa Rican women. Unfortunately, the hustlers are the easiest girls to meet in many instances and a good number of men fall into this trap.

A very small number of these women will become good wives, find religion, etc. They are often women who have been sexually or otherwise abused at a very young age, so the problem is very deeply rooted. Your realistic chances of converting them are very slim. No matter how gorgeous the girl is, it is just not worth it.

The best way to spot a bad girl is her profile. They never have a job, never live with their parents, never have phone numbers and never invite you to their home or introduce you to their friends or family. They do not want to leave any trail for you to track them down later. They typically come from very poor backgrounds and have very little education, rarely completing high school.

They are quite aggressive and target older Americans. Often they speak a little English and will start up a conversation with you or smile at you until you make the first move. They will appear friendly and sincerely interested in you. They are always attractive or very young. They will always ask for your phone number.

The best way to politely get rid of one of these women is to ask them to loan you a little money. You will immediately see their interest disappear. Actually, a nice woman in Costa Rica might just loan you the money.

Women you see working in stores are usually poorly educated and from poor families. Some may show an interest in an older American who is friendly with them, but the relationship is likely to be overly influenced by a poor woman looking for a rich American husband.

Foreign men should beware of the so-called "Costa Rican set-up." We have heard countless stories where Costa Rican women get pregnant as a ploy to get a foreigner to marry them. We believe it is our duty to alert men about this underhanded and self-centered method of ensnaring them into an unwanted relationship.

In general, a nice Costa Rica woman typically lives with her parents until she gets married. Single daughters are not encouraged to get jobs unless the parents are very poor. Instead, they are expected to help with taking care of the house or study.

Quality Costa Rican women from traditional family backgrounds are raised to take care of their man. They can be quite possessive and jealous at times, but this is only because they are very emotional and deeply in love with their man. They tend to seek out long-term relationships, starting at a very young age. It is quite rare for Costa Rican women to have any interest in casually dating many different men.

When approached by strangers, they are friendly and helpful by nature; this is their culture. All Costa Ricans value making new friends. Americans often misread this friendliness and think the woman has a romantic interest in them. In order for the woman to develop any romantic interest in you at all, they have to first know from a trusted third party that you are looking for a long-term relationship. After a brief encounter, a decent woman will never ask for your phone number. If you ask for her number, she will always give you the wrong number in order to avoid appearing rude. Nice women live with their parents and would never want to have strange men calling their house. From a romantic interest point of view, quality Latin women are very difficult to meet.

As we alluded to earlier, some Costa Rican women prefer older men. Most Costa Rican women meet a boy in high school and are only interested in men their own age. However, about 40% do seriously prefer older men. We have met many Costa Rican friends who are happily married to women 10 to 25 years younger than them.

If the woman is convinced you are seriously looking for a long-term relationship, she will then start to show an interest in getting to know you better. Her initial physical attraction to you will usually be of very minor importance to her. Her main interest will be focused on your personality: Are you are a kind person? Can you offer minimum security to raise a family? Do you sincerely care about her family? Would you make a good father?

Over the years we have encountered a lot of foreigners who end up not using common sense and end up getting involved with people with whom they would probably never associate back home. This brings us to the story of "Dumb and Dumber."

Dumb came to Costa Rica about twelve years ago from the U.S. where he was a successful businessman. Almost upon arriving here he became romantically involved with a woman of ill- repute. He was basically too lazy and busy getting drunk to find a quality mate. Over the course of his relationship he lost about $300,000 because he entrusted his business dealings to his girlfriend. After splitting up with her and having to give her half of everything he owned because of their common law situation, he goes and gets involved with another women who will probably "take him to the cleaners" someday.

Dumber is even more stupid than dumb. He came to the country as a millionaire. The first thing he did was get romantically involved with a woman of the night. Dumber also spent most of his time in bars like

How I Found Love in Costa Rica

By Brian

My name is Brian and right now I am about to take a beautiful lady on tour of Southern California. And, at the end of our drive, she will come home with me. She is my lovely Tica wife, Yanory and this is her first dayin her new home. I met Yanory a year ago in San Jose at an agency called Spanish Eyes.

I first heard of Spanish Eyes through a fellow surfer during one of my trips to Playa Hermosa to surf. He said it was a great way to meet ladies from Costa Rica. Having been a widower 6 years, I was feeling lonely and wanted to find a woman who was kind, sweet, gentle and loving but was not sure how to approach the ladies of Costa Rica.

Once I contacted Spanish Eyes and met Tom and Purita, I felt comfortable and sure that together we would find that perfect lady for me. I met some beautiful women and made some lifetime friends. About a year ago, Purita introduced me to Yanory, a quiet, soft spoken wonderful young woman who captured my mind and heart. We dated and I found myself coming back to

Costa Rica as often as I could to see her. We spent Christmas together and I knew that we were meant for each other so I asked her to marry me. We married in April and began the process for her spousal visa. The process took only 3 months which is unusually fast.

In less than a year, I met my future wife, married her and she is now with me in our home in California. It all seems so easy. But, every step of the way, Purita and Tom were there to answer questions for me, to take my phone calls and answer my questions and to help in any way they could.

Spanish Eyes Introductions is about service. I still do not understand how they find the time to give every client the personalized service that they do. And, how they can recommend the perfect ladies for you to meet. Yanory was not one of my first choices, but a recommendation made by Purita. To this day I do not know how she knew that Yanory would be so perfect for me.

Dumb. Consequently, when he broke up with his lady friend, after a few years together, he had to pay her around $50,000. He is now with another woman and most likely supporting her whole family. He will probably end up broke like dumb. Neither Dumb nor Dumber speak Spanish nor have made any effort to understand the locals and constantly refer to them in derogatory terms.

The majority of foreign men who come to Costa Rica don't share Dumb and Dumber's fate. Nevertheless they should learn a lesson from this story.

Probably the most effective way to meet quality Costa Rica women is through an introduction service. **Spainsh Eyes Introductions** provides this services and screens their women very carefully to protect their clients. In addition to there standard services, they offer parties for their members to meet women. We have several friends who are members and rave about this service. You may contact them at: Tel: 011-506-289-5271/228-7389, e-mail: **info@spanisheyesccostarica.com** or see **www.spanisheyescostarica.com**.

A Walk on the Wild Side

The author of this guidebook feels it is his responsibility to paint a realistic picture of all of the aspects of living in Costa Rica. He would not be doing a service to our readers if he did not cover the subject of prostitution. However, let it be known that in no way does he condone the sexual exploitation of minors. In this section he only provides information about sexual relationships between consenting adults.

For some people Costa Rica is a sexual paradise. Like Thailand, the Philippines and many other countries outside of the U.S., prostitution is permitted and looked upon with general acceptance in Costa Rica. As in the rest of Latin America, many males have their first sexual experience with prostitutes. In order to control the propagation of venereal disease and AIDS, prostitutes are required by the government to undergo regular health checkups by the Ministry of Health or *Ministerio de Salud* in order to practice their trade legally. Most upscale brothels make sure their employees have their health papers and tests up to date.

It is not therefore surprising that many foreigners are attracted to Costa Rica because of the availability of women. In San José there is a myriad of bordellos, cabarets, escort services, massage parlors and bars where you can find female company. One Costa Rican remarked jokingly when questioned about the number of whorehouses in San José, " In order to put a roof over all of the houses of ill repute, you would have to cover the whole city."

We have interviewed a few tight-fisted residents and retirees who think just because they live here they should pay less for sex than tourists. Consequently, many of them go to the "houses of ill repute" which dot Calle 6, just north of the Central Market. Prices are "rock bottom" and you probably get what you end up paying for. We don't recommend venturing into this area at night. However, none of the people interviewed have ever had problems during the day.

The infamous **Park Hotel**, 50 meters west of San Jose's Central park, is an institution that thrived during the 70's and 80's. In the old days the place was frequented by soldiers of fortune, expatriates and an odd assortment of other seedy characters. Its popularity waned in recent times but recently has become popular again.

In the "Gringo Gulch" area near Morazán Park two places come to mind. **Key Largo** is an institution and has been around for over 25 years. Located in a beautiful colonial mansion directly across from Parque Morazán, the place looks like a scene taken right out of a Humphrey Bogart movie. It has recently been remodeled and offers live music and dancing nightly.

The Blue Marlin Bar at the Hotel Del Rey is under the same ownership as the Key Largo and is the place to meet women of the night. Most evenings there is standing room only in the bar. During the day the bar is a gathering place where local expats and tourists "shoot the bull". The Hotel Del Rey also offers a casino and fine dining

There are a number of cabarets and nightclubs where men can also find female companionship. Most of these establishments try to get you to buy expensive drinks and run up a large tab. It is not unusual to be stuck with a large bill in a short period of time. To avoid surprises we suggest you do not buy any women more that one or two drinks. The management can be very nasty if you complain about your bill. Here are the most popular cabarets and night clubs: **Club Hollywood** (232-8932), across from the south side of the Sabana Park, **Pure Platinum** (256-9989), Ave. 3 between 10 and 12 Streets, and **Night Club Olympus** (233-4058), Central Street one block north of Hotel Europa. Most of these establishments offer floorshows, Jacuzzis, massage rooms, V.I.P. rooms, exotic dancing and a stable of women from which to choose. **Tango India** (290-1235) www.tangoindia.net, and **KRISIS** (222-7640) are other hot spots worth checking out.

There are a dozen escort services operating in the San José area. Most of these services advertise in local newspapers. You may find many of the local escort services by going to the search engines like yahoo, google or altavista and typing in the keywords "costa rica escorts."

If you are looking for a relaxing massage and steam bath, there are a number of massage parlors to cater to your needs. Prices range from about $15 for a straight hour-long therapeutic massage to $35 for a massage with "the works"or *masaje completo*. As a rule these places are very clean and provide a secure discrete atmosphere. **New Fantasy** (Tel: (506) 221-4916), located two blocks north of Morazán Park in San José is very popular among foreign residents. It is located in Barrio Amon, on Avenida 9 and Calle 7. From the Parque Morazan (front of the Holiday Inn) 200 meters or 2 blocks to the north, a right turn and we are there. It is frequented by foreign residents, Costa Rican men of means and tourists. The **747**, located on Calle 6 one block south of Avenida 7, is also a favorite. **Idem**, Ave. 8-10 and Calle 11, has beautiful women and is considered one of the best massage parlors in the San José area.

There is a good online book which can be used as a guide to all of San José's erotic places called *Passion in Paradise*. See www.passioninparadise.com to find out how to order this publication.

An interesting phenomenon are Central America's famous "love motels." Several dozen are found around San José and the suburbs and do a very business. Many foreigners do not know the difference between a 'hotel' and 'motel'. In Costa Rica and the rest of Central America motels are for making love and serve no other purpose.

These establishments exist for discrete liaisons between adults. Bosses and their secretaries, men with prostitutes, young lovers who still live at home, and others enjoy these convenient establishments. Patrons can hide their car as well as their lovers in one of these places. Rooms may be rented for several hours. Fresh towels, sheets, food drink and even a condom are provided. Each room also has a small waist-level window for you to pay and for staff to hand you alcoholic beverages, soft drinks, food, towels, and more. Clients and staff of the motel never see each others faces.

Most rooms also have a TV, some with pornographic movies, and music. There is a big curtain or door which is closed immediately to hide the identity of the couple and their vehicle. On weekend nights and during lunch the country's love motels fill up quickly. It is very easy to find one of these motels once you have lived in Costa Rica for a while. Just ask a taxi driver or one of your friends.

Nightlife and Entertainment

There are countless open-air restaurants, bars, dance halls and discotheques all over San José and in most other parts of the country. Costa Ricans love to party and dance. Most of these nightspots will appeal to anyone from 16 to 50, give or take a little for the young at heart.

After you have lived in the country for a while, the dance bug will bite you. There are numerous dance academies in the San José area that offer classes for all levels of experience in various styles of Latin American dance. If you want to learn how to dance like a Costa Rican, call **El Malecón Escuela de Bailes Populares** 255-0378 or **Merecumbé** 220-8511 in Rohrmoser, 289-4774 in Escazú, 240-8511 in Tibás, 237-0851 in Heredia, 442-3536 in Alajuela and 219-8787 in Desamoarados. The latter has schools all over the San José area in Alajuela, Heredia, Pavas, Escazú, Tibás and San Pedro. Other s dance schools are: **Academia de Bailes Latinos** 233-8938, **Kinesis Academia de Baile** 440-0852, **Inovación Latina** 255-1460 and **Academia Salsabor Estudio** 224-1943.

Once you have mastered the basic dance steps and can dance to the rhythms of salsa, merengue, cumbia and other Latin dances, put on your best pair of dancing shoes and go to either **El Higuerón** or El **Azteca** dance halls in the suburb of Desamparados. They have large dance floors and really fill up on the weekends. **El Garabaldi** and **El Buen Día** are other dancehalls in the southern part of the city.

San José´s many discotheques and dance halls play music for all tastes until the wee hours of the morning; admission is inexpensive or free. International liquors and cocktails as well as all local beers and beverages are served. Also, keep in mind that many of these clubs serve food and the traditional heaping plates of delicious local appetizers or hôrs d'oeuvres, called *bocas*.

Most of these establishments are quiet by day and artistically decorated. Many have adjoining restaurants, live music or a disc- jockey and well-lighted dance floors. **El Centro Comercial El Pueblo** has two of the country's best discotheques: **La Plaza** and **Infinito**. Both have huge dance floors and play a mix of American pop, salsa and reggae.

The city of Heredia boasts several excellent watering holes. **El Bulevar, Rancho Fofos** and **La Choza** in the vicinity of the national University of Heredia, are *the* places to party. **Hooligan's Bar** on the road to Heredia, in front of the Atlas Factory, features a Ladies' Night and 2 for 1 nights.

Bohemian types should check out **El Cuartel de La Boca del Monte**. Old hippies and Costa Rican yuppies mingle there. It is one of San José's oldest and most popular bar and restaurant combinations. They have a good mix of Latin and American music. The place really fills up on Mondays and Wednesdays when they feature live music. The bar is known for its truly authentic cuisine.

For lovers of jazz there are several good clubs in the San José area. **The Jazz Café** in San Pedro is the best spot to hear the rhythms of soul, blues and jazz. The décor will make you feel like you are in a jazz club back home.

The quiet **Shakespeare Bar**, near the Sala Garbo movie theater, is a good place to have a couple of drinks.

If you like the university atmosphere, the college crowd and bar - hopping, then the suburb of San Pedro is just the place for you. Start by checking out the **Planet Mall Disco** located in the San Pedro Mall. The **Sand Rock Bar** around the corner is popular with the younger crowd.

The area around the University of Costa Rica in San Pedro is packed with college-type hangouts. Most of these places are full any night of the week. There is some entertainment here for everyone.

For those of you who do not like loud music, sports bars, large crowds or a boisterous atmosphere, some more sedate establishments let you relax with friends and enjoy conversation. Most hotels bars have a laid-back ambience. **The Hotel Grano de Oro** has a lovely patio where you may sit and nurse your favorite beverage. Also check out the bar on the second floor of the **Holiday Inn**. It has a great view of Morazán Park.

Where to go for nightlife and entertainment

Antojitos..Good Mexican food
Bar Mexico..Live music
Chelles...People watching hangout
El Cocoloco ....Good dancing to a Latin beat
Infinito......................... Has two dance floors, all types of music
Mirador Ram Luna......................Family style, jukebox, dancing
La Plaza ....Elegant with large dance floor
Friday's..........................In San Pedro, great American style food

*See the *Tico Times* or *La Nación* for more entertainment.

The Gringo Bar Scene

There are several gringo bars, that cater almost exclusively to expatriates in downtown San José or nearby. Although we do not recommend hanging out at these places 24-hours a day, there is no better way to hear stories about life in the tropics, keep up on local gossip, meet some colorful local characters and gather tips about living in Costa Rica while you sip your favorite beverage.

The Hotel Presidente's new bar, the **News Café,** is the new happening place in San José. The food and drinks are great and it is a fantastic spot to "people watch". Thousands of people walk by this spot each day.

The New York Bar is one of our favorite watering holes. The congenial female bartenders will make you feel right at home.

Another *gringo* hangout is the bar at the **Dunn Inn Hotel.** You can always meet expatriates there. The owner, Pat "Tex" Dunn used to run Nashville South and a couple of other *gringo* bars. He is a congenial man who can provide you with information about living in Costa Rica.

As previously mentioned a great gringo spot is the **Blue Marlin Bar** Sport enthusiasts frequented this bar. You'll hear a bit of friendly boasting and some tall fish tales at this unique bar. If you want to make some acquaintances, this bar is worth visiting.

There is always plenty of action in the "Gringo Gulch" area.

Pat Dunn also owns **Lucky's Piano Bar** next door to the Hotel Balmoral. It is another excellent people- watching bar due to its large plate glass window provides a view of busy Avenida Central.

Nashville South is a country western bar in downtown San José with an interesting clientele, western decor and country music in the background.

Mac's American Bar and **Restaurant**, south of the Sabana Park is another famous *gringo* hangout. Doña Carmen of Tiny's Tropical bar fame is the cook. You can savour her great cooking and watch major spoting events.

Tex Mex restaurant in Santa Ana is another favorite drinking spot with Americans. A lot of golfers go there after playing at the nearby Valle de Sol golf course.

More Good Bars

Most bars open at 11 a.m. and close at 2 a.m—7 days per week. Some have happy hours.

The Boulevard ....College atmosphere in Heredia
Hotel Corobicí...Good bar
Holiday Inn ....Across from Morazán Park
La Soda Tapia ....Nice place across from Sabana Park
Hotel Balmoral ....Nice quiet bar
Gran Hotel...................Nice outdoor patio In the heart of San José
KS Brewery ....Another micro brewery in Curridabat
Chango ....Bar-restaurant in Escazú
Tapachula ....Gringo bar near soccer stadium in Alajuela

---

Gambling

Costa Rica has about twenty casinos, most are in the San José area and a few at beach resorts. Rules differ slightly than in the U.S.A. or Europe, but gambling is fun to learn the Costa Rican way. There are four legal casino games. Rummy, a variation of black jack or 21, is the most popular of these casino games. The remaining games are craps, roulette (played lottery style rather than with a wheel), and *tute*, a type of poker played against the house. Slot machines are legal. Most casinos give free drinks while you play and are opened from 6 p.m. to 3 or 4 a.m. Many casinos offer 24-hour gambling.

The **Fiesta Casino**, the **Gran Hotel Costa Rica Casino** and **Club Colonial** are casinos located in the heart of San José. They are by far the best places to gamble. The casino on the top floor of the **Holiday Inn** offers a spectacular panoramic view of the city of San José. If for no other reason, you should go to this casino to take in the view and snap a few photos. You may also gamble on the Internet through a local company called **Grand Central Casino** and **Sports book** (see www.gcsports.com or call 1-800-213-3370).

The most popular form of gambling in Costa Rica is the national lottery or *lotería*. This game of chance is played a couple of times each week. You can purchase a whole sheet of tickets or a fraction of a sheet from any street vendor. A substantial amount of money may be won. If you are lucky enough to win the huge annual Christmas Lottery, or *Gordo Navideño*, you will become very rich and will probably be set up for life. To find the results of the lottery look in the local newspaper. There is also an instant winner lottery similar to that played in the U.S., called *raspa*. In this game you scrape off an area on the ticket with a coin to see if you have matching symbols or numbers.

Betting on horses is legal in Costa Rica, but the local track closed in 1995 due to financial problems. At the Casino Club Colonial and Hotel Del Rey there is betting on most major sporting events. In November of 2001, betting on Costa Rican soccer games was legalized.

One of San José's popular casinos.

A Bookmaker in Paradise
By Redstone Brimely

The life I led in the States wasn't working for me. My last business venture ended in failure and I was being evicted from my home. The country health inspector, alerted by my nosey neighbor, posted the notice on my front door citing me with excessive refuse from fast food establishments. If that wasn't enough, I was down to my last pair of pants, I had outgrown Big and Tall. I needed a change.

Watching infomercials at four in the morning, I heard testimony from a West Virginian illiterate expounding of teaching English overseas. I sent for the delux package. The exotic destinations offered were many, but I decided Costa Rica was going to be my new home. There's something about change that gives a young man a bounce to his step. I sensed good things ahead and I was right.

I went to work as an English teacher for a language institute in San José, tutoring local exectives. My first week there I instructed a group of Costa Ricans who spoke excellent English but needed to brush up on their grammar. Interesting work but my biweekly stipend would barely keep me in rice and beans. A compamy called Grand Central Sports, an offshore Las Vegas-style sportsbook operating in San José, had sent their employees to the class. The top student in the class happened to be a supervisor in the wagering department. At the end of the term he offered me a job.

I had never before worked in the gambling business, however I knew something about gambling— my father was a generate gambler.

When I completed my training I was placed in the betting department along with fifty other clerks where the phones were literally "ringing off the hook." Native beauties with cocoa butter skin and pearly white teeth in halter-tops and sarongs answered the phones speaking perfect English. I was in shock!

My main concern when I took this job was whether or not I was breaking any laws. I did some investigating and found out offshore bookmaking is legal and beyond the juristiction of the United States government. The company's growth during the past football season has been phenomenal. In fact, we've both grown. I was made a betting supervisor and was given a couple of weeks off before the start of the basketball season. Until then I'll be at the beach where I've traded in my Oshkosh for Bermuda shorts and a Panama hat with the radio at my feet to keep track of his numerous plays.

Where to Gamble
- Fiesta (downtown casino in the Hotel Presidente)
- Gran Hotel Costa Rica (another good place to gamble)
- Hotel Del Rey
- Casino Tropical
- Cheetah's
- Club Colonial (sports betting)
- Holiday Inn
- San José Palacio
- Hotel Cariari
- Balmoral Hotel
- Hotel Corobicí
- Hotel Irazú
- Club Triángulo
- Hotel Sheraton Herradura

Movies and Theaters in San José and Other Areas

There are movie theaters all over the San José area and in other large cities. Most of these theaters show first-run movies usually within a month after they first are released in the United States.

The **Sala Garbo** shows first-rate films from Europe with Spanish subtitles. About 40 percent of all current hit movies shown in the United States make their way to Costa Rica sooner or later. You should not worry about understanding these movies since they are all in English with Spanish subtitles except movies for children. You can read the local newspapers to see what movies are currently playing. At present, admission is around three dollars. Several theaters have more than one screen. To find out what is playing look in the *Tico Times* or any of the Spanish newspapers like *La Nación*. Information about movies may also be accessed at **www.entretenimiento.co.cr (in Spainsh).**

In the Central Valley you can experience everything from old-time Paramount-style theater palaces to ultra-modern movie complexes in suburban malls. The Cine **Variedades**, up the street from the Plaza de la Cultura, is one of the oldest. The **Cine Magaly** in Barrio California, is a great theater for that old-time big-movie experience. It has over 1,000 seats and second story balconies. The parent company of the Magaly runs other movie theaters in the country.

The first of Costa Rica's megatheaters is found in the San Pedro Mall. It has five-screens and is located on the second floor of the mall. The **Real Cariari** Shopping center boasts the six-screen Cariari Movie Theater. **Cinemark** is a new U.S. style movie theater with 8 screens located at the **Multiplaza Mall,** west of Escazú. This theater boasts a top-quality digital sound system and stadium seating . It is one of the best places to see a movie in the country. They serve snacks and candies from the U.S. and even offer hot buttered popcorn with real butter and free refills if you purchase the large size. **Cineápolis** at the new **Terramall,** also has a state of the art theater.

The Magaly theater chain has a movie theater with three screens on the third floor of the new **Outlet Mall** in San Pedro. These theaters show nontraditional foreign films and have state-of-the-art DTS Digital and Dolby sound systems. You can purchase and reserve tickets by telephone with a credit card.

The Magaly movie chain also recently opened several movie theaters at the **Mall Paraíso** near the city of Cartago.

San José is purported to have more theaters and theater companies per capita than any other city in the world. Most live plays are in Spanish but there are occasional plays in English at the North American Cultural Center. The Little Theatre Group is Costa Rica's only English-language acting troupe and frequently presents plays in English. However, by going to plays in Spanish, you can improve your language skills. Current stage plays are also listed in the activities section of local newspapers.

Movies ((INES)

```
Cinépolis................................................................278-3506
    Terramall
Cine Cariari (6 screens)......................................293-3300
    Plaza Real Cariari, across from the
    Sheraton Herradura Hotel
Cine Colonial 1 & 2 (2 screens).......................289-9000
    Centro Comercial Plaza Colonial, Escazú
Cine Magaly.........................................................223-0085
    Calle 23, Ave. Central & 1 Barrio California
CineEl Semáforo (alterntive movies).............253-9126
    San Pedro
Cinemark (8 screens)........................................288-1111
    Multiplaza, Escazú
```

Cinemark (8 screens)..224-8383
    Multiplaza del Este
Cine Omni..221-7903
    Behind MacDonald's and the Plaza de la Cultura
Cine Variedades 222-6104
    Ave. Central & 1 Calle 5
International (4 screens)...442-6100
    Mall International, Alajuela
Laurence Olivier...222-1034
    Ave. 2, Calle 28
Libería 223-0085
    Guanacaste
Magaly Outlet Mall (3 screens foreign movies) 234-8868
    San Pedro across from la Plaza Roosevelt and Kennedy Park
Mall Paraíso 592-3133
    Cartago
Multiplex...460-6733
    San Carlos
Nuevo Guáplies 710-0894
Plaza Mayor 1-2 (2 screens)...232-3271
    Main Road, Rohrmoser
Sala Garbo...222-1034
    Ave. 2 Calle Cale 28 100 meters south of
    Pizza Hut Paseo Colón
San Pedro Mall (5 screens) 221-6272
    Mall San Pedro
Cinematec..207-5732
    Auditorium of the School of General Strudies, U.C.R.
Cine Universitario..207-4271
    At the U.C.R. Law School Auditorium
Cine en el Campus, Teatro Centro de Arte del Cidea,
    Universidad Nacional, 200 meters north of McDonald's,
    Heredia

Theaters (Teatros) In And Around San José

Teatro de Esquina...257-0223
    100 meters south of the old Atlantic Train Station

Teatro Laurence Olivier 222-1034
    Ave. 2, Calle 28
Teatro Arlequin...222-0792
    Calle 13, Ave. Central
Teatro del Angel..222-8258
    Ave. Central & Plaza de la Democracia
Teatro Melico Salazar 221-4952
    Ave. 2, Calle Central
Teatro de La Aduana 223-4563
    Calle 25, Avenidas 3 & 5
Teatro Capra 234-2866
    Calles 29 & 33, Ave. 1
Teatro Chaplin...223-2919
    Paseo de Los Estudiantes
Teatro Máscara 255-4250
    Calle 13, Avenidas 2 & 4
Teatro Nacional... 221-5341
    Ave. 2, Calles 3 & 5
Teatro Giratablas 253-6001
    Diagonal to Kentucky Fried Chicken on
    the road to San Pedro
Teatro Tiempo...222-0792
    Ave. Central & 2, Calle 13
Teatro Eugene O'Neil 253-5527

Recently-released movies with subtitles are shown here.

COMMUNICATIONS

Telephone Service

Costa Rica has the greatest number of telephones per capita of any Latin American country and boasts one of the world's best telephone systems, with direct dialing to more than 60 countries. The country has 1,500,000 regular telephones, 930,000 cellular phones and 20 thousand public phones. Calls within the country are a bargain; you can call any place in the country for only a few cents. If your house or apartment does not have a phone, don't worry. Public telephones are just about everywhere in Costa Rica and use 5, 10, and 20 silver *colón* coins. Phones accepting pre-paid phone cards are slowly replacing coin-operated phones.

If you do not have your own phone and want to make a direct international call, go to the **Radiográfica (287-0087)** telephone office, (open 7 a.m. to 10 p.m.) in downtown San José at Calle 1, Ave. 7. Long distance calls from may be made from any phone booth by dialing 114. You can also make long distance calls from most hotels. From private phones in homes or offices, the procedure is just like in the U. S. by direct dialing or first talking to the operator *(operadora)*. The access numbers for calling Costa Rica from North America are 011-506 plus the rest of the number. To call or fax the U.S. from Costa Rica dial 001+area code+number. You may purchase prepaid phone cards for local or international direct-dial calls. Three types of cards may be purchased from Costa Rica Electricity (ICE) offices, *Correos de Costa Rica,* or businesses displaying a gold and blue sign which says "Tarjetas Telefónicas." **CHIP cards** sold in denominations of 300 to 2000 *colones*, may be used for local calls. **Servicio 197** cards come in denominations of 300, 500 and 1000 *colones* and provide domestic calls. **Servicio 199** cards are in $10, $20 or 3000 and 10000 *colón* denominations and may be used for international calls and have instructions in English.

In April of 1994, all phone numbers in Costa Rica were changed from six to seven digits. Most phone numbers now have an additional digit before the first number.

Purchasing a telephone can be a real "pain in the neck" depending on where you live and the number of available lines. You can expect to wait from one to three months for phone installation after paying around $100 for this service.

You can request a number and service from anywhere in Costa Rica by calling 115. Place your request with one of the operators or ask where the nearest ICE office is to order the service. If you need assistance in English, there are several English-speaking operators available to help you.

By the way, the Costa Rican Yellow Pages are found online at www.superpages.co.cr.

To get on the waiting list for phone service, you'll need a telephone number of the nearest building to the place where you want your phone line installed so the phone company can verify if a phone can be installed

San José's old post office.

and how long it will take. Your passport, identification or cellular phone number may be used to identify you for your account information. Finally, a postal address or directions where phone bills and other information about phone service may be sent. When you have given this information to ICE, they will give you a personal identification number to be used for paying the installation fee and to make any change in your service.

The next step is to pay the one-time fee to get on the waiting list for phone service. The fee ranges from $80 to $150, depending on the area for which you are requesting service. This payment can be made at any ICE office or the phone company will send a messenger at no cost to pick up the payment.

If you are having problems with the line or need to make changes in your service, call 119. No English-speaking operators work at this extension and a lot of transactions are done by computer, so it might be better to go directly to an ICE office for this kind of assistance. Or you may call the international phone service number at 124, where operators speak English and are often willing to help foreigners having problems with their telephone service. All of this information is clearly explained in Spanish at the beginning of the local phone book.

To have a phone installed, go to one of the following ICE offices: north side of the Sabana Park— 220-7720, Pavas Centro — 296-0303, La Florida, Tibás — 240-6466, San Pedro — 225-0123, San José — 221-0123. Phone bills may be paid at the ICE office in downtown San José or any of their other offices in Costa Rica. You can also pay your phone and electric bills (*recibos*) at many supermarkets and online through banks like the Banco Nacional.

Cellular phone service is available in Costa Rica. Cellular phones have become a "status symbol" here. Most middle and all upper-class *ticos* and many businessmen are using cellular phones. We even saw a street fruit vendor with a cellular phone. The basic cost is around $30 per month.

Phones are more expensive than in the States and there are no super deals where you get a free phone by just signing up for a year's service. Nevertheless, business is booming for the companies that sell cell phones here. Stores selling cell phones are found all over San José and most of the large shopping malls. You can get hooked up by the store that sells you your phone. You can save money by purchasing your phone in the States and then getting connected to the service here. However, not only certain types of phones from the U.S. work here. Cell phone rentals are available from **Rent a Cell Phone** at 800-967-1111 or see www.costaricarentacellphone.com, **M & M Cell Service** at Tel: 394-

5904/296-5553, Fax: 291-1851, E-mail: cellservcostarica@yahoo.com or **www.cellphonescr.com** at 293-5892.

Sending a FAX is very easy in Costa Rica. You can go to **Radiográfica** (Tel: 287-0513, 287-0511) or **Telecomunicaciones Internacionales** (Tel: 257-2272). At the Radiográfica office you can send a fax or have one sent to you. You can call their office to see if they have received a fax for you. They will even call when a fax comes in if they have your phone number. Many private businesses offer fax services to individuals. You can usually find their number in the classified section of the *Tico Times* or *Central America Weekly*.

Internet Service

Computer buffs will be pleased to know Internet services are available throughout Costa Rica. Costa Rica has Central America's highest Internet connection rate, with 20 of 1,000 citizens regularly going online. This compares with less than one percent per 1,000 in every other Latin American country except Chile. At the begining 2004 Costa Rica had more than 100,000 Internet accounts. It is predicted that soon one-quarter of the country's population will be frequent users of the Internet.

To get connected to Internet just go to the **Radiográfica** offices and open a **RACSAPAC** account. Recently, using the Internet became less expensive and the hours more flexible.

Rates for home Internet users is $10 to$15 per month. The new $15 unlimited-hours rate does not include the basic telephone rate of $.55 per hour online. The extra charge will be added to Internet client's telephone. For further information about these services call 011-(506) 287-0321 or 011-(506) 287-0087; Fax: (506) 223-1609, or e-mail: tarifas@sol.racsa.co.cr.

Internet service cable TV hookup is also available in Costa Rica through a couple of cable TV companies. This service is faster than regular dial-up service. **Cable Tica** (210-1450) and **Amnet** (210-2929) now offer two-way high-speed cable modem Internat service in some areas of the San José area. The monthly cost ranges between $40 to $80 depending on the speed of the connection you choose. At present, this service is available only in San José and some of the surrounding suburbs.

The Costa Rican Electricity Institute (ICE) now offers that ADSL Broadband Internet. Initially there will be 80,000 high-speed connections throughout the country by the end of the year. Eventually there will be enough lines for 650,000 users. Broadband Internet will enable homes, schools and businesses to connect to the internet at high speeds at a fraction of the current cost without using regular telephone lines. The monthly cost of this service will range from $35 for 128-Kbps connection , $50 for a 256-Kbps connection and$70 for a 512-Kbps connection. A connection speed of 1024 Kbps will aslo be available. To sign up for this service call 800-800-ADSL.

Although the sound quality is not too good, Internet users can now make long distance telephone calls with their computers. Net calls are dirt-cheap. All you need is a headset and to hook up with a company like **www.dialpad.com** and you are in business.

Many private Internet companies offer private services such as hoasting and web design. For a small hourly fee of $1 to $1.50 you may send and receive mail and surf the web at any of the many local Internet Cafés like **Ciber Cafe Las Arcadas** below the Hotel Costa Rica in downtown San José . The **Radiográfica** office also has computers you can use to surf the web. They even have printers so you can download and print out information from the web. The central post office in downtown San José offers seven computers with Internet and E-mail connection for about $1.50 per hour. Costa Rica's postal services hopes to have nearly 150 post offices branches online over the next few years.

Mail Service

Costa Rica's postal system or *Correos de Costa Rica* offers postal services comparable to that in many countries abroad. The country's first mail service was officially established in December of 1839.

Curbside boxes for mail pick up are almost nonexistent in Costa Rica. You will have to mail your letters from the post office or from a hotel if you are a guest. Just as in the United States, mail may be received and sent from the post office *(correo or casa de correos.)* The main post office is in the heart of downtown San José at Calle 2, Ave. 1-3 (223-9766). Other small cities and towns in rural areas have their own centrally located post offices. Airmail between the United States or Europe and Costa Rica usually takes about five to ten days. At present, an airmail letter to the U.S. or Canada costs 30 cents or 100 *colones.* A postcard to North America is around 20 cents or 70 *colones.* An airmail stamp to Europe is about 35 cents or 120 *colones.* The post office also provides other services, including M-bags for sending large quantities of books or other printed matter abroad, telegrams, fax service, courier services and delivery of documents.

As stated above, mail boxes are few and far between as are house numbers, so we recommend using your nearest post office for all postal related matters. The country's charming but exasperating "100-meters-east-of-the-church" present style addresses makes getting a post office box for local mail delivery a necessity. Obtaining a post office box *(apartado)* from your local post office in Costa Rica ensures prompt and efficient mail service.

Getting a post office box is a straightforward process, but vacant boxes can sometimes be hard to come by. These P.O. boxes are in great demand, but you can usually get one in January, when most people give up leases on their boxes when annual renewal fees are due. If a box's annual renewal fee isn't paid by mid-February, it is sold to those on the waiting list at that time. Popular branches like San José's Central Post office or Escazú have long waiting lists, so it is much easier to find a box in suburban or rural areas.

Many people deal with the shortage of boxes by sharing with friends, neighbors, extended family or a business associate. In theory, said practice isn't permitted, but many people do it and nobody seems to check closely.

To apply for a post office box, go to the post office nearest your office or home to fill out an application *(solicitud de apartado)*. The annual rental fee ranges between $10, $30 or $40 dollars in the San Jose metropolitan area and provincial capitals depending on the size of the post office box. There are three size boxes: small, medium and large. In rural post offices, the costs are about half.

Once you fill out the paperwork and pay your annual fee, you are given an address that reads something like this: José López, Apdo. 7289-1000, San José, Costa Rica, Central America. The number before the hyphen is the *apartado* (P.O. Box) and the number after the hyphen is the post office's code.

You may also receive mail in the general delivery section *(lista de correos)* of your local post office. This is especially useful in isolated regions of the country. Register at the nearest post office and they will put your name on the local *lista de correos*. When you pick up your mail, you pay a few cents per letter for this service. All letters must have your name, the phrase *lista de correos* and the name of the nearest post office.

The worst time to receive any correspondence through the regular Costa Rican mail is between November 20 and January 1st. Letters can be delayed up to a month by the enormous volume of Christmas mail and the vacations of postal workers during the month of December.

You should avoid having anything larger than a letter or a magazine sent to you in Costa Rica. Any item bigger than that will be sent to the customs warehouse (*aduana*) and you will make several trips to get it out. On the first trip to customs your package or parcel is unwrapped so you can fill out a declaration of its contents. On the second trip you usually will have to pay an exorbitant duty equivalent to the value of the item plus the mailing cost. If you refuse to pay, your package will be confiscated, not sent back, just confiscated.

So as you can see, due to the costs involved and wasted time, it is better to have friends bring you large items, pick them up when you're visiting the States, or use one of the private mail companies mentioned in this section.

In an effort to win back some of its customers, the government recently privatized the **Costa Rican Postal Service (CORTEL)**. The service has officially shed its public status and was reborn as Correos de Costa Rica S.A. The overhaul aims to transform the notoriously slow service into an efficient operation. The country's archaic street address system will be changed to a systematic numbering of streets, avenues and buildings.

For information about the Correos de Costa Rica's services contact them at: Tel: 800-900-2000, 253-3375 extension 343 and 345 or go to **www.correos.go.cr**.

Receiving Money from Abroad

Do you plan on having money from abroad sent to you in Costa Rica? Perhaps the cheapest and easiest way to get money is the ATM machine available at almost all banks and supermarkets.

Western Union in Costa Rica boasts that they offer the fastest money transfers in the country. Call Western Union at 1-800-777-7777, Tel: 283-6336 or E-mail: bvib@western-union.co.crfor additional information or go to one of their local agencies in San José, Liberia, San Isidro General, Puntarenas or other parts of the country. You'll have to show some form of valid identification to pick up your money. **Moneygram** 1-800-328-5678, Tel: 295-9595, www.moneygram.com offers similar services.

One of the safest way to receive money while visiting or residing in Costa Rica is to have an international money order or any other type of important merchandise or document shipped to you by one of the worldwide courier services, such as DHL or UPS. Letters and small packages usually take about two working days (Mon.–Fri.) to reach Costa Rica from the United States or Canada.

Many worldwide air couriers have offices in San José, such as **DHL** (290-3010), **Federal Express** (255-4567), **UPS** (257-7447), **TNT** (233-5678), **Jetex** (293-5838) and **Skynet** (232-5678). The latter two are probably the cheapest options. Until recently, Costa Rica's postal service, **Correos de Costa Rica**, was the slowest and least safe option. Its "non-priority" mail was too slow to even consider as a valid option. The Costa Rican postal Service does offer Priority Mail Service Tel: 253-3375, 800-9002000 or E-mail: pacc_prioritymail@correos.go.cr."Priority" mail *(certificado)* supposedly takes 12 days to reach any destination in the U.S., three weeks for Europe and the rest of the world. Rates are very affordable at about $5.35 per kilo and $4.75 for each additional kilo.

However, Correos de Costa Rica just inaugurated **EMS Courier** — a national and international courier service with 127 offices throughout the country. They hope to compete with private courier companies. You may contact them at Tel: 221-2136, Fax: 221-1737, E-mail: ems@correos.go.cr.

U. S. banks can wire money to banks in Costa Rica. This method is safe, but can be slow at times, as many bureaucratic delays can develop while waiting for checks to clear. You are also charged a fee for the transfer. We had a money order sent from England to our account in the Banco Nacional de Costa Rica and didn't experience much delay or any problems. Once we followed the correct procedure our money arrived promptly.

One of many offices for sending receiving money from abroad.

Necessity Begets An Inernational Mail Service
By Chuck Swett

Back in the good old days, the early sixties Jimn Fendell had been here 10 plus years (arrived with parents in 1951), and I was just getting over the caravan like, Pan-American Airways milk-run through Central America, things were a lot different here. The nearest beach, Puntarenas, was four hours away, via Cambronero, with fog so thick you had to ride on the hood of the car and guide the driver. You could go to the movies for a few colones, fill up a VW for almost nothing, and a popuplar priced a liter of milk cost a little over one colón. The train ride to Puntarenas was one big long party. And you could walk down any street in San José at any hour without ever considering yourself to be in danger.

But the one thing you wouldn't even consider doing , unless you really felt generous toward the customs officer population, was subscribe to National Geographic, The Saturday Evening Post or Life Magazine. Playboy would probably not even make it off the plane, much less through the postal system. The custom was to find out who was travelling and ask them to bring that car part or special shampoo or the latest Beatles album, when they came back.

As the country and the expatriate colony grew, communications media began to introduce new goodies and remind the foreigners of things they were accustomed to at home but couldn't easily get on the local market.

Our innovative friend Jim began to recognize the need for an alternative means of establishing and regaining that "link to home" that was missing. A reliable way to get peoples' important mail safely to its destination, and to allow them to enjoy a "taste of home" in their adopted country. That need finally took shape in Aerocasillas, twelve years ago.

Envisioned as becoming "The best personalized network for receiving and sending documents and mechandise between the rest of the world and our country," This way both national and international markets were opened to our clients.

Pioneering the field of private international mail service in this country, Aerocasillas has built a growing user base of 25,000 satisfied customers, with over 3,000 active accounts. This is the result of over twelve years of constant dedication to fulfilling the needs of our clients and seeking ways to improve on the service we provide.

The Costa Rican postal service is planning to start a money order service allowing money orders to be sent from the U.S. to Costa Rica. This service promises to be much faster and much more economical than getting money wired to your bank in Costa Rica.

You can always have a trustworthy friend or relative bring you up to $10,000 when they come to Costa Rica.

Automatic Teller Machines (ATMs) are found all over the country. You can't transfer money directly but can get cash advances from one of your credit or debit cards. Use of ATMs along with cashing a personal check are perhaps the fastest way to get money.

Many money changers (*cambistas*) have private offices near the central post office and banks in downtown San José. Some of these money changers will cash personal checks from your U. S. checking account when they know you. You can get the name of a money changer from other retirees or residents.

Another safe way of having checks sent to you is through one of the private mail services we list in the next section.

Once you have established a permanent residence in Costa Rica you can have Social Security and Veteran's benefits mailed to you directly through the U.S. Embassy.

The worst way to send money is through the regular mail. People report that many checks have been lost or stolen. Postal thieves are very sophisticated in Costa Rica and may work with some unscrupulous black market money changers. The postal system has received numerous complaints and has promised to do something about them.

If you need to file a complaint about lost or stolen mail, go to *Correo de Costa Rica's* complaint department (*Departamento de Reclamaciones*) in downtown San José on Ave. 6, between Calles 17 and 19. If you live outside San José, you can file a complaint at any local post office and it will be forwarded to San José.

If you still choose to use the regular mail system after reading the above, be sure to have your checks or money orders sent to you in secure, non-transparent manila envelopes—ones that can't be seen through when held up to a light.

A rash of postal thefts has prompted more and more people to use the private-mail companies which offer a variety of postal related services.

Private Mail Services

There are a few of the mail companies which provide clients with a mail drop and P.O. Box in Miami and a physical address where they can send or receive packages. This enables customers living in Costa Rica to have their mail sent to the Miami address where the companies forward the mail to Costa Rica. **Aerocasillas** (P.O. Box 4567–1000, San José, Costa Rica, Tel: 208-4868, Fax: 257-1187, E-mail: servicesjo@aerocasillas.com or see www.aerocasillas.com) is the oldest of these companies. Besides their main office they have other branches in the suburbs and in other areas of the country: La Uruca, San José 232-6892, Curridatbat, San José 224-6381, Novacentro in Guadalupe 224-9843, Cartago 592-0000, Limón 798-0606 ext. 6, Ciudad Quesada 460-7454 and Quepos 777-1925.

Trans-Express "Interlink" (P.O. Box 02-5635, Miami, FL 33102, Tel: 296-3973/296-3974; Fax; 232-3979), **AAA Express Mail** (Tel: 233-4993; Fax: 221-5056), **Star Box** (P.O. Box 405–1000, San José, Tel: 257-3443, Fax: 233-5624), **Jet Box** (tel: 231-5592 in Pavas, 253-5400 in Guadalupe, 281-3208 in Curridabat and 665-0017 in Liberia see www.jetbox.com) and **Daily Mail** (Tel: 233-4993; Fax: 221-5046) are other companies offering similar services.

Mail Boxes Etc. (Tel: 232-2925, Fax: 231-7325, E-mail: infombecr.com, www.mbecr.com), has a store near the U.S. Embassy in the suburb of Pavas

Mail Boxes Etc. offers a full ranger of postal related services.

and another in the Real Cariari Mall. They provide the same services as the companies above plus packing and shipping, office supplies, a photocopy center and much more.

These companies provide much faster service than the Costa Rican mail system to access mail order products from the U.S., to enable clients to subscribe to magazines and newspapers at U.S. domestic rates, to help obtain replacement parts from abroad and to order directly from mail order catalogs like Land's End, J.C. Penny and L.L. Bean. Large automobile parts may also be ordered from the U.S. You can pick up your correspondence directly from their offices or have your letters and packages picked up and delivered to your home or office at any time you decide. They will also get packages out of customs for you and save you a lot of headaches.

We have used one of these services for over four years and in general their service has been good. Because of the nature of our book business, we have an unusually high volume of incoming and outgoing mail. Our letters, books, packages, monies and other mail reach their U.S. destinations almost as fast as if they were mailed from another city in the States. This reliable service makes doing business from Costa Rica very easy.

Most of the private mail companies offer Certified Mail, RegisteredMail, Express Mail and FEDEX, UPS, DHL or other courier services.

Rates at any of these private mail services run from about $15.00 to $60.00 or more per month depending on the amount of mail you receive and whether you have a business or personal account.

EDUCATION

How to Learn Spanish

Although many of Costa Rica's well-educated people speak English, (and more than 30,000 English-speaking foreigners live permanently in Costa Rica), Spanish is the official language. Anyone who seriously plans to live or retire in Costa Rica should know Spanish — the more the better. Frankly, you will be disadvantaged, handicapped and be considered a foreigner to some degree without Spanish. Part of the fun of living in another country is communicating with the local people, making new friends and enjoying the culture. Speaking Spanish will enable you to achieve these ends, have a more rewarding life, and open the door for many new, interesting experiences. Knowing some Spanish also saves you money when you're shopping and, in some cases, keeps people from taking advantage of you.

If you take our advice and choose to study Spanish, you can enroll at one of Costa Rica's intensive conversational language schools for a modest fee. In addition to language instruction, most of these schools offer exciting field trips, interesting activities and room and board with local families, all of which are optional. Living with a family that speaks little—or preferably no—English is a wonderful way to improve your language skills, make new friends and learn about Costa Rican culture at the same time.

Spanish is not a difficult language to learn. With a little self-discipline and motivation, anyone can acquire a basic Spanish survival vocabulary of between 200 and 3000 words in a relatively short time. Many Spanish words are similar enough to English, so you can guess their meanings by just looking at them. The Spanish alphabet is almost like the English one, with a few minor exceptions. Pronunciation is easier than in English because you say words as they look like they should be said. Spanish grammar is somewhat complicated but can be made easier if you are familiar with English grammar and find a good Spanish teacher. Practicing with native speakers improves your Spanish because you can hear how Spanish is spoken in everyday conversation. You will learn many new words and expressions not ordinarily found in your standard dictionary.

Watching Spanish television and listening to the radio and language cassettes can also improve your Spanish. We suggest that if you have little or no knowledge of spoken Spanish, you purchase the one-of-a-kind *Christopher Howard's Guide to Costa Rican Spanish*. It is designed especially for people planning to retire or live in Costa Rica. It makes learning easy because the student learns the natural way, by listening and repeating as a child does, without the complications of grammar. If you are interested in a deeper study of Spanish, we include a list of language schools at the end of this section. Please check first with the school of your choice for current prices.

The Spanish spoken in Costa Rica is more or less the same as standard Castillian Spanish except for one big difference which confuses beginning students. Spanish has two forms for addressing a person: *usted* and *tú*. However, in Costa Rica *vos* is used instead of *tú*. The verb form used with *vos* is formed by changing the *r* at the end of a verb infinitive to *s* and adding an accent to the last syllable. This form is seldom taught because it is considered a colloquial form, used only in Central America and some parts of South America (Argentina and Uruguay). It is not found in most Spanish textbooks.

Don't worry! Once you live in Costa Rica for a while and get used to the Costa Rican way of speaking, you will learn to use the *vos* form almost automatically. If you do makes mistakes and use the *tú* form, most Costa Ricans overlook it because they know you are not a native speaker. Costa Ricans appreciate any effort you make to speak their language.

You will notice that Costa Ricans frequently use local expressions called *tiquismos* that are not used in other Latin American countries. Some of these common expressions are *pura vida* (fantastic, super, great), *tuanis* (very good), *buena nota* (good, OK), *salado* (tough luck, too bad), and many others. One saying in particular, *hijo de puta* (roughly translated as "Son of a B——"), is considered offensive and vulgar in most Spanish speaking countries, but usually not in Costa Rica . You will be shocked hearing this expression used so frequently in everyday conversation. Even children and old women can sometimes be heard uttering this phrase. We don't

Super Tips For Learning Spanish
by Christopher Howard M.A.

1) Build your vocabulary. Try to learn a minimum of five new words daily.
2) Watch Spanish TV programs. Keep a note pad by your side and jot down new words and expressions. Later use the dictionary to look up any words and expressions you don't understand.
(3) Pay attention to the way the locals speak the language.
(4) Listen to Spanish music.
(5) Talk with as many different Spanish speakers as you can. You will learn something from everyone. Carry a small notebook and write down new words when you hear them.
(6) Read aloud in Spanish for five minutes a day to improve your accent.
(7) Try to imitate native speakers when you talk.
(8) Don't be afraid of making mistakes.
(9) Practice using your new vocabulary words in complete sentences.
10) When you learn something new, form a mental picture to go along with it—visualize the action.
11) Try to talk in simple sentences. Remember, your Spanish is not at the same level as your English, so simplify what you are trying to say.
12) If you get stuck or tongue-tied, try using nouns instead of complete sentences.
13) Remember Spanish and English are more similar than different. There are many cognates (words that are the same of almost the same in both languages).
14) Learn all of the basic verb tenses and memorize the important regular and irregular verbs in each tense.
15) Study Spanish grammar, but don't get bogged down in it.
16) Read the newspaper. The comic strips are great because they have a lot of dialog.
17) It takes time to learn another language. Don't be impatient. Most English speakers are in a hurry to learn foreign languages and get frustrated easily because the process is slow. Study a little bit everyday, be dedicated, persist and most of all enjoy the learning process.

¡Buena suerte! Good luck!

Getting a Head Start
by Christopher Howard M.A.

If you are seriously considering moving to a Latin American country, you should begin to study Spanish as soon as possible.

Here are a few suggestions that will give you a head start in learning the language. Look for some type of Spanish course that emphasizes conversation as well as grammar and enroll as soon as possible. University extension, junior colleges and night schools usually offer a wide range of Spanish classes.

You should also consider studying at a private language school like Berlitz if there is one near where you reside. Many of these schools allow the students to work at their own pace.

Another excellent way to learn Spanish, if you can afford it, is to hire a private language tutor. Like private schools this type of instruction can be expensive, but is very worthwhile. The student has the opportunity of working one-on-one with a teacher and usually progresses much faster than in a large group situation.

If you happen to reside in an area where there are no schools that offer Spanish classes, you should go to your local bookstore and purchase some type of language cassette. This way, at least you will have a chance to learn correct pronunciation and train your ear by listening to how the language is spoken.

Listening to radio programs in Spanish and watching Spanish television are other ways to learn the language, if you are fortunate enough to live in an area where there are some of these stations.

You can also spend your summer or work vacations studying Spanish in Mexico or Costa Rica. This way you will experience language in real life situations. These language vacations can be enjoyable and rewarding experiences.

Finally, try befriending as many native Spainsh speakers as you can who live in the area where you reside. Besides making new friends, you will have someone to practice with and ask questions about the language.

By following the advice above and making an effort to learn the language, you should be able to acquire enough basic language skills to prepare you for living in a Spanish speaking country. Best of all, you will acquire the life-long hobby of learning a new language in the process.

encourage you to use this expression. However, be aware that it is a local custom and is usually used with no malice in mind.

Another trait of the Costa Ricans is the common use of *don* (for a man) and doña (for a woman) when addressing a middle age or older person formally. These forms are used with the first name, as in the case of the famous "don Juan." However, you will usually hear the more traditional *señor* or *señora* used instead of *don* or *doña*. Teachers in Costa Rica are addressed *Profesor* or *Maestro*, an engineer as *Ingeniero* and Attorney as *Licenciado*. Using these titles is a sign of respect and to do not is considered rude. Anyone with a bachelor's degree from the university is also entitled to be addressed as *Licenciado*.

In Costa Rica as in the rest of Latin America, the father's and mother's surname comes after a person's given name. For example, if Carlos is born to José García López and Marta Lara Pérez, his complete name would be followed by his father's first surname and then by his mother's, or Carlos García Lara. All official documents must have both surnames.

For some basic Spanish phrases and more *tiquismos*, see the section titled "Important Phrases and Vocabulary."

Language Schools

Centro Lingüístico Conversa has an excellent conversational program at the main school in San José and another campus west of town in a rural setting. See their display ad in this book. Write to Apdo. 17-1007, Centro Colón, San José, Costa Rica. Tel: 506- 221-7649;   Fax   506- 233-2418 E-mail conversa@racsa.co.cr   , www.conversa.co.cr.

Instituto De La Lengua Española is an excellent intensive program. Six hours daily for 15 weeks for $635. Terms begin in January, May and September. Apdo. 100-2350, San José, Costa Rica. Tel: 506- 227-7366; Fax: 506 -227-0211.

Forester Institute International offers a variety of classes. Prices range from $600 to $1150 depending on the program. Apdo. 6945-1000, San José, Costa Rica. Tel: 506- 225-1649; Fax: 506-225-9236 E-mail: forester@racsa.co.cr.

Intensa has two, three and four week programs with home- stays available. Prices range from $260 to $545. Apdo. 8110-1000, San José.   Tel: 506-   281-1818;   Fax: 506   253-4337   E-mail:intensa@racsa.co.cr, www.intensa.com.

Academia de Español Intercultura has an excellent reputataion and is located in Heredia. Tel: 260-8480, Fax: 260-9243, www.interculturacostarica.com.

Centro Cultural Costarricense Norteamericana has five-week courses, three hours daily for $280. Apdo. 1489-1000, San José, Costa Rica. Tel: 506-207-7500; Fax: 506-224-1480, www.cccnr.com.

Instituto Británico offers a three-week course, three hours a day, with field trips for $1000 includes home-stay. Apdo. 8184-1000, San José, Costa Rica. Tel: 506-234-9054; Fax: 253-1894, www.institutobritanico.co.cr.

Instituto Universal de Idiomas has various programs. Apdo. 751-2150, San Pedro, Moravia, Costa Rica. Ave. 2, Calle 9 Tel. 506-223-9917; Fax: 506- 223-9917; E-mail: info@universal-edu.com, www.universaledu.com.

Institute for Central American Development Studies which offers one-month programs, five hours a day, for $892, includes classes, lectures, field trips, and home-stay with a Costa Rican family. Apdo. 3-2070 Sabanilla, San José, Costa Rica. Tel: 506- 234-1381; Fax: 506- 234-1337; E-mail: icads@netbox.com.

Academia Costarricense de Lenguaje has intensive classes and many cultural activities for $975 a month. Apdo. 336-2070, San José, Costa Rica. Tel: 506-221-1624; Fax: 506-233-8670E-mail: crlang@racsa.co.cr

Centro Panamericano de Idiomas is a new school in a beautiful rural setting. The cost is around $1000 monthly and covers instruction, home-stay and excursions. Apdo. 151-3007, Heredia, Costa Rica. Tel: 506- 265-6866; Fax: 506- 265-6213.

Mesoamerica Language Institute gives four hours of instruction each day for $80 a week. Apdo. 1524-2050, San Pedro, Costa Rica. Tel: 506-234-7682 E-mail: mesoamer@racsa.co.cr.

Lisa Tec, Tel: 506-239-2225 Fax: 506-293-2894 E-mail: mkcarney@itspanish.com, www.itspanish.com.

IPEE Spanish Language School, Tel; 506-283-7731 Fax: 506-225-7860 E-mail: ipee@gate.net, www.ipee.com.

Academia Tica's various courses and home-stays cost between $120 and $180 for twenty hours of instruction. Apdo. 1294-2100, Guadalupe, San José, Costa Rica. Tel: 506-229-0013 e-mail: toyopan@intercentro.net.

ILISA, Instituto Latinoamericano de Idiomas. Apdo. 1011, 2050 San Pedro, Costa Rica or Dept. 1420, P. O. Box 25216, Miami, FL 33102-5216Tel: 506-225-2495 Fax: 506-225-4665. In U.S. and Canada: 800-454-7248 E-mail: spanish@ilisa.com

Centro Lingüístico Latinoamericano teaches intensive courses five hours per day for four weeks, including home-stay for $295 weekly. Apdo. 425-4005, San Antonio de Belen, Costa Rica. Tel: 506- 293—0128 Fax: 506-239-1869.

Central American Institute of International Affairs (ICAI) specializes in workshops and conferences, all levels of Spanish and also offers deluxe tours and college credits. Apdo. 10302, San José, Costa Rica. Tel: 506-233-8571; Fax: 506-221-5238 E-mail: icai@expreso.co.cr, www.expreso.co.cr/icai/index.htm

University of Costa Rica now offers Spanish courses as a foreign language through the School of Philology, Linguistics and Literature. This program lasts four months and the space is limited. The cost is around $450. Tel: 506-207-5634 Fax: 506-207-5089 E-mail: espanucr@cariari.ucr.ac.cr.

Berlitz offers different language programs to meet all of your needs.Tel:(506)-204-7555, (506)-253-9191 Fax: (506)-204-7444, (506)-253-1115or http:www.berlitz.com.

This list should start you on your way. Private, individualized language classes are also available. For listings look in the classified section of the *Tico Times*.

There is a Spanish conversational club for foreigners wanting to improve their Spanish skills. Call 254-1433 or 235-7026 for all of the details. The Instituto Universal de Idiomas (Ave. 2, Calles 7/9) has an exchange club where you can practice Spanish with a native speaker in exchange for help with English (Tel: 257-0441). Centro Cultural also has free Spanish social- conversation classes through a program called"Simply Spanish"

You can now combine language study with one of **Christopher Howard's Relocation / Retirement Tours**. Please see www.travel.costaricabooks.com or call toll free 800 365-2342.

Frequently Used Tiquismos
(Costa Rican Expressions)

Alimentar las pulgas — To sleep

Birra — Beer

Brete — work

Pura Vida — Great, Fantastic

Caerle la peseta — To get the idea, understand.

Campo — Space (in line, on a bus etc.)

Chepe — Slang for the city of San José

Chile — A joke

Chinamo — A booth or stand where things aree sold

Chuica — A rag or old clothes

Cien metros — One city block

Clavar el pico — To fall asleep

Con el moco caído — Sad

¿Diay? — What can be done about it?

Guaro — Moonshine

Harina — Slang for money

Jalado — Dissipated, pale

Jarana — A debt

Jetonear — To lie

lo duda — You said it! You're right!

Macho - Any fair skin or haired person

Montarse en la carreta — To get drunk

Pachuco — A type of street slang

Pinche - A tight-fisted person

Platero — Money hungry person

Porta amí — Who cares

Rajar — To brag

Tata - Father

Torta — An error or screw-up

Vieras — If you only knew; sure; would you believe

Vino — A snoopy person

Volar pico — To talk a lot

2005
Costa Rica Books Catalog
More Great Books to Buy!

These highly specialized guides are availables through our catalog.
On special request some can be ordered from bookstores
in the U.S. Canada or Europe

"Living and Investing in the 'NEW' Nicaragua"
By Christopher Howard

"This visionary work will help anyone thinking of living or making money in Nicaragua. It promises to become a Classic.".

This one-of-a-kind guidebook provides you with all the tools for living and investing in Nicaragua - Central America's "Sleeping Giant" and Land of Oportunity.

"Living and Investing in Panama"
By Christopher Howard

This one-one-of-a-kind definitive guidebook will tell you everything you need know about living and investing Latin America's most underrated country. Panama best benefits for retires of any country south of the border. It also has the most attractive financing for real estate purchases.

Speak Sanish Like a Costa Rican!
"Christopher Howard's Guide to Costa Rican Spanish"
By the author of **The Golden Door to Retirement and Living in Costa Rica**, Christopher Howard

"A must if you plan to live in Costa Rica."
Bestselling book.

FAST, EASY, PROVEN METHOD!
GUARANTEED RESULTS!

Excellent Books for Learning Spanish

Costa Rica Spanish Phrasebook, by Thomas B. Kohnstamm. Lonely Planet. A handy pocket-size book for Costa Rica.

Madrigal's Magic Key to Spanish, by Margarita Madrigal. Dell Publishing Group , 666 Fifth Ave, New York, NY 10103. Provides an easy method of learning Spanish based on the many similarities between Spanish and English. This book is a "must" for the beginner.

Open Door to Spanish - A Conversation Course for Beginners by Margarita Madrigal. Regent Publishing Company. (books 1 and 2). Two other great books for the beginner.

Spanish for Gringos, by William C. Harvey. Barron's Press. This is an amusing book that will help you improve your Spanish.

Breaking Out of Beginning Spanish, by Joseph J. Keenan. University of Texas Press. This helpful book is written by a native English speaker who learned Spanish the hard way. It contains hundreds of practical tips.

Barron's Spanish Idioms, by Eugene Savaia and Lynn W. Winget. This book has more than 2,000 idiomatic words and expressions. It is a helpful handbook for students of Spanish, tourists and business people who want to increase their general comprehension of the language.

Guide to Spanish Idioms, by Raymond H. Pierson. Passport Books, 4255 West Touchy Ave, Chicago, Illinois, 60646. Contains over 2,500 expressions to help you speak like a native.

Barron's Basic Spanish Grammar, by Christopher Kendris. An in-depth study of Spanish grammar.

Nice n' Easy Spanish Grammar, by Sandra Truscott. Passport Books. Basic grammar.

A New Reference Grammar of Modern Spanish, by John Butt and Carmen Benjamin. NTC Publishing Group. This one of the best reference books ever written in Spanish grammar. It is very easy to use and understand.

Talk Spanish Today, 2470 Impala Dr., Carsbad, CA 92008. Call 800-748-54804.
Grammar for serious students.

Barron's Spanish Vocabulary, also by Julianne Dueber. A good book for building vocabulary.

Household Spanish, by William C. Harvey. Barron's Press. A user-friendly book especially for English-speakers who need to communicate with Spanish-speaking employees.

Useful Reference Books

Dictionary of Spoken Spanish Words, *Phrases and Sentences.* Dover Publications Inc., New York, NY. ISBN 0-486-20495-2. This is the best of all phrase dictionaries. It contains over 18,000 immediately useable sentences and idioms. We recommend it highly.

Cassell's Spanish Dictionary -New World Edition by Anthony Gooch and Angelica García de Paredes. Macmillan Publishing Company., Inc. An excellent Spanish dictionary.

Webster's New World Spanish Dictionary, by Mike Gonzalez. Prentice Hall. Also covers Latin American usage.

The New World English/Spanish Dictionary, by Salvatore Ramondino. A Signet Book. Another excellent dictionary of Latin American Spanish.

Latin-American Spanish Dictionary, by David Gold. Ballantine Books. A good dictionary of Spanish used in Latin America.

Gran Diccionario CUYAS, Ediciones Hymsa, Barcelona Spain. One of the most extensive dictionaries ever printed.

Business Books

Just Enough Business Spanish, Passport Books. Full of phrases to help the businessman.

Talking Business in Spanish, by Bruce Fryer and Hugo J. Faria. Barron's Educational Series. Has over 3,000 business terms and phrases. A must for any person planning to do business in the Spanish speaking world.

Just Enough Spanish, Passport books. ISBN 0-8442-9500-0. As the title implies, this phrase book shows how to get by in most situations.

Costa Rica's Institutions of Higher Learning

If you wish to continue your education, university level courses are available to foreigners in subjects such as business, art, history, political science, biology, psychology, literature, and Spanish, as well as all other major academic areas.

Foreigners can enroll directly as special students for their first two years at the University of Costa Rica. Tuition is much lower than in most U.S. universities. Students can also audit classes for a nominal fee. Contact the **University of Costa Rica** (UCR), Tel: 506-207-4000 Fax: 506-225-6950 www.ucr.ac.cr. Another excellent public university is **The University Nacional** (UNA) in Heredia. Tel: 506-261-0101 Fax: 506-237-7593, E-mail: webmaster@una.co.ac.cr, www.una.accr. **National Correspondence University** (UNED) offers correspondence programs. Tel: 506-253-2121 Fax: 506-253-4990, E-mail: cendocu@arenal.uned.ac.cr, www.uned.ac.cr.

During the last ten years there has been a proliferation of private universities. They are mainly for those students who can't qualify academically for the University of Costa Rica or National University of Heredia. These schools are more expensive than the public universities and their degrees aren't quite as prestigious. **Autonomous University of Central America** or UACA, as it is more commonly known here, is the oldest of these private universities and has an excellent reputation. Tel: 506-234-0701 Fax: 506-224-0391, E-mail: lauaca@racsa.co.cr. Please see the local phone book for a listing of the many private universities found in the San José area.

Some U.S. universities offer programs in Costa Rica where you can get university credit. We understand the University of California offers one such program. However, you are better off surfing the Internet to see what is available if you want to continue your education here and receive credits towards a degree in the United States or Canada.

Public Universities

- **Technical Institute of Costa Rica** (ITCR), Apdo. 159-7050, CartagoTel:551-5333, Fax:551-5348

Private Universities

- **Adventist University of Central America,** Tel: (506) 441-5622, Fax: (506) 441-3465, E-mail: unadeca@racsa.co.cr
- **Escuela de Agricultura de la Región Tropical Húmedo** (EARTH),Tel: (506) 255-2000, Fax: (5060 255-2726, E-mail: relext@ns.earth.acca, www.earth.accr.
- **Latin American University of Science and Technology (ULACIT)** Tel:(506) 257-5767, Fax: (506) 222-4542, E-mail: info@ulacit.ac.cr
- **Inter-American University of Costa Rica**, Apdo. 6495-1000, San José. Tel: (506) 234-6262, Fax: (506) 253-8744
- **International University of the Americas (UIA)**, Apdo. 1447-1002, San José) Tel:(506) 233-5304, Fax: (506)222-3216, E-mail:infomatri@uia.ac.cr, www.uia.ac.cr

The University of Costa Rica in San Pedro.

- **Instituto Centroamericano Para la Administration de Empresa (INCAE).** Apdo. 960-4050, Alajuela. Tel: (506) 433-0506, Fax: (506) 433-9101.
- **University for Peace,** Apdo. 138, Ciudad Colón.Tel: (506) 249-1072, Fax: (506) 249-1929
- **University Mundial,** Tel: (506) 240-7057, Fax: (506) 236-6537

Of course, certain requirements for these schools of higher learning must be met. Once again, remember that private universities are generally more expensive than public universities.

Outstanding Private Schools

If you have small children or teenagers you will be pleased that Costa Rica has a variety of schools from which to choose. There are many public schools, numerous private bilingual schools and four English-language, or American schools.

Public schools tend to be crowded but legal foreign residents are entitled to attend public schools. However, since all instruction is in Spanish, you shouldn't even think of enrolling your children in a public school unless they speak, read and write Spanish fluently. If your children are not Spanish speakers you may have to enroll them in a private school.

The school week is Monday through Friday, and the day begins about 7:30 a.m. and ends about 2:00 p.m. in private schools. Schedules vary according to the school and age of the students. Public schools are on a similar schedule unless the are operating two shifts, in which case the second shift may not end before 5:00 or 6:00 p.m.

Most schools include pre-Kinder to 12th grade. The school structure is further divided into pre-kinder, Kinder, *primaria* (1st to 6th), *secundaria* (7th to 12th) grades. Some private schools have a middle school (7th and 8th) and high school (9th through 12th grade). Class size in private schools range from 20 to 30 students, depending on the age of the students and the school. Public schools tend to have much larger classes, ranging from 40 to 60 students.

Students are graded on a scale of 100 being the highest possible score and 70 being the minimum passing grade. Grading system is not on a ABCDF system as in many schools in the United States.

Students from pre-kinder through twelfth grade are required to wear uniforms established by each school. Even private schools require the use of uniforms. There is usually an emblem on the chest of each school's shirt with the name of the particular institution.

Costa Rica's private English-language American schools are exceptional, have high academic standards and four are accredited in the U.S.: **Lincoln School, Marian Baker School, Country Day School** and **American International School**. Some follow the U.S. school year schedule with vacations in June, July and August. Others follow the Latin American academic calendar, which begins sometime in February and ends in November or December. Changing from the U.S. calendar to one of these schools may require that your children move back half a year and start the grade over. Likewise schools are also free to move students up a half-year if they are academically and mature enough to handle the change.

These schools are academically oriented and prepare students for admittance to colleges in the U.S. as well as in Costa Rica. They teach English as a primary language and offer Spanish as a second language. In some ways these schools are better than similar institutions in the U.S.A. because not as many harmful distractions or bad influences exist in Costa Rica. Children also have the opportunity to learn a new language which is of great value to them. The cost of some of these private schools can be more than $300 per month.

It is a good idea to visit a number of schools before deciding which one is right for your child. You should ask to visit a couple of classrooms as well as see all of the facilities. This way you may view the school's infrastructure.

A class of busy students at the Lincoln School

Make a list of the pros and cons of each school before making your final decision. Do not forget to see if the school is accredited in the U.S. Also find out about the teacher-student ratio. Be sure to see what percentage of the students graduate and go on to universities in Costa Rica and the U.S. Finally, try to talk to other foreigners who have children enrolled in private schools to see if they are satisfied with the quality of education their children receive.

We talked with one couple from the U.S. who did not have the resources to afford a private school so they opted for home schooling. They recommended several programs which you can find on the Internet: **www.calvertschool.edu, www.unl.edu** and **www.keystonehighschool.com**.

Our son attends the **Lincoln School** in Moravia. He has learned more than at the private school he attended in the States. All subjects are taught in English except for an hour a day of Spanish. There are special courses of Spanish as a second language for students new to the country and advanced classes for foreign students and Costa Ricans who have mastered the language. We have seen children who move to the country learn to speak fluent Spanish in a couple of years. Conversely, Costa Rican children are able to master English in a short period of time. If you listen to the high school students speak English you would think they grew up in the U.S. or Canada. It must be pointed out that generally, the younger the student, the more quickly a second language can be learned. Junior and senior high school students take much longer to learn a new language than preschool and elementary students.

The following schools are accredited in the U.S. Some follow the U.S. schedule, September to June. Others follow the Costa Rican academic year which begins in March and ends in November:

Lincoln School: Pre-kindergarden through grade 12 with classes in English. Tuition about $350 monthly: Apdo. 1919, San José, Costa Rica. Tel: 506- 247-0800; Fax: 506- 247-0900 E-mail: director@ns.lincoln.ed.cr, www.lincoln.ed.cr. Follows the U.S. academic year.

American International School: Pre-kindergarten through grade 12. Classes taught in English, U.S. style education. Annual tuition: $1,070 pre-kindergarten, $3,130 per year for kindergarten to grade 12. Apdo. 4941-1000, San José, Costa Rica. Tel: 506- 239-2567; Fax: 239-0625 E-mail: aiscr@cra.ed.cr. Follows the U.S. school year.

Country Day School: Kindergarten through grade 12 in Escazú. Annual tuition: Pre-kindergarten $3,245; grades 1 to 12, $6,510. Apdo.

8-6170, San José, Costa Rica. Tel: 506- 289-8406; Fax: 506-228-2076 E-mail: codasch@racsa.co.cr; www.cds.ed.cr. Follows the U.S. school year.

Country Day School Guanacaste: This new branch of the Country Day School offers a curriculum similar to the main campus in Escazú. Since the school is located near Flamingo, a surfing class is available for high school students. All subjects are taught in English except for Spanish. Future boarding facilities are being considered. Tel: 506 654-5042, Fax: 506 654-5044, E-mail; cdsgte@costarica.net, www.cds.ed.cr.

Marian Baker School: Kindergarten through grade 12. U.S. curriculum with classes in English. Annual tuition: Kindergarten, $3,550; preparatory to grade 6, grades 7 - 12, $6,610. Apdo. 4269, San José, Costa Rica, Tel: 506- 273-3426; Fax: 506- 234-4609; E-mail: mbschool@racsa.co.cr; www.marianbakerschool.com. Follows the U.S. school year.

Blue Valley School: Preschool to grade 12. Tel: 506-289-8653;Fax: 506-228-8653; E-mail: bvschool@racsa.co.cr. Follows both U.S. and Costa Rica calendars.

The European School: Pre-kindergarten through 6. Apdo. 177, Heredia, Costa Rica. Tel: 506- 261-0717; Fax: 506- 237-4063, E-mail: aaronson@racsa.co.cr, www.eupeanschool.com

The less expensive bilingual private schools below also prepare students for U.S. colleges and universities but follow the Costa Rican academic year that begins in March and ends in November.

Anglo American School: Kindergarten through grade 6. Costs about $100 a month. Apdo. 3188-1000, San José, Costa Rica. Tel: 506-225-1723.

Canadian International School: Pre-kindergarten through grade 2. About $100 monthly. Apdo. 622-2300. San José, Costa Rica. Tel: 506-272-7097; Fax: 506-272-6634.

Colegio Bilingue Santa Cecilia: Preschool to grade 11. Tel: 506-237-7733; Fax: 506-237-4557; colsuper@racsa.co.

Colegio Humboldt: Kindergarten through grade 12. Classes half in German, half in Spanish. Tuition is about $70 monthly. Apdo. 3749, San José, Costa Rica. Tel: 506- 232-1455; Fax: 506-232-0093; E-mail: humboldt@racsa.co.cr, www.infoweb.co.cr/humbolt.

Colegio Internacional: Grades 7 through 10. Apdo. 963, 2050 San Pedro, Costa Rica. Tel: 506- 224-3136 Fax: 506- 253-9762; sekerdir@racsa.co.cr; www.sek.net.

Colegio Metodista: Kindergarten through grade 12. Classes in English and Spanish. Apdo. 931-1000, San José, Costa Rica. Tel: 506- 225-0655 Fax: 506-225-0621.

Escuela Británica: Kindergarten through grade 11, classes half in English, half in Spanish. $150 per month. Apdo. 8184-1000 San José, Costa Rica. Tel: 506- 220-0131 Fax: 506-232-7833; british@racsa.co.cr; www.infoweb.co.cr/british..

Kiwi Kinder: Pre-school for two and a half to five-year olds. Apdo. 549-6150, Santa Ana, Costa Rica. Tel: 506-282-6512; **Fax: 506-282-4319; klc@edenia.com; www.edenia.com/kiwi.**

Liceo Franco-Costarricense: Classes in French, English and Spanish. Concepción de Tres Ríos. Tel: 506- 273-4543; Fax: 506-279-6615; lyfrancos@racsa.co.cr; www.lefranco.ac.cr.

International Christan School: Pre-kindergarten through grade 12. Annual tuition: Pre-kindergarten, $990; Preparatory and kindergarten, $1,300; Grades 1 - 6, $2,200; Grades 7 - 8, $2,300; Grades 9 - 12, $2,500. Apdo. 3512-1000, San José, Costa Rica. Tel: 506-236-7879 Fax: 506-235-1518.

Pan American School: Pre-kinder through 12. Tel: 506-293-7393, Fax: 506-293-7392, E-mail: cpcrsa@racsa.co.cr. Located in San Antonio de Belén.

Saint Anthony School: Pre-school through grade 6. Classes half in English, half in Spanish. Apdo. 29-2150, Moravia, Costa Rica. Tel: 235-1017; Fax: 506-235-2325; santhony@racsa.co.cr.

Saint Claire: Grades 7 - 10, classes in English and in Spanish. Tuition $125 per month. Apdo. 53-2150, Moravia, Costa Rica, Tel: 506- 235-7244.

Saint Francis: Kindergarten through grade 11, classes in English and Spanish. Inquire about rates. Apdo. 4405-1000, San José Costa Rica. Tel: 506- 297-1704 Fax: 240-9672 E-mail: sfc@stfrancis.ed.cr.

Saint Joseph's Primary School: Pre-school through grade 6, classes half in Spanish, half in English, $70 per month. Apdo. 132-2150, Moravia, Costa Rica. Tel: 506- 235-7214.

Saint Mary's: Pre- kindergarten through Grade 6, around $100 monthly. Classes in English, and Spanish. Apdo. 229-1250, Escazu, Costa Rica. Tel: 506- 228-2003.

Summerhill Latinoamericano: Pre-school, elementary school and weekend camp programs. Tel: 506-280-1933, Fax: 506-283-0146.

*See the yellow pages for more listings.

GETTING AROUND

Air Travel to, in, and around Costa Rica

Most direct flights from Miami cost less, however there are flights from your home city to San José by way of Los Angeles, Houston, New Orleans or Panama.

Most flights arrive at **Juan Santamaría Internations Airport** (Tel: 443-262) the country's main airport, located about a half-hour northwest of San José. The airport now boasts a new terminal with restaurants and many shops. Many travelers choose to fly into **Daniel Oduber International Airport**, the country's other main airport, located near the city of Liberia. The main attraction here is the airport's proximity to the excellent Pacific beaches in the northern province of Guanacaste. Many U.S. carriers now offer daily flights to this area. Delta, Air Canada and American West are now flying to Guanacaste.

However, the vast majority of flights continue to land at Juan Santamaría Airport. The airlines currently offering service from the United States to San José, Costa Rica are **Aviateca** (800-327-9832), **Sasha** (800-327-1225), **Continental** (800-231-0856), **Mexicana** (531-7921), **Grupo Taca** (800-535-8780), **American** (800-433-7300), **Delta** (800-241-4141), **United** (800-538-2929) and **LACSA** Costa Rica's national airline. Lacsa's toll-free number is 800-225-2272 in the U.S.A. and 800-663-2444 in Canada.

Some airline tickets are good for a year, but you need permission from the Costa Rican Immigration Department to stay in the country longer than 90 days unless you are a Costa Rican resident or *pensionado.*

Most airlines offer excursion rates and three-or-four week packages. Others, especially Canadian airlines, offer special group and charter rates. Fares are subject to availability, change and restrictions including advanced purchase requirements, minimum stops or cancellation penalties. Remember, the main tourist season in Costa Rica runs from about Thanksgiving to Easter. This period approximately coincides with local vacations so it is hard to find available space at this time of year. If you are planning to travel to or from Costa Rica during December you may have to buy a ticket months in advance because of the Christmas holidays. However, if you get into a jam you can sometimes find space on a flight via Panama.

If you plan to travel or explore South America from Costa Rica, you can usually save money by flying to Miami and then buying a round-trip ticket to your destination. For instance, a one-way ticket from San José to Buenos Aires, Argentina can cost more than a round trip ticket from Miami to Buenos Aires.

The **Travel Store** (www.allcostaricatravel.com E-mail: travel@costaricatravelstore.com) and **Tico Travel** (800-493-8426) specialize in trips to Costa Rica.

International Airlines Located In San José Costa Rica

American Airlines, La Sabana	257-1266
Avianca/SAM, Ave. 5, Calle 1	233-3066
Aviateca	257-9444
Continental, Juan Santamaria Airport	296-4911
COPA, Ave. 5, Calle 1	222-6640
Delta	257-4141
Grupo Taca	257-9444
Iberia, Ave. 2-4, Calle 1	257-8266
KLM	220-4119
Mexicana	257-6334
Nica	257-9444
Sasha, Ave. 5, Calle 1-3	221-5774
TACA	257-9444
United	220-4844

A Travel Business is Born
By Robert Hodel

So there I was, preparing for the culmination of three years of law when I realized that sinking feeling just was not going to go away.

That feeling I was referring to was the fact that I did not want to spend the rest of my life, nor even one minute for that matter, as a lawyer.

As soon as I accepted that fact I was in a quandry. What was I to do?

It was then I remembered from somewhere that the key to any successful business venture one may choose is to: 1) do what you like and 2) do what you know or do well.

With that in mind I pondered my future both day and night. Finally, I realized the thing I liked most to do was travel and the place I knew best, other than my home town, was Costa Rica.

I knew where was the best place to go and when. I also knew how to get the best prices on airfare, rental cars and hotels. So after a long phone call with my brother, who was even more knowledgeable than myself, I had a plan.

We would start a travel company dedicated primarily to Costa Rica and we would call it Tico Travel. I would move back to Costa Rica and introduce myself to the hotels, car rental companies and tour operators that we wanted to work with plus stay on top of any new developments that would be of interest to our clients. My brother moved to Florida and opened our office and was able to give our clients expert information on Costa Rica with a "gringo" point of view.

Within a short amount of time we became the agency of choice for people that travel frequently to Costa Rica and also for the first time visitor.

Along the way we learned many things. For instance, just because it makes sense does not mean it works that way.

We also found no matter how much we advertised, that over 80% of our clients were either clients' referals or repeat customers, as a testimony to how important one's reputation is in this part of the world.

I have been told many times that one could make many times more money with the same effort if we were in the United States.

That may be so but I have been told something else by a longtime resident here,"We are not here for the money, we are here for the lifestyle."

See Tico Travel on the Internet at **www.ticotravel.com**.

Domestic Airlines

Smaller domestic airlines like **SANSA, Nature Air** or chartered planes called air taxis, are used for flights within the country. Domestic airlines use four-to-15-passenger planes. The latter can cost up to a few hundred dollars an hour. SANSA, the national airline, is more reasonably priced ($15 to $30, depending on your destination). SANSA flies to the beach cities of Golfito, Quepos, Barra del Colorado, Sámara, Nosara, and Tamarindo. We recommend purchasing your tickets in advance, especially during the heavy tourist season (December to May.) These flights get you to your designation quickly and economically, save you time, and give you the thrill of viewing Costa Rica's spectacular landscape from above.

SANSA's office is in the Grupo Taca building diagonal to the northeast corner of the Sabana Park. Telephone 221-9414 or E-mail; info@flysansa.com or sansa@lacsa.atlas-com or see www.flysansa.com for flight times and reservations. Some travel agencies in San José also make reservations.

Nature Air offers domestic flights. Call (506) 220-3054 or see www.natureair.com. Charters are available at Tel: 011-(506) 257-0766 or www.costaricacharters.com. Also look in the yellow pages under "Taxis Aereos."

Traveling by City Bus

As you already know, bus fares from San José to the surrounding suburbs are very cheap. On urban and inter-urban buses you pay the driver as you board.

Here is a list of where to catch a bus from the center of San José to the surrounding neighborhoods.

Alajuela	Ave. 2 Across from the Parque Merced
Alajuelita	Ave. 6 and 8, Calle 8
Aserrí	Ave. 4 and 6, Calle 7
Barrio México	Ave. 3, Calle 3
Barrio Luján	Ave 2, Calles 5 and 7
Calle Blancos	Ave. 5, Calles 1 and 3
Coronado	Ave. 7, Calle 0
Curridabat	Ave. 6, Calles 3 and 5
Desamparados	Ave. 4, Calles 5 and 7
Escazú	Ave. 0-1, Calle 16
Guadalupe	Ave.3, Calle 0
Hatillos	Ave. 2 and 6 Calle 6, Ave. 4 Calle 2

Heredia ....Ave 2 next to Merced Church
Moravia...Ave. 3 Calles 3 and 5
Paso AnchoAve .... 4 and 6, Calle 2
Pavas ....Ave. 1, Calles 16 and 20
Sabana Cementerio ....Ave. 2, Calles 8 and 10
Sabana Estadio...Ave.2, Calles 2 and 4
Sabanilla..Ave. 0-2, Calle 9
San Pedro...Ave. 0, Calles 9 and 11
Santana Ana ....Ave. 1 and 3, Calle16
Santo Domingo..................................Ave. 7 and 9, Calles 2
Tibás...Ave. 5 and 7, Calle 13
Tres Riós ....Avenida Central and 2, Calle 13
Zapote...Ave. 2 and 4, Calle 5

Traveling by bus around San José or to the surrounding suburbs may seem quite difficult to a newcomer. However, once you get the hang of it, you will find it surprisingly easy and an affordable way to travel. Most expatriates who do not have cars use the city's excellent bus system. A few who own cars prefer taking buses to avoid traffic and paying for parking.

If you do not know where to catch a specific city bus to your destination, then you will have to ask someone. If you cannot find an English speaker who knows or your Spanish is not adequate, then go to the tourism office below La Plaza de La Cultura in the heart of San José. They will provide you for a free map of San José's bus stops. Also you might want to ask a policeman who can usually help.

When you finally find your bus stop, you should not assume that every bus that stops there goes to your destination. It is not unusual to have several buses with different routes using the same bus stop. When in doubt try to ask someone who is waiting, *"A dónde va este autobús?"* (Where does this bus go?). Another thing you can do is to look at the sign displayed horizontally above the windshield or at the lower left-hand-corner of the front window. These signs will list the final destination of every bus.

Once you figure out which bus to take, have your change in hand and be ready to pay the bus fare. You can usually find out how much the fare is by asking one of the people who is waiting or by looking at the sign the buses' window. Do not be in a hurry to board, since some passengers may exit through the front door.

When you get inside the bus hand the driver your fare. If you do not have the exact amount the driver will make change. Try to avoid giving the driver anything larger than a 2000 *colón* bill. Be careful not to stand between the electronic counter or the driver will get mad. They were installed to replace the turnstiles most buses used to have. These devices have an electric eye and count the number of people who use the bus. Once a friend of mine boarded a bus, and his young son accidentally stood in front of the electric counter. The driver made my friend pay an extra fare or he would have had to pay the amount out of his own pocket.

Next, you will need to find a seat. It is advisable not to sit on the sunny side of the bus. A large number of buses have large windows with no curtains. If you sit on the side the sun hits, you may feel like you are under a magnifying glass. However, many of the newer buses have curtains you can draw to keep out the sun.

During rush hour buses tend to be very crowded and you often have to stand up if you cannot find a seat. In that case take hold of one of the horizontal bars. Most buses start and stop with a jerky motion and it is easy to fall if you are standing and not holding on to something.

Be sure to let the driver know about a block before you want to get off. You can do this by pulling the horizontal cord next to the window or by pressing an overhead button. Buses usually have one these devices. If you cannot locate the cord or button or if either one of them does not work, then yell, *"Parada!"* (Stop!), so the driver will know let you off at the next stop. If you do not know at which bus stop to get off, ask the driver or someone else on the bus. Usually the name of a street, a neighborhood or a landmark will suffice. When boarding a bus if you let the driver know where you want to be let off he will usually remember to tell you when you reach you stop.

Bus Travel Around Costa Rica

For a very low cost ($2– $6, or about $1 per hour of driving time) you can take a bus to almost anywhere in the country. Most Costa Ricans do not own cars, so they depend on buses for traveling to other parts of the country. Riding a bus provides the perfect opportunity to get to know people on a personal basis, see the lovely countryside and learn something about the country and the culture. Most buses used for these longer trips are modern and very comfortable. Unlike some parts of Latin America, Costa Rica's buses are not filled with chickens and other small animals and standing is NOT allowed. Buses are crowded on weekends and holidays, so buy your tickets in advance or get to the station early. Be sure to check for schedule changes.

Alajuela (A bus every 20 minutes or so) Ave. 2,
  Calle 12 and 14 222-5325
Arenal (Buses at 4:15, 8:40, 11:30 am) Calle 16, Ave. 1 and 3
Cartago (A bus every 10 minutes) Calle 5,
  Central Ave.18-20 233-5350
Golfito (Get tickets in advance) Ave. 3-5, Calle 14................221-4214
Heredia (A bus every 5 minutes) Calle 1, Ave. 7 and 9 233-8392
Heredia (Small buses or Busetas) Ave.2, Calles 12 and14 261-7171
Liberia (Get tickets in advance) Calle 14, Ave. 1 and 3...........222-1650
Limón (Hourly get tickets in advance on holidays) Calle Central,
six blocks north of the Metropolitan Cathedral ...221-2596 or 223-7811
Nicoya (Get tickets in advance) Calle 14, Ave. 3 and 5...........222-2666
Puntarenas (Every 30 minutes. Be early on holidays.)
Calle16, Ave. 10 and 12..222-0064
Quepos (Get tickets in advance inside the market)
  Coca Cola Terminal..223-5567
San Carlos (A bus every hour) Coca Cola Terminal................255-4318
Santa Cruz Calle 20, Ave.3 and 4...221-7202
San Isidro del General (Get tickets in advance)
  Calle 16, Ave. 1 and 3.. 222-2422
San Ramón Calle16, Avenidas 10 and 12 222-0064
Sarchí (Coca Cola Terminal, every hour)
  Calle 16 and 18, Ave. 1 and 5...494-2139
Southern Border (Paso Canoas, leaves daily)
  Ave. 3 and 5, Calle 14 221-4214
Tilarán - (Daily) Calle 12, Ave. 7 and 9................................222-3854
Turrialba Calle 13, Ave. 6 and 8 556-0073

* If your destination is not listed, check with a local travel agency or some knowledgeable person who is familiar with bus schedules and knows the different bus stops. There is an Intercity Buses Web page which gives a complete bus schedule. It may be found at: **www.yellowweb.co.cr/crbuses.hmtl**.

Bus tickets may be purchased on online at: **www.Costa RicaBusTicket.com**. This company covers most areas north and west of San José. You may contact them at: **011-(506) 365-9678.**

Interbus (Tel: 283-5573,Fax: 283-7655, E-mailvsftrip@racsa.co.cr, www.interbusonline.com) and **Fantasy Tour/Gray Line** (Tel: 220-2126, Fax: 220-2393, E-mail: fantasy@racsa.co.cr, www.graylinecostarica.com), offer direct tours between many of the country's major tourist attractions. Both companies offer transportation to over 40 destinations and have offices around the country.

Bus Travel to and from Costa Rica

If you want to travel to Guatemala, Panama or other Central American countries, you can use the bus services listed. Those wanting to live in Costa Rica permanently without being legal residents can take a bus to Panama or Nicaragua, return to Costa Rica after 72 hours, and thus renew your papers so you can remain legally in the country for another 90 days. Many foreigners living as perpetual tourists in Costa Rica go through this procedure every few months in order to avoid immigration hassles.

From time to time the immigration department asks to see a return ticket before extending tourist cards. So it is a good idea to buy an inexpensive bus ticket to a neighboring country to prove you can leave the country.

Tica Bus (Tel: 2218954), Avenidas 2 and 4 between Calles 9 and 11, offers bus service to the rest of Central America.

San José to Panama City leaves daily at 10 p.m. from the Tica Bus Terminal. The 542-mile journey takes eighteen hours.

San José to David (Panama) leaves daily at 7:30 a.m. from Avenida 5, Calle 14. It makes the 240 mile-trip in 9 hours.

San José to Managua leaves the **Sirca Bus Company** at 6 a.m. The 270-mile trip takes about 10 hours.

San José to Guatemala leaves daily at 6:00 a.m. from Avenida 4 between Calles 9 and 11. This trip takes 2-1/2 days.

San José to Honduras leaves at 6:00 a.m. daily.

Buses provide inexpensive transportation to any destination in the country.

Round Trip Back to Paradise
By Jay Trettien

"I never had more money or had more fun than when I lived in Costa Rica," was my response when a fellow bartender friend from southern California suggested we open a bar in Baja California.

"If you're heading South of the Border, you may as well go to Costa Rica, where the weather is nicer and the people more friendly," I said.

I was first invited to Costa Rica in 1973 by a college friend who worked for the Bank of America. Through the bank he had met an American who needed help with a bar he had just bought. My friend suggested that maybe I would come to Costa Rica to help out. A late-night phone call, and two weeks later I arrived from New York. After a few weeks of working together, the bar owner and I had developed trust and a friendship and, on the strength of a handshake, I became a partner in what was to become Central America's most popular "Gringo" rock and roll bar, Ye Pub. Gringos and ticos loved the place. After living in Costa Rica for a while, I was granted a cédula, or Costa Rican "green card."

But the time came to sell. Costa Rica had been enjoying a spectacular boom but with small countries as fast as it goes up, it can go down. After three years we sold.

With a girlfriend that was driving me nuts it was easy to leave Costa Rica. I visited every country in South America. I had already seen almost all of Europe, most of the United States and Canada. So, I ended up in Australia and New Zealand for about four years, finally washing up on the shores of southern California.

I began thinking about Costa Rica again and made a brief visit about 12 years ago to be pleasantly surprised that I still had friends in the country. I returned to California, loaded up the old Pontiac and ended up back in Costa Rica.

A lucky coincidence got me my cédula back when the Costa Rican government declared an amnesty for all foreigners, trying to get a grip on all the illegal Nicaraguans in the country.

Now I'm working at a popular San José hotel bar. I think I have about $150 under my mattress, but I have a good time and a lot of fun.

When guests ask me how long I've been in Costa Rica, I say, " I don't remember...10-12 years." And that's the truth, I don't really remember.

Guest, "Do you like Costa Rica?" "NO! I'm here on the United States Witness Protection Program, but they could only find this low-profile job for me!"

Traveling by Train

In 1995 regular passenger train service on Costa Rica's two main rail lines was shut down due to economic loss. The famous "Jungle Train" that ran from San José to the Caribbean port of Limón was discontinued because of earthquake-caused landslides. Starting this year the Railroad Institute (INCOFER) offered limited passenger service to Puntarenas. With any luck full train service to both coasts will resume soon.

Costa Rica's Taxis

As we mentioned in Chapter 2, it is not necessary to own an automobile if you live in or near San José because taxis are plentiful and inexpensive. San Jose's buses are cheaper, but taxis are the best way to get from point A to point B.

Taxis registered with the Ministry of Public Works and Transportation (MOPT) are red with a yellow triangle on both front doors. The triangle contains the taxi's license number, which begins with the letter(s) of the province where the cab is licensed and registered, followed by a "P" for province. For example, a taxi registered in San José province has a license plate number beginning with "SJP."

Taxis charge 265 colones (61 cents) for the first kilometer and 150 *colones* (30 cents) per kilometer thereafter. You can rent cabs by the hour for 1000 to 1500 *colones*. There is also a charge for stopping time equivalent to the charge for one kilometer on the meter. If you take a taxi between 10 p.m. and 5 a.m., the driver can charge 20 % more than the meter fare. If you want the driver to wait while you do an errand or some other business, there is an hourly rate of around 1,120 *colones*. If you have to go more than 12 kilometers outside the metropolitan area, there is another rate. In this case the driver and the passenger should negotiate the fare (Do this in advance). Nearly all taxis have computerized meters called **marías**. Always insist that your taxi driver use his meter, and be sure to ask about rates before traveling anywhere. Drivers are required to use their meters, even if they tell you they are not. If the *maría* is missing or broken, you might be overcharged for the trip. Always tell the driver, *"Ponga la maría por favor."* (Please turn on the meter).

Many city cab drivers get upset if you try to pay with large bills. If you intend to pay with a big bill ask the driver if he has change before boarding the cab to avoid last minute misunderstandings. If you tell a driver beforehand you are oing to pay with a large bill, he'll usually stop along the way to get change at a gas station.

Most taxi drivers are polite, but if you are overcharged or dissatisfied with service, you can take the driver's permit number usually on the visor of his taxi or his license number and complain to the MOPT Office (**Ministerio de Obras Públicas y Transporte**) at Plaza Víquez. You can do this in person, by letter or over the telephone (Tel: 257-7798, ext. 2512).

Taxies can be found around every public square and park, outside discotheques, on most busy streets, and in front of government buildings and most hotels. Be careful since many taxis parked in front of hotels may overcharge. Some of the drivers claim they work exclusively for the hotel and will overcharge you.

They will try to double the fare to account for driving back to the hotel, their home base, empty. Many times the explanation is fair and the driver is honest. Also, if you have a complaint and the driver works for the hotel you have immediate recourse, the hotel's management.

It is difficult to find a taxi during the rainy season, especially in the afternoon when it usually rains. You may also have trouble getting a cab on weekdays or during rush hour between 7 a.m. and 9 a.m. and 4:30 p.m. to 6:30 p.m.,as in most cities.

To hail a taxi just yell, "Taxi!" If a taxi is parked just say "*libre*" (free) to the driver to see if a cab is available. If the taxi is available, he will usually nod or say, "*sí*" (yes). If you want to stay on a taxi driver's good

Taxis are a bargain in Costa Rica.

side, NEVER slam the taxi's doors; taxis are expensive in Costa Rica and drivers try to keep them in good shape.

Some people moonlight as taxi drivers using their own unmarked cars. Many look like regular cabs but without the yellow triangles on the front doors. They are called *piratas* (pirates) by the locals, and will often approach if they see you looking for a taxi. Since they do not have meters, we advise you not to hire any of these vehicles for transportation. Most do not have insurance to cover their passengers in the event of an accident. If you do have to take one, remember there is no meter, so negotiate the fare <u>before</u> you get in or you may run the risk of being overcharged.

If you call a taxi, be able to give your exact location in Spanish so the taxi driver knows where to pick you up. If your command of Spanish is limited, have a Spanish speaker write down directions to your destination. We know one old grouchy *gringo* who has never made an effort to learn a word of Spanish. He has all the directions of the places he has to go written in Spanish for taxi drivers. If you phone for a taxi, the driver can turn on the meter when he gets the call and charge for the driving time to your location.

Airport pick-ups can be arranged in advance by calling one of the taxi companies. We recommend doing this, especially during the rainy season, when it is difficult to get a taxi when you need one.

Telephone numbers of the local taxi companies are in the yellow pages of the telephone book under the heading "Taxi." **Alfaro** (221-8466), **Copeguaria** (226-1366), **Coopeirazú** (254-3211 and **Coopetico** (224-7979) have taxis available 24-hours a day. (See the directory in the back of this book for a list of taxi companies.)

Many of these companies also rent big trucks, or *Taxis de Carga*, at a very low hourly rate. These vehicles can be very helpful if you ever have to move furniture.

Automobile Rentals

Major international car rental agencies and private car rentals are conveniently located all over San José. Most rental agencies operate like those in the United States. The cost of renting a vehicle depends on the year, model and make of car. You must be at least 18 years old and have a valid driver's license, an American Express, Visa or Master Card or be able to leave a large deposit. Remember, insurance is extra.

Always phone or make arrangements for car rentals well in advance. For a list of car rental agencies, see the phone directory we have provided in the back of this book, the yellow pages or the *Tico Times* for ads. We recommend **Prego Rent-A-Car**. They offer all kinds of vehicles to meet your every need. Unlike many car rental companies they give generous discounts.

Tico Times has ads for private drivers or chauffeurs. This is a good alternative to taxis but can be expensive. We know quite a few people who do not like to drive and prefer to hire private drivers instead of taking taxis whenever they have to do errands or other business.

Driving in Costa Rica

You may use your current driver's license for up to 90 days if you are a tourist. After 90 days you must get a Costa Rican driver's license. At present foreigners can obtain a Costa Rican license if the possess a valid U.S. license. All permanent residents and *pensionados* must have a Costa Rican license to drive in Costa Rica.

It is relatively easy to obtain a license if you meet the requirements. First, go to San Jose's central driver's license office where licenses are issued. It is located one block west of Plaza Víquez on the southwest corner (Ave. 18 and Calle 5, Tel: 227-2188). You can also obtain a license from the regional offices in Liberia, Limón, Perez Zeldón, San Carlos and San Ramón

Good news! The days of long lines to renew a Costa Rican driver's license are over, thanks to new digital equipment which now processes licenses in a few minutes.

If you have a license from your own country, it is only a matter of taking an eye exam, transferring information, paying a small processing fee, having a little—or a lot of— patience and you will have your license in an hour. First, go across the street to one of the businesses with a sign outside saying, " *Dictamen* or *Examen Médico*". You will have to fill out a questionnaire about your medical history, read an eye chart and pay about $10 dollars to a doctor to get a "medical certificate." In the past, only people over fifty had to go through this cursory medical exam. Now people of all ages have to take it in order to get a license.

Next, cross the street and go to a window where you show a clerk your driver's license from your country and pay about $15 dollars U.S. You also have to leave your passport or residency card with the clerk. Then go to the next window and wait until your name is called. The employee hands you a piece of paper and you go to have your photo taken for your license, at which time your passport or residency card is returned. Finally, you sit and wait for about fifteen minutes to a half hour. When your name is called you go to the counter and receive your Costa Rican license "hot off the press." It is actually hot from the laminating machine. It is valid for three years. To renew your license, the procedure is similar to the steps described above.

If you do not have a current license or if your license has expired, you have to take a driver's test and written exam as in the U.S. The first step involves learning the basic traffic laws, road signs and driver's etiquette that are slightly different here. There are several courses through the Ministry of Public Works and Transportation designed to help you learn about driving in Costa Rica and pass the written test. Courses cost about $5.00 and the required test costs a little over $3.00. After passing the written exam, you have to take the driving test. Once you pass both tests you may get your license. To find out about courses and test sites nearest you call the Ministry at 226-4201, 226-4213, 226-7944, 227-5158 or 228-9297. This is all worthwhile if you plan to live and drive in Costa Rica.

One thing we would like to point out is that in most cases a driver's license is not a valid form of identification as in the U.S. In order to cash checks or identify yourself you need a passport or a *cédula*. The latter is issued only when you have permanent residency in Costa Rica.

Whether you are renting a car or using your own automobile, always keep the proper documents in your car. Check with your lawyer to see what documents are required. If you are a *pensionado* and your car has special *pensionado* plates, the police will occasionally stop you to see if your paperwork is in order. If a policeman should stop you, above all be polite, stay calm, and do not be verbally abusive. Most traffic police are courteous and helpful. However, if you commit a traffic violation, some policemen will try to have you pay for your ticket on the spot. Be advised this is not the standard procedure. If this happens to you, there are two offices where you can complain. You can file your complaints with the Judicial Police (O.I.J.) or with the Legal Department of the Transit Police (227-2188). Finally, if you are involved in a traffic accident, **do not move your car!** Be sure to contact the local traffic police (222-7150, 227-8030) so they can make out a report.

Be very careful when driving in San José or any other city. Most streets in San José are narrow, one-way and very crowded due to heavy traffic. Names of streets are not on signposts on the street corners as in the United States. Most streets' names are on small blue signs on the sides of buildings. Some streets do not even have signs.

On Driving in Costa Rica
By Carlos Morton

After nearly two years of living (and Driving) on Costa Rica's scenic highways, I feel inspired to submit the following wisdom to my fellow gringos. I speak with the voice of experience, having been a taxi driver in Chicago and New York City. I've also lived in mexico, driven there and other parts of Central America.

So, without any hyperbole whatsoever, I give the following advice.

1. DON'T WORRY ABOUT THE POTHOLES: Three are too many of them! Trying to avoid the potholes will only cause you to crash into other cars and/or pedestrians.Best thing to do is buy yourself a monster Sports Utility Vehicle (or Hum-vee, tank, dump truck, etc.) and drive over all obstacles, including beaches, ditches and animals.

2. IGNORE ALL STOP SIGNS, TRAFFIC LIGHTS AND SIGNS: Everyone else does! Besides, the traffic lights are usually positioned in awkward places too hard to see. Stop signs are bent, broken, faded or hidden behind shrubbery. Translations: "Alto" "means speed," "Ceda el paso" means "get the hell out of my way!" If you find yourself in a rotunda, pretend you are in the bumper-car rides at the Parque de Diversiones (local amusement park).

3. PARK WHERE YOU WANT: That's right! In the middle of the street, on the sidewalk, anywhere your little heart desires. No one will give you a ticket; no one will tow your car away. Continue talking with your car in idle to Don Profundo while other frustrated motorists honk their horns and curse.

4. DRIVE AS FAST AS POSSIBLE: When in Rome, do as the Romans do. You may pass on the right, drive on the sidewalk, pass on the left going up hills against oncoming traffic, it's all fair game. Furthermore, this is a free country, and you don't have to wear a seatbelt if you don't want!

5. DO NOT TRY TO BRIBE A TRAFFIC COP: It will cost you more! Yes, he'll think your just another rich Gringo who overstayed your tourist visa. Wait until he offers to let you give him the propina (tip). The barter, always barter. Show him the certified Tico driver's license you procured from a cereal box.

6. DISCARD YOUR MAPS: Maps are usless without strret signs or addresses. if you want directions, stop and ask three or four different people, who will probably tell you three or four different ways to get there.

7. DON'T LET THE PEDESTRIAN HAVE THE RIGHT OF WAY: People think they own the roads! Run them over! That also includes kamikazes on motorbikes, people on bicycles, horseback riders and oxen pulling colorful oaxcarts.

There is some car theft in Costa Rica. To discourage thieves you should always park your car in your garage or public parking lots. If you park on the street make sure there is someone like a guard who can watch your car. Always lock your car and set the alarm system.

When driving in the countryside, drive only during the day, watch out for livestock, and be sure to use some kind of map. Do not get off the main paved road unless absolutely necessary during the rainy season if your car does not have four-wheel drive. You may end up getting stuck in the mud. Unfortunately, the only way to many of Costa Rica's best beaches and mountain resorts is by unpaved roads. So be careful!

While on this subject, let us say a word about potholes or *huecos* as they are commonly known here. The Costa Rican government tries to keep its paved roads in good shape but cannot keep up with the workload. So watch out for potholes and ruts in the pavement. Your car's shocks and suspension system will be grateful.

Driving Times in and around Costa Rica

Driving times from San José are based on 43 km an hour
which is about 27 mph.

LOCATION	DISTANCE (KM)	TIME
Alajuela	18	25 minutes
Atenas	45	1 hour 10 minutes
Cahuita	195	3 hours 15 minutes
Cartago	20	25 minutes
Cañas	182	2 hours 50 minutes
Cd Quesada	100	2 hours 40 minutes
Golfito	330	8 hours 30 minutes
Grecia	43	1 hour
Heredia	12	25 minutes
Jacó	102	2 hours
Liberia	228	3 hours 30 minutes
Limón	153	2 hours 15 minutes
Monteverde	162	4 hours
Nicoya via Liberia	318	4 hours
Parrita via Jacó	243	3 hours 15 minutes
Paso Canoas	349	8 hours
Peñas Blancas	292	4 hours
Playas de Cocos	262	4 hours
Puntarenas	105	1 hour 15 minutes
Quepos via Jacó	268	3 hours 15 minutes

San Isidro de El General	131	3 hours
Tamarindo	301	4 hours 15 minutes
Tilarán	209	3 hours 15 minutes
Volcán Irazú	53	1 hour 40 minutes
Volcán Poas	55	1 hour 30 minutes

For your information there is a new book, "The Essential Road Guide for Costa Rica" by Bill Baker, designed to make driving easier. This book is also available through Costa Rica Books. *Driving the Pan)american Highway to Mexico and Central America* is another helpful publication. You may order it throuhg **Amazon.com** or see **www.drivetocentralamerica.com**.

Keeping Your Bearings Straight

You can get confused in Costa Rica trying to find your way around especially in San José. Except for the center of San José, most streets have no names or numbers, or they are not in a visible place. People use known landmarks to get around, to locate addresses, and give directions. If you are unfamiliar with this system it is almost impossible to find your way around, and easy to get lost. Don't worry. After you have lived in Costa Rica awhile you will get used to this system. In the event you get lost, you can always ask Costa Ricans for directions—provided you understand a little Spanish or they speak some English.

As you know, Costa Ricans are generally very friendly and are usually happy to help you find the address you are seeking. However, it is always a good idea to ask a second person, because most *Ticos* are embarrassed to admit they don't know an address and will sometimes give you directions whether they know where you want to go or not.

Here are some basic tips on how to get around Costa Rica and understand how the street numbering works. It is somewhat easier to find your way in downtown San José because of the layout of the city. Avenues, or *Avenidas*, run east to west. All the odd numbered avenues are north of Central Avenue (*Avenida Central*). The even numbered avenues are south. Streets, or *Calles*, run north to south, with odd numbered streets east of Calle Central, and even numbered streets to the west.

If you get lost, looking for a street sign on the side of a building and counting by two's will usually help you get your bearings. Keep in mind that the word avenue is often abbreviated as *A* and streets as *C* when you

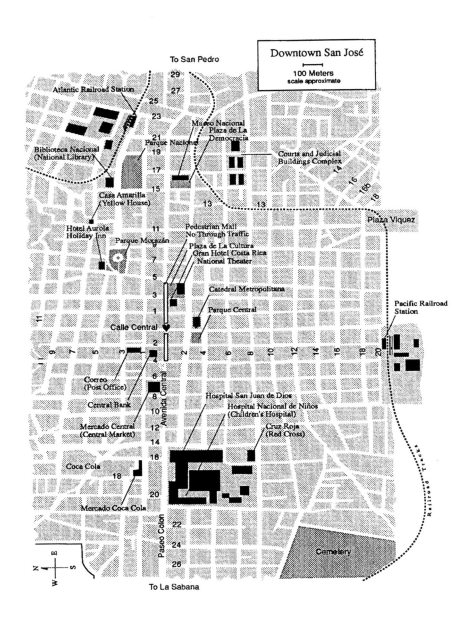

* Courtesy of Bill Baker

get written directions. To find your way around Costa Rica, you also need to know that 100 meters (*cien metros*) is another way of saying one block. Likewise, 50 meters (*cincuenta metros*) is a half-block and 150 meters (*ciento cincuenta metros*) a block and a half. The word *varas* (an old Spanish unit of measurement almost a yard) is slang and often used instead of the word *metros*-meters, when giving directions.

Landmarks, such as corner grocery stores (*pulperías*), churches, schools and other buildings are usually used with this metric block system to locate addresses. For example, in finding a house someone might say, "From Saint Paul's Church, 200 meters west and 300 meters south." In interpreting written directions you should also know that "M" stands for meters.

An old trick Costa Ricans often use for finding the four compass points may make it easier for you to get your bearings straight. The front doors of all churches in Costa Rica face west. So, if there is a church nearby, imagine yourself with your back to the entrance of the church—you are facing west.

If you live in San José, there is another method for finding the compass points. Volcano Poás is north, the Cruz de Alajuela mountain, approximately south, the direction of Cartago is east and the general direction of the Sabana or Rohrmoser is west. This system of using landmarks should make it easier for you to find your way around the city.

Street signs are few and far between in Costa Rica.

The time wasted searching for a house or building in Costa Rica may be a thing of the past. The Costa Rica Postal system plans to initiate a new plan which will introduce a uniform system of street and house numbers.

Signs will be posted on street corners following a coordinated system of colors, sign sizes and symbols. Blue signs will mark international thoroughfares, yellow will be used to indicate inter-provincial highways and white will denote interurban roads. Homeowners will be told where to place their number signs. This system will be tested in several areas with the hope of extending it to all parts of the country within three years. Let us hope this system becomes a reality to make everyone's life easier.

MORE USEFUL INFORMATION

Where to find Affordable Foods

A wide variety of delicious tropical fruits and vegetables grow in Costa Rica. It is amazing that every fruit and vegetable you can think of besides some exotic native varieties flourish here. More common tropical fruits such as pineapples, mangoes and papayas cost about a third of what they do in the United States. Bananas can be purchased at any local fruit stand or street market for about five cents each.

Once you have lived in Costa Rica you can do as many Costa Ricans do and eat a few slices of mouth-watering fruit for breakfast at one of the many sidewalk *fruterías* or fruit stands all over the country. For people living on a tight budget, this healthy, fresh fruit breakfast will cost about 50 or 60 cents. There are also many *sodas*, or small cafes, where you can eat a more typical Costa Rican breakfast for around a dollar.

Besides fruits and vegetables, many other bargain foods are available in Costa Rica. Bakeries sell fresh homemade breads and pastries. Other foods such as eggs, chicken, meat and honey are available at most small neighborhood grocery stores, *pulperías*, as well as large supermarkets. These supermarkets are much like markets in the U.S.; everything is under one roof, but the selection of products is smaller. There are even 24-hour mini-markets in gas stations like the 7-Eleven, Circle-K types found in the U.S.

Some imported packaged products found in Costa Rican supermarkets can be expensive. It is usual to pay more for your favorite breakfast cereal, certain canned foods or liquor. Do not worry because there are local products to substitute for your favorite U.S. brand. However, if you absolutely cannot live without your foods from the States, you can usually find them at, at the Auto Mercado supermarkets and Hipermás stores. You stock-up on these items on shopping trips to the States and bring them back with you by plane.

Since most foods are so affordable in Costa Rica, you will be better off changing your eating habits and buying more local products so you can keep your food bill low. You can save more money by shopping at the Central Market in Heredia or the one in San José, *Mercado Central*, as many cost-conscious Costa Ricans do. The latter covers a whole city block in the heart of downtown San José, near the banking district. Under one roof are hundreds of shops where you can buy fresh fruits, vegetables, grains and much more. You can also go to an open-air street market found in most every large town, called *feria del agricultor*, on any Saturday or Sunday morning. Farmers bring their fresh produce to these street markets each week, so you can find a variety of produce, meats and eggs at low prices. There is a weekly list that appears in *La Nación* newspaper listing the suggested prices of all fruits and vegetables sold at the various *ferias*.

Inexpensive fruits and vegetables can be found at any of the country's weekend outdoor markets or ferias.

CEVICHE DE CORVINA
(Marinated White Seabass)

1 lb. seabass, cut in small pieces
3 tablespoons omion, finely chopped
1 tablespoon celery, finely chopped
2 tablespoons fresh coriander, chopped
2 cups lemon juice
Salt, pepper and Tabasco Sauce
1/2 teaspoon Worcester Sauce

Combine all ingredients in a glass bowl. Let it stand for at least four hours in the refrigerator.
Serve chilled in small bowls topped with catsup and soda crackers on the side. Serves 8.

TRES LECHES
(Three Milk Cake)

Cake Base
5 eggs
1 teaspoon baking powder
1 cup sugar
1/2 teaspoon vanilla
1 1/2 cups of flower
Preheat oven at 350 F. Sift baking powder. Set aside. Cream butter and sugar until fluffy. Add eggs and vanilla and beat well. Add flour to the butter mixture 2 tablespoons at a time, until well blended. Pour into greased rectangular Pyrex dish and bake at 350 F for 30 minutes. Let cool. Pierce with a fork and cover. For the filling combine 2 cups of milk, 1 can of condensed milk and one can of evaporated milk. Pour this mixture over the cool cake. To make the topping, mix 1 1/2 cups of half & half, 1 teaspoon vanilla and a cup of sugar. Whip together until thick. Spread over the top of the cake. Keep refrigerated. Serves 12.

A few words about Costa Rica's excellent seafood. With oceans on both sides, Costa Rica has a huge variety of fresh seafood. Tuna, dorado, corvina, abound as well as lobster, shrimp of all sizes and some crab. All of these can be purchased at any *pescadería* (fish market) in and around San José's Central Market at low prices. While you're there, try a heaping plate of *ceviche* (fish cocktail) at one of the many fish restaurants called *marisquerías.*

Typical Costa Rican food is similar to that of Mexico and other Central American countries. Tortillas often, but not always, are eaten with a meal of rice, beans, fruit, eggs, vegetables and a little meat. The most common dish, *gallo pinto,* is made with rice and black beans as a base and fried with red bell peppers and cilantro.

Some other popular Costa Rican foods include *casado,* the blue-plate special in Spanish (fish, chicken, or meat with beans and chopped cabbage), *empanadas* (a type of stuffed bread turnover), *arreglados* (a kind of sandwich) and *palmito* (heart of palm), which is usually eaten in salads.

The major supermarkets in the Central Valley are **Periférico** (several locations in the San José area), **Más por Menos** (a large chain), **Auto Mercado** (upscale with home delivery service), and **Palí Supermercados** (discount warehouses). **Mega Super** is the newest chain with huge stores virtually all over the Central Valley.

Modern U.S. -style supermarkets abound in Costa Rica

Where to Eat

Many excellent restaurants serving a wide variety of international foods are scattered all over the San José area. Most of these restaurants are incredible bargains when compared to similar establishments in the United States. You will be happy to know that Costa Rica's restaurants are clean and health codes are strictly enforced by the Health Department (*Ministerio de Salud*). For your convenience we have included a list of our favorite places to eat but you are sure to discover many on your own or by word of mouth once you have lived in Costa Rica for a while.

Some of the best sea food you will ever savor may be found at **La Fuente de Los Mariscos** behind the Hotel Irazú in the San José 2000 Shopping Center. **El Banco de Mariscos** in Santa Barbara de Heredia and **El Balcón de Maricos** in Curridabat round out our list of affordable seafood eateries. **La Cascada** in Los Anonos has very tasty fish and meat dishes.

There are also many Italian restaurants. The **Balcón de Europa** serves about the best pasta dishes in San José. If you like U.S.-style food and beer served in foot-tall mugs, try **Fridays** near the university in San Pedro. **La Soda Tapia** is famous for its gigantic fruit salads and typical breakfasts. **Restaurante Grano de Oro**, in the charming hotel with the same name, offers an excellent menu.

You can dine, watch TV and read an assortment of newspapers at The **News Café** in the Hotel Presidente. They just installed a new street-side bar which is great spot for people watching. **Chelles** (Ave. Central, Calle 9) serves great sandwiches. **Café Parisien**, in the Gran Hotel Costa Rica, never closes and is one of the best locations in town to people watch. The **City Café**, is one of many all-night restaurants and popular North American hangout. If you get a case of the munchies and want to grab a late-night snack, there is a lot of action here with the adjacent gambling area and swinging bar. Rounding out our list of all-night eateries is **Manolo's** outdoor café .

Good Spanish food is served at **Casino Español** (222-9440) and at **La Masia de Triquell** (296-3524). **Zermatt** (222-0604) serves European style dishes.

Chinese restaurants abound in the San José area. It seems as if there is one on every block. The oriental food served here is not as tasty as what you will find in San Francisco's China Town, but it is inexpensive. If you want something other than chopsuey, chow mein and rice dishes, try the **Tin Jo** (221-7605) restaurant. They have a wide selection including tasty Mandarin, Szechuan and even Thai food. **Shil La** is a new restaurant in the suburb of Rohrmoser which features authentic Korean and Japanese food including sushi, sashimi and tempura. **Villa Bonita** in Pavas is famous for its oriental food.

Lovers of Mexican food should try any of the **El Fogoncito** (several locations), **Antojitos** (four locations) restaurants, **Las Tunas** in Sabana Norte and **Los Panchos** in Zapote. The latter has a great atmosphere together with roving mariachis to serenade you. **Tex Mex** in Santa Ana has become very popular with foreigners.

Excellent French cuisine is available at **El Refugio del Chef Jaques** located in a beautiful mountain setting above Heredia.

The **Pops** ice cream parlors sell every imaginable flavor of your favorite ice cream. **TCBY**, the U.S. frozen yogurt chain, even has a couple of stores here. The **Spoon** pastry shops sell the best cakes and pastries in the country. They have four locations in the San José area. Bagels can even be found in Costa Rica. **Haagaen Dazs** now has stores in Escazú and Curridabat and is available in many super markets.

Baglemans in San Pedroand Escazú offers a wide selection of fresh baked bagels, sandwiches and excellent coffee.

La Fuente de Mariscos offers some of the best saefood you will ever savor.

Coffee connoisseurs can savor a cup of their favorite local brew and grab a bite to eat at the **Café Parisien** in the Gran Hotel Costa Rica, **La Esquina del Café** or **La Casa Verde** in Barrio Amón. Coffee lovers should also try **Café Britt's** coffee. They offer a great coffee tour of their farm in the hills of Heredia. We recommend this excursion to tourists as well as permanent residents. They explain every step of how coffee is grown and processed and relate the history of coffee in Costa Rica.

If you like to eat-on-the-run, you can, all of the American fast food restaurant chains operate in Costa Rica. **Pizza Hut, Papa John's, MacDonald's, Taco Bell, Burger King, Kentucky Fried Chicken** and **Subway** sandwiches all have restaurants conveniently located in San José, the suburbs and several shopping malls.

However, the best chicken is served at the **Rosti Pollos** restaurants in downtown San José, San Pedro, Escazú and Guadalupe. They cook their chicken over coffee branches, which gives it an incredibly delicious flavor.

Denny's has one 24-hour restaurant next to the Hotel Irazú. Two more restaurants will open during the next couple of years. The chain offers breakfast specials just as they do in the States.

Most U.S. fast-food chains can be found in Costa Rica.

Meat lovers will be pleased to know that **Tony Roma's Barbecue** famous for its ribs opened restaurant in Escazú. The same owners plan to bring the **Wendy's** (hamburger chain) to Costa Rica.

Goya in downtown San José and **La Masía de Triquell** in Sabana Norte offer a wide variety of Spanish and International dishes.

For the best Costa Rican style cooking try **La Casa de Doña Lela** located on the main highway to Limón about a mile past the Saprissa Soccer Stadium. Since it is located somewhat off the tourist path, not many foreigners have discovered this great restaurant. The food is delicious and a steal. **The Rústico,** a local chain, also offers a wide selection of Costa Rican style dishes. They have restaurants in Multiplaza, San Pedro Mall and El Real Cariari Mall. **La Casona del Cafetal** is a real find. This restaurant is located about 45 minutes from San José in the heart of the Orosi Valley and has a great Sunday buffet. The setting is incredible. It is located next to a lake and surrounded by a coffee plantation.

Sodas are plentiful and found all over. You can be assured almost any small shop displaying the sign *soda* serves affordable food since the majority of working class *ticos* eat in these establishments. Most big towns and cities have a central market where a lot of sodas can be found. Both San Jose's and Heredia's central markets have dozens of sodas where you can find

The Vishnu Natural Food Restaurante offer affordable cusine.

almost every imaginable dish at rock bottom prices. We have eaten at the market in Heredia and many a time couldn't finish the huge amount of food that was served to us. The bill usually never runs over three dollars.

There are of vegetarian restaurants all over San José and surprisingly in remote areas of the country like Montezuma Beach. As more and more Costa Ricans become health conscious these establishments grow in popularity. Prices are generally low priced and the servings are huge. One establishment in San José offers soups, salad, rice, a vegetable dish, dessert and a natural fruit juice drink for under three dollars. **Restaurante Vegetariano** of San Pedro, located near the University of Costa Rica in San Pedro, is one of our favorites and popular with the college crowd. **SIGLO XXI, 300** meters west of POP'S ice cream in west Sabana, is a vegetarian Chinese food restaurant. **Vishnu** has a couple of locations in downtown San José and another in Heredia. The **Mango Verde** also in downtown Herdia completes our list of vegetarian eateries.

The *Tico Times* and *Costa Rica Today* both carry advertisements for restaurants and feature occasional restaurant reviews.

Religion

Although 90% of Costa Ricans are Roman Catholic, there is freedom of religion and other religious views are permitted.

We hope the list of churches we have provided below will help you. Call the number of your denomination to be directed to your nearest house of worship in the San José area. Some churches in the San José area have services in English.

Baptist (San Pedro)	253-7911
Beit Menschem	296-6565
Bilingual Christian Fellowship.	442-3663
B'nai Israel	257-1785
Catholic (Downtown Cathedral)	221-3820
Catholic (Escazú)	228-0635
Catholic (Los Yoses)	225-6778
Catholic (Rohrmoser)	232-2128
Catholic (Barrio San Bosco)	221-3748
Cathloic (San Rafael)	232-6847
Christian Science	221-0840

Episcopal	225-0209
International Baptist Church	253-7911
Jehova's Witness	221-1436
Methodist	222-0360
Morman (Santos de Los Ultimos Días)	234-1945
Protestant	228-0553
Quaker	233-6168
Seventh Day Adventists	223-7759
Saint Mary's(Catholic)	239-0033
Synagogue Shaare Zion	222-5449
Unitarian	228-1020 or 228-4196
Union Church	235-6709
Unity	228-6051
Unity Church (Escazú)	228-6051

One of Costa Rica's houses of worship.

Costa Rica's Holidays

Costa Ricans are very nationalistic and proudly celebrate their official holidays, called *feriados*. Plan your activities around these holidays and do not count on getting business of any kind done since most government and private offices will be closed. In fact, the whole country shuts down during *Semana Santa* (the week before Easter) and the week between Christmas and New Year's Day. Asterisks indicate paid holidays and days for workers.

January 1	New Year's Day*
March 19	Saint Joseph's Day
Holy Week	Holy Thursday and Good Friday*
April 11	Juan Santa Maria's Day (local hero)*
May 1	Labor Day
May	University Week (held in San Pedro)
June	Father's Day (the third Sunday)
July 25	Annexation of Guanacaste Province*
August 2	Virgin of LosAngeles Day
August 15	Mother's Day*
September 15	Independence Day*
October 12	Columbus Day - Discovery of America
October 12	Limón Carnival
October 31	Halloween
November 2	Day of the Dead
December 8	Immaculate Conception
December 25	Christmas*
December 25	Feria de Zapote (December 25th to January 2nd)
December 25	Fiestas del Fin del Año

Bringing Your Pet to Costa Rica

We did not forget those of you who have pets. There are procedures for bringing your pets into the country that require very little except patience, some paperwork and a small fee.

First, a registered veterinarian from your hometown must certify that your pets are free of internal and external parasites. It is necessary that your pet has up-to-date vaccinations against rabies (The rabies vaccination must

NOT be older than one year), distemper, leptospirosis, hepatitis and parvovirus vaccination within the last three years. Remember, all of these required documents are indispensable and must be certified by the Costa Rican consulate nearest your home- town. These papers are only good for thirty days. If you do not renew them within this period of time, you will have to make another trip to the vet's office and the airline will not accept your animal. If you are bringing an exotic animal to Costa Rica —parakeet, macaw or other—you will need special permits from the Convention of International Species in Danger of Extinction and the Costa Rican Natural Resources Ministry.

If all of this paperwork is too much for you, the Association of Residents of Costa Rica (ARCR) can take care of everything, including the airport pick up for around $100. If you have no place to keep your pet, they offer boarding at $20 a day.

If you fail to comply with these regulations and do not provide the required documents, your pet(s) can be refused entry, placed in quarantine or even put to sleep. But don't worry, if worse comes to worst, there is a 30-day grace period to straighten things out.

If the animal is traveling with you as part of your luggage, the average rate is $50 U.S. from one destination to the next (i.e. Los Angeles—Miami—San José). If your pet travels alone, depending on size and weight, the average rate is between $100 to $200 U.S. Please consult your airline for the actual price. Call the 800 toll-free cargo section of American Airlines and they will tell you the cost.

Whether your pet is traveling with you or separately, be aware that the weather can delay your animals arrival in Costa Rica. If the temperature is above 85 degrees or below 40 degrees at either your point of departure or a layover, your animal will not be able to travel. We know of several people who have arrived at the airport only to find out their animals could not travel due to a change in the weather. Call your airline the day you intend to ship your animal and again an hour or two before departure to see if your animal will be allowed to travel. This way you can avoid unpleasant surprises.

Also make sure your dog or cat has an airline approved portable kennel. These rules are very strict and the kennel must be the appropriate size for your animal or it will not be allowed to travel. Some airlines rent kennels. Make sure your kennel has a small tray so your pet can have food and water during the journey. Two to eight hours is a long time to go without food or water.

If there is a layover involved, the baggage handlers will give water to your pet. The operator at American Airlines told us about a special service which will walk your dog for an extra charge at some airports. Some people suggest tranquilizing dogs and cats when shipping them by plane. We talked to our vet when we were going to ship our large Siberian husky, and he did not seem to think it was a good idea. We also asked a friend who ships show dogs all over the U.S. and he said to use our own judgment since tranquilizers can make an animal ill.

Some airlines allow small pets to rravel in kennels in the passenger cabin. A few airlines have restrictions on certain breeds of dogs, including Doberman Pinscher, Rottweiler and pit bull. Be sure to check with the airline if you have one of these breeds.

If you want to take your pet out of Costa Rica you will need a special permit, a certificate from a local veterinarian, and proof that all vaccinations are up-to-date. When you obtain these documents, take them to the Ministry of Health and your pet is free to leave the country. The day you leave plan on being at the airport at least two and a half hours early, since all your pet's papers must be stamped before departure. Do not for get to make sure that your papers comply with the rules and regulations of your home country or destination.

These requirements and additional information are available from the Agriculture Minister's **Animal Sanitation Department** Tel: 260-9046.

Veterinarians

Dr. Federico Patiño (Rohrmoser)	231-5276
Clinica Echandi	223-3111
Dr. Adrián Molina	228-1909
Dr. Federico Piza	248-7166
Dr. Douglas Lutz	225-6784
Dr. L. Starkey	253-7142
Tecnología Veterinaria (clinic, pharmacy, and boarding)	228-9347
Dr. Lorena Guerra (makes house-calls, also boarding)	228-9887

If you have to travel, the Clínica Echandi will care for your dog, cat or other pet. They charge about $7 per day U.S. for this boarding service. For additional veterinarians, look under the heading *"VETERINARIA"* in the yellow pages.

Services for the Disabled

Getting around in the U.S. or Canada is hard enough when a person is disabled, but it can be even harder in a foreign country.

Handicapped and disabled persons should find living in Costa Rica not much of an obstacle. Presently, some places have wheel chair access. A few hotels like the Hampton Inn in Alajuela and the Hotel del Sur in San Isidro, have fully equipped rooms for disabled persons.

During the rainy season the terrain can sometimes be hard to negotiate. Recently the government has increased the construction of sidewalk ramps, special marked parking spaces and telephones for those people with physical limitations. In 1998, the Costa Rican Law for the Equality of Opportunities for Persons with Disabilities went into effect. It mandates every public space in the country to be wheelchair-accessible by 2008, thus improving accessibility for the disabled.

As we mention in Chapter 2, medical care is affordable in Costa Rica and should not be a problem. Also, keep in mind that taxis are inexpensive and the best way to travel for people with physical impediments. Since hired help is such a bargain, a full-time employee may be hired as a companion or as a nurse for a very reasonable price. We even know several men confined to wheelchairs who have even found love and married in Costa Rica. There is a social club for disabled veterans that meets once a month. Call 443-9870 for more information.

We suggest that you pick up the book, *Access to the World: A Travel Guide For the Handicapped*, by Louise Weiss, Published by Chatham Square Press, 401 Broadway, New York, NY 10013. This book contains good information and suggestions for disabled travelers.

For Our Canadian Readers

In order to escape Canada's cold winters, many Canadians live in Costa Rica on a full or part-time basis. It is therefore not surprising that many businesses and services catering to Canadians have been created.

Canadians may stay in Costa Rica for up to 90 days without a visa, however a passport is required. Extensions may be obtained from the office of *migración*. If you overstay your visa or entry stamp, you will have to pay a nominal fine for each extra month you've stayed.

Currently there is a **Canadian Club** which helps make life easier for Canadians living or planning to live in Costa Rica. By attending club meetings people can make new friendships and establish some good contacts.

This organization provides information about acquiring residency, starting a business, transferring ownership of a car, names of doctors and lawyers and will assist with purchasing medical, automobile and home insurance in Costa Rica. All Canadian visitors and residents are urged to attend. They meet at the King's Garden Restaurant over the Yaohan Supermarket the 3rd Wednesday of every month at 12 noon. You can find a schedule of their activities and meetings in the *Tico Times*.

The **Canada Costa Rica Trust Company Limited (CCTC)** offers a variety of financial services for Canadians. They are located in Casa Canada, Ave. 4 and Calle 40 in San José. For more information, you may contact them at; P.O. Box 232-1007, Centro Colon, San José, Costa Rica, Tel: 011-(506) 255-1723 or 255-1592, Fax: 011-(506) 255-0061.

If you are a Canadian non-resident living in Costa Rica, you should think about receiving the *CRA Magazines's Canadian Expat Quarterly*. It sends out a periodic update newsletter covering topics of tax and financial interest to Canadians overseas. If you should have an expatriate-related tax or investment question, send it to them and they will try to research the answer for you. Contact Canadian Residents Abroad Inc., 305 Lakeshore Road East, Oakville, Ontario, Canada L6J 1J3. Tel: 905-842-0080 Fax: 905-842-9814, E-mail: cra@canadiansresidentabroad or see www.canadiansresidentabroad.com.

The Canadian Embassay is now located in the Oficentro office complex in the Sabana Sur area of San José in building 5, on the third floor behind the Contraloría. Their address and phone are: Apartado 351-1007 Centro Colón, San José, Costa Rica, Tel: (506)-296-4149, Fax: (506)-296-4270.

If you have any questions about Costa Rica or need a visa, you may contact any of the following Costa Rican Embassies and Consulates in Canada:

Montreal, 1155 Dorchester Blvd. West, Suite 2902, Montreal, Quebec H3B 2L3, Tel: (514) 866-8159.

Ottawa, 15 Argule St., Ottawa, ON K2P 1B7, Tel: (613) 234-5762 or 562-2855 Fax: 230-2656.

Toronto, 164 Avenue Rd., Toronto, ON M5R 2H9, Tel: (416) 961-6773, Fax: 961-6771.

Understanding the Metric System

If you plan to live in Costa Rica, it is in your best interest to understand the metric system. You will soon notice those automobile speedometers, road mileage signs, the contents of bottles, and rulers are in metric measurements. Since you probably did not study this system when you were in school and it is almost never used in the U.S., you could become confused.

The conversion guide below will help you.

To Convert:	To:	Multiply by:
Centigrade	Fahrenheit	1.8 then add 32
Square km	Square miles	0.3861
Square km	Acres	247.1
Meters	Yards	1.094
Meters	Feet	3.281
Liters	Pints	2.113
Liters	Gallons	0.2642
Kilometers	Miles	0.6214
Kilograms	Pounds	2.205
Hectares	Acres	2.471
Grams	Ounce	0.03527
Centimeter	Inches	0.3937

* Courtesy of *Central America Weekly*.

PARTING THOUGHTS AND ADVICE

Personal Safety in Costa Rica

Living in Costa Rica is much safer than residing in most large cities in the United States or Latin American, but you should take some precautions and use common sense to ensure your own safety. Remember, you should be careful in any third world country.

In Costa Rica, the rate for violent crimes is very low, but there is a problem with theft, especially in the larger cities. Thieves tend to look for easy targets, especially fore igners, so you cannot be too cautious. Make sure your house or apartment has steel bars on both the windows and garage. The best bars are narrowly spaced because some thieves use small children as accomplices as they can squeeze through the bars to burglarize your residence or open doors.

Make sure your neighborhood has a night watchman if you live in the city. Some male domestic employees are willing to work in this capacity. However, ask for references and closely screen any person you hire. Also, report suspicious people loitering around your premises. Thieves are very patient and often case a residence for a long time to observe your comings and goings. They can and will strike at the most opportune moment for them.

You should take added precautions if you live in a neighborhood where there are many foreigners. Thieves associate foreigners with wealth and look for areas where they cluster together. One possible deterrent, in addition to a night watchman, is to organize a neighborhood watch group in your area.

If you leave town, get a friend or other trustworthy person to house-sit.

Mountain areas offer some spectacular views and tranquility but are less populated and usually more isolated. This makes them prime targets for burglars and other thieves. We have a friend who moved to a beautiful home in the hills, but was burglarized a couple of times. Out of desperation he had to hire a watchman and buy guard dogs. Unfortunately, a few weeks later he was robbed while doing an errand in town. This is the down side to living off the beaten path.

If you are really concerned about protecting your valuables, you would be better off living in a condominium complex or an apartment. Both are less susceptible to burglary due to their design and the fact that, as the saying goes, there is safety in numbers.

Private home security patrols can provide an alarm system and patrol your area for a monthly fee. There are a few companies that specialize in security systems for the home and office. Some even offer very sophisticated monitored surveillance systems. You should contact **ADT** at 257-7373 if interested in one of these services. We just installed a complete ADT security system in our home in Heredia for less than $600.00.

The National Insurance Institute offers insurance policies that protect your home against burglary. However, the coverage is limited to certain items; there are stipulations, a lot of paperwork involved and there is a 10% deductible on the value of stolen items. All items must be listed as well as their serial numbers. Premiums run from 1 to 1.5 % of the total on the list depending on where you live. Homes in more secure areas receive the lower rates. Less protected homes in remote areas have higher rates. If your home is to be unoccupied for more than 48 hours, it must be placed under the care of a guard and you must notify the insurance company one week in advance.

If you own an automobile, you should be especially careful if you have *pensionado* (retiree) license plates. These plates identify you as a foreigner and, in some cases, make you a sitting duck for car burglars who relish breaking into your car and stealing your valuables. Thieves can pop open a locked trunk and clean it out in a few minutes. Make sure your house or apartment has a garage with iron bars so your car is off the street.

When parking away from your house, always park in parking lots or where there is a watchman. He will look after your car for a few cents an hour when you park it on the street. It is not difficult to find watchman since they usually approach and offer their services as soon as you park your car.

Never park your vehicle or walk in a poorly lit area. Avoid walking alone at night and during the day, and stay alert for pickpockets. Pickpockets like to hang around bus stops, parks and crowded marketplaces, especially the Central Market (between Calles 6 and 8, Aves. 1 and Central). You should never flaunt your wealth by wearing expensive jewelry or carrying cameras loosely around your neck because they make you an easy mark on the street. Keep a good watch on any valuable items you may be carrying. It is advisable to find a good way to conceal your money and never carry it in your back pocket. It is best to carry money in front pockets. It is also a good idea to always carry small amounts of money in several places rather than all your money in one place. If you carry large amounts of money, use traveler's checks. Be very discreet with your money. Do not flash large amounts of money in public. Every time you finish a transaction in a bank or store, put away all money in your purse or wallet before going out into the street.

Never carry any original documents, such as passports or visas. Make a photocopy of your passport and carry it with you at all times. The authorities will accept most photocopies as a valid form of identification.

Avoid the dangerous parts of San José, especially the area near the Coca-Cola bus terminal and the *"Zona Roja"* south of Parque Central. Keep alert. Be aware of who is around you and what they are doing. Thieves often work in teams. One will distract you while the other makes off with your valuables. Never accept help from strangers and ignore and never accept business propositions or other offers from people you encounter on the street. Never pick up hitchhikers.

Men should also watch out for prostitutes who are often expert pickpockets and can relieve the unsuspecting of their valuables before they realize it. Men, especially when inebriated or alone, should be careful—or avoid—the *"Gringo Gulch"* area in the vicinity of Morazán Park, the Holiday Inn and the Key Largo Bar. Many muggings have been reported in this area at night.

If you are a single woman living by yourself, never walk alone at night. If you do go out at night, be sure to take a taxi or have a friend go along.

White-collar crime exists in Costa Rica and a few dishonest individuals—Americans, Canadians and Costa Ricans included—are always waiting to take your money. Over the years many unscrupulous individuals have set up shop here. We have heard of naive foreigners losing their hard-earned savings to ingenious schemes. Con men prey on newcomers. One crook bilked countless people out of their money by selling a series of non-existent gold mines here and abroad. The guy is still walking the streets today and dreaming up new ways to make money.

One "dangerous breed of animal" you may encounter are a few foreigners between 30 and 60 years of age who are in business but do not have pensions. Most of said people are struggling to survive and have to really hustle to make a living in Costa Rica. In general, they are desperate and will go to almost any means to make money. They may even have a legitimate business but most certainly try to take advantage of you to make a few extra dollars. Most complaints we hear concerning people being "ripped off" are caused by individuals who fit this description.

On your first trip to Costa Rica you will probably be besieged by con-artists who are anxious to help you make an investment. Be wary of blue ribbon business deals seemingly too good to be true, or any other get-rich quick schemes i.e. non-existent land, fantastic sounding real estate projects, phony high-interest bank investments or property not belonging to the person selling it. If potential profit sounds too good to be true, it probably is. However most of the high interest yielding investments we mention in Chapter 3 have proven to be perfectly safe. These types of investments have good track records.

Always do your homework and talk to other expats before you make any type of investment. There seems to be something about the ambience here that causes one to trust total strangers. The secret is to be cautious without being afraid to invest. Before jumping into what seems to be a once-in-a-lifetime investment opportunity, ask yourself this question: Would I make the same investment in my hometown? Do not do anything with your money in Costa Rica that you wouldn't do at home. A friend and long-time resident here always says jokingly when referring to the business logic of foreigners who come to Costa Rica, "When they step off the plane they seem to go brain dead."

Most people in Costa Rica are honest, hard-working individuals. However, do not assume people are honest just because they are nice. Remember it does not hurt to be overly cautious.

If you are robbed or swindled under any circumstances, contact the police or the O.I.J. (*Organización de Investigación Judicial*), a special, highly efficient investigative unit like the FBI (between Aves. 8 and 10 and Calles 15 and 17 in the middle building of the court house complex, 295-3271). The O.I.J. 20 more offices around the country. All of them are open 24 hours a day. You may also want to contact the Security Ministry, *Ministerio de Seguridad* at 227-4866. You may not recover your money, but you may prevent others from being victimized.

HANDGUNS

We have received numerous requests from people about Costa Rica's handgun laws. First check with your airline about their policy on packing guns in your luggage. In order to legally have a handgun it must be registered with the *Departmamento de Armas y Explosivos* (Department of Arms and Explosives). If you bring your weapon from the States you will have to pay taxes. They can range sometimes from 50 to 100 percent of the new value of the weapon.

If you don't have proof or a receipt of ownership or you want to reduce the taxes on an imported weapon , you should obtain a sworn statement (*declaración jurdada*) from a lawyer saying someone gave you your weapon. This way you will not have to pay the taxes. However, if you purchase your weapon in Costa Rica, the taxes are included in the price. Expect to pay about double for a handgun in Costa Rica. If you fail to register your gun you there will be serious legal repercussions if you are caught with an unregistered weapon. To register your handgun take the proof of purchase/declaration of ownership papers and your residency *cédula* to the **Departmento de Armas y Explosivos** in Zapote.

Once you have registered a handgun, it is illegal to carry it unless you have a special permit or *Permiso de Portación de Armas*. In order to get a permit you have to be a legal resident or have a Costa Rican Corporation. You may register the gun through the latter. In addition, you have to take a psychological test in Spanish to see if you are suited to own a gun. The cost of this exam is around 5000 to 7000 *colones*. Finally, you have to show a qualified instructor that you know how to use your gun by shooting at some targets. You need to score 80% (ten rounds fired from 10 meters). The cost of this exam is 2500 *colones*. You may take shooting lessons from a certified instructor at the **Club de Tiro** Tel: 220-0188 located next to the national Soccer Stadium at the west end of the Sabana Park. The results of both the psychologial and shooting test will be filed with the Departmento de Armas y Explosivos.

DEATH OF A FRIEND OR LOVED ONE OVERSEAS

Facing the death of a friend or loved one is difficult under any circumstances, let alone when it occurs in a foreign country. Since a majority of Americans living in Costa Rica are middle-aged or seniors, it is advisable that they know what procedures to follow if their spouse or a friend passes away.

First, you should contact the U.S. Embassy to report the death of an American citizen. If necessary, they will contact family members, hold valuables for the family, act as a liaison to help the family make funeral and/or cremation arrangements, and help with repatriation of the body (this cost is covered by the government if the deceased was an active member of the military, if so desired). They will also issue a Certificate of Death Abroad, an official copy of which is sent to the State department in Washington, D.C. This document may be important for both insurance, tax and probate purposes.

Note: If your spouse passes away while at home, the police will come and make a report. You will have to get a death certificate from a doctor before the body can be sent to a funeral home. Without a death certificate the body will be taken to the judicial morgue no matter under what circumstances your relative died. Then you'll have to go though a bureacratic proces to get it released. If your relative dies in the hospital then you do not have to worry about this. You can find out additional information by calling the U.S. embassy at 220-3050

Life As An Expatriate

Throughout this book we have provided the most up-to-date information available on living and retirement in Costa Rica. We have also provided many useful suggestions to make your life in Costa Rica more enjoyable and help you avoid inconveniences. Adjusting to a new, culture can be difficult for some people. Our aim is to make this transition easier so you can enjoy all of the marvelous things that Costa Rica offers.

Before moving permanently to Costa Rica, we highly recommend spending time there on a trial basis to see if it is the place for you. We are talking about a couple of months or longer, so you can experience Costa Rican life as it is. Remember visiting Costa Rica as a tourist is quite another

Getting Past Cultural Shock
By Eric Liljenstrope

Unlike twenty years ago, the majority of people (especially travelers) know the term Culture Shock. However, there still exists an "it won't happen to me" attitude in many who move overseas. The symptoms can be severe, including difficulty sleeping, loss of appetite, paranoia and depression. Denial of the possibility of Culture Shock and ignorance of its symptoms can result in increased difficulty in adjusting to a new life overseas. A basic understanding of the reasons why it happens and what you can do about it are essential when making an international transition.

Culture shock occurs when people find that their ways of doing things just don't work in the new culture. It is a struggle to communicate, to fulfill the most basic needs, and many find that they are not as effective or efficient as before in their jobs and in their personal lives. All this loss of competence threatens a person's sense of identity.

The abilities and relationships that we relied on to tell us who we are, are absent, and we find ourselves a little lost in our new homes. To re-establish ourselves in a new context requires proactive planning in a number of different areas of life.

There are four basic areas of Culture Shock, like four legs to a chair. They are the physical, intellectual, emotional and social. To have the smoothest possible transition, one needs to employ a balanced approach in each of the areas.

After a transition such as an overseas move, the rhythms of everyday life are interrupted, including our exercise and eating habits. Often people neglect their exercise regiment because they don't know where to find a gym or they don't feel safe running or exercising in public places. Similarly, diets are neglected or some begin drinking too much alcohol. The way that our bodies feel physically directly affects our emotional health. A healthy diet and consistent exercise can help balance our emotional lives when confronting the difficulties of an international move.

The second area of concern is the intellectual dimension. When we step into a new culture we often find that we understand very little about the local customs and history. Due to our lack of understanding we sometimes assume that people think like us and value the same things we do. Reading and inquiring about the history and the culture of Costa Rica can help one to see things from a Costa Rican's perspective and develop greater empathy for their culture and ways of thinking.

Tending to emotional needs when moving overseas will help us to weather the ups and downs of the adjustment period. Finding people that are in similar positions that you can talk to and confide in helps to alleviate some of the loneliness that one feels.

When a person begins to feel down, sometimes they are listening to negative "tapes" in their head. One's "tapes" consist of the things we tell ourselves or the conversations that we have in our own mind. The negative tapes need to be consciously changed to positive hopeful messages. From "I am a failure and I hate this place" to "things are getting better every day." It may seem somewhat Pollyanna, but it really works.

Finding a group of friends, learning the language, and getting involved in clubs or activities helps to fill the social needs that we have when changing our latitude. This requires time and dedication, especially if one wants to meet locals. Meeting locals is essential for long-term happiness overseas, but it can take a long period of time and a great deal of proactive planning. It may sound harsh, but it's important to remember that the locals don't really need you. They have their families and friends from their whole lives. You need to insert yourselves in their lives.

In my time working with people in international transition I have seen may cases of fabulous success, but I have also seen many spectacular failures. If a person develops a plan and proactively carries it out, it is very probable that you will find success and happiness in your new Latin home.

Eric Liljenstolpe is president and founder of the **GLOBALSOLUTIONS GROUP (GSG),** an organization based in San José, Costa Rica, is committed to enhancing intercultural understanding. GSG offer seminars and workshops to help people during the cultural adjustment process. You can check out upcoming events and learn more about what GSG offers at **www.gsgintercultural.com.**

thing from living there on a permanent basis. It is also good to visit for extended periods during both the wet and dry seasons, so you have an idea of what the country is like at all times of the year. During your visits, talk to many retirees and gather as much information as possible before making your final decision. Get involved in as many activities as you can during your time in the country. This will help give you an idea of what the country is really like.

It is a good idea to attend one of the monthly Newcomer's Seminars offered by the **Association of Residents of Costa Rica (ARCR)**. Besides gathering information, you will learn from other residents and make some good contacts. Please see page 131 for more details.

The final step in deciding if you want to make Costa Rica your home is to try living there for at least a year. That's sufficient time to get an idea of what living in Costa Rica is really like and what problems may confront you while trying to adapt to living in a new culture. It may also allow you to adjust to the climate and new foods. You can learn all the dos and don'ts, ins and outs and places to go or places to avoid before making your final decision.

You may decide to try seasonal living for a few months a year. Many people spend the summer in the U.S. or Canada and the winter in Costa Rica (which is its summer), so they can enjoy the best of both worlds—the endless summer. As we mentioned in Chapter 4, it's easy to do, since you can legally stay in the country up to six months as a tourist without having to get any type of permanent residency.

Whether you choose to reside in Costa Rica on a full or part-time basis, keep in mind the cultural differences and new customs. First, life in Costa Rica is very different. If you expect all things to be exactly as they are in the United States, you are deceiving yourself. The concept of time and punctuality are not important in Latin America. It is not unusual and not considered in bad taste for a person to arrive late for a business appointment or a dinner engagement. This custom can be incomprehensible and infuriating to North Americans but will not change since it is a deeply rooted tradition.

As we previously mentioned, in most cases bureaucracy moves at a snail's pace in Costa Rica that can be equally maddening to a foreigner. In addition, the Latin mentality, *machismo*, apparent illogical reasoning, traditions, different laws and ways of doing business seem incomprehensible to a newcomer.

You will notice countless other different customs and cultural idiosyncrasies after living in Costa Rica for a while. No matter how psychologically secure you are, some culture shock in the new living situation will confront you. The best thing to do is respect the different cultural values, be understanding and patient, and go with the flow. Learning Spanish will ease your way.

The fastest way to fit in with the locals is to speak the native language. You do not have to be fluent in Spanish. The locals will recognize your interest; doors will open and friendships will blossom.

Whatever you do try to avoid being the Ugly American. We know cases where Americans have caused themselves a lot of problems by their obnoxious behavior and by trying to impose their American ways on the locals.

You should also read *Survival Kit for Overseas Living,* by L. Robert Kohls, Intercultural Press, P.O. Box 700, Yarmouth, Maine 04096. This guide is filled with useful information about adjusting to life abroad.

Costa Rica is an exciting place to live but poses many obstacles for the newcomer. Don't expect everything to go smoothly, or be perfect at first. By taking the advice we offer throughout this book and adjusting to the many challenges, you should be able to enjoy all of Costa Rica's wonders.

Our recommendation is do not burn your bridges or sever your ties with your home country; you may want to return home.

Finally, try taking the adaptability test on the next page to see if you are suited for living abroad.

Communicating with Costa Ricans
by Eric Liljenstrope

On many occasions I have been engaged in a conversation with a Costa Rican friend or acquaintance when a very basic conversational miscue occurs. I ask a question and my friend responds by saying *yes*. I assume that the *yes* I receive meant an affirmative response, i.e. *Yes, I'll be there, yes, I'll do it*, or *Yes you can dress like that in public without people laughing at you*. However, my experience in Costa Rica and other Latin American countries has taught me a different meaning of the word *yes* of which I was not previously aware . *Yes*, can be merely an acknowledgement of the fact that I am talking, that the listener has heard me, or a reflection of what I want to hear. *Yes* does not necessarily mean an affirmative, positive response. The person may not show up, may not do what you thought they would do, and you may be dressed ridiculously and shouldn't be allowed to go out in public.

Costa Rican playwright Melvin Méndez from the book, *The Ticos*, expands on this point. He writes of his fellow Costa Ricans, "We beat around the bush to avoid saying 'No', a syllable which seems almost rude to us. And rather than hurt someone, we say one thing and do another." I had an experience recently that illustrates this point. I was supposed to meet a friend at a party and when I called him after arriving at the party he assured me that, *yes*, he'd be right over. When I called again, an hour later, he said, *yes*, he was almost ready and was just leaving the house. He never showed up. The truth was that he was waiting for a phone call from a girl that he wanted to go out with but didn't want to tell me that he was choosing her over me, so in order not to hurt my feelings he just told me what I wanted to hear. This was not the first time I had experienced such difficulties in basic communication, and experience has taught me to take such snubs in stride. Remembering that no disrespect or injury was intended. My friend was doing the culturally acceptable, correct and polite thing by expressing to me that he wanted to be at the party with me and that he liked me. He was answering a different question than the one I was asking. I was literally asking, "Are you coming to the party?" But he was answering a question much like, "Would you like to come to the party with me if you could?" So, how in the world can a person adjust to such conversational conundrums? Understanding the basic differences between the communication styles of indirect culture direct culture can be helpful. A person from a culture with direct communication style values "putting all the cards on the table" and "cutting to the chase." Direct communicators do not place as much emphasis on context or on body language to get their point across. For direct communicators, if it is not verbally stated, it is not communicated. In contrast, indirect communicators place a heavy emphasis on context and often consider stating what appears to be obvious as insulting. It is assumed that an intelligent person will read the context and body language in communication, whereas direct communicators assume that if something is important then it will be stated clearly with no room from misinterpretation.

Perhaps you are left feeling a little overwhelmed at the prospect of having to reinterpret what people are saying to you with the added complexity of communication in a foreign language. The good news is that one gets better at interpreting indirect speech patterns as well as adjusting expectations appropriately. In the example above, I knew after the second phone call that my friend was not going to be coming. or at least I knew there was a strong possibility he wouldn't be there. Something in his tone of voice tipped me off. Of course, the ability to read those subtleties took years to develop, so one must have patience during the process.

What well-adapted Costa Rican residents know adapting their communication style.

(1) *Give people an option*. Sometimes one doesn't know Ticos are sincere until you give another option.

(2) *Ask in another way, using qualified speech*. You might try to say something like, "Is it difficult for you to come tonight?"

(3) *Ask a third party*. Sometimes a friend of a friend or someone else who is familiar with the situation is the only way to get accurate information.

(4) *Ask a Costa Rica*. Costa Ricans will always be able to interpret their compatriots much better than foreigners.

M.R.T.A. Overseas Living Adaptability Test

Using the figures 1 (below average), 2 (average) or 3 (above average), ask yourself the following questions and rate your answer accordingly. Couples should take the test separately. As you take the test, write your selected numbers down, then add them together. When completed, refer to the Score Comments Box at the bottom of this page.

1) Open to new adventures
        select one: 1 2 3
2) Flexible in your lifestyle
        select one: 1 2 3
3) Enthusiastic to new things in a new and different culture
        select one: 1 2 3
4) Able to make and enjoy new friends:
        select one: 1 2 3
5) Willing to learn at least basic phrases in a new language
        select one: 1 2 3
6) Healthy enough mentally and physically not to see family, friends and favorite doctor for occasional visits
        select one: 1 2 3
7) Confident enough to be in a "minority" position as a foreigner in a different culture
        select one: 1 2 3
8) Independent and self-confident enough not to be influenced by negative and often ignorant comments against a possible move to a foreign country
        select one: 1 2 3
9) Patient with a slower pace of life
        select one: 1 2 3
10) Usually optimistic
        select one: 1 2 3
11) Eager to travel to a new country
        select one: 1 2 3
12) Open mind to dealing with a different type of bureaucracy
        select one: 1 2 3
13) Understand enought to look at things in a different light without being critical and accepting the differences
        select one: 1 2 3
14) Financially stable without needing to work
        select one: 1 2 3

Score Comments:	
Your Score	Evaluation
37-45	Great move abroad
30--36	Will have a few problems
22-32	Some problems but possible
Less than 22	Forget it, stay home!

Courtesy of Opportunities Abroad. This test taken from the book "Mexico Retirement Travel Assistance." To order wrtie M.R.T.A., 6301 S. Squaw Valley Rd., Suite 23, Pahrump, NV 89648-7949

23 Things Every Prospective Expatriate Should Know
by Shannon Roxborough

When moving to a foreign country, making adequate pre-departure preparations is essential. Here are some tips to make your international move easier.

1) Be sure to undergo a complete medical check-up before leaving to avoid dealing with a major health issue overseas.

2) Take one or more advance trips to your destination to familiarize yourself. It's worth the investment.

3) Take the appropriate documents on the advance trip to start the immigration paperwork. Consulate personnel in the country can secure the visa and residency permit more efficiently than those working thousands of miles away.

4) If you have dependent children, in your pre-departure research, be thorough in seeking the availability of education in your host country.

5) Make sure you and your family understand the country's culture so that they know what will be accepted in terms of volunteer and leisure activities at your new home.

6) In case of health emergencies, make sure you know good health-care providers and how to contact them.

7) Use a travel agency for booking en-route travel so you may search for low-cost fares.

8) Check into purchasing round-trip tickets for en-route travel. They may be less expensive than one-way. And the return ticket may be used for other travel.

9) Remember the sale of your Stateside home increases year-end tax costs due to lost interest deduction.

10) Cancel regular services and utilities. Pay the closing bill for garbage collecting, telephone, electricity, water, gas, cable TV, newspapers, magazines (or send them a change of address), memberships such as library and clubs, store accounts (or notify them that your account is inactive), and credit or check - cashing cards that will not be used.

11) Leave forwarding address with the Post Office or arrange for a mail forwarding service to handle all your U.S. mail.

12) Give notice to your landlord or make applicable arrangements for the sale of your home.

13) Have jewelry, art, or valuables properly appraised, especially if they will be taken abroad. Register cameras, jewelry and other similar items with customs so that there will be no problem when reentering the U.S.

14) Make sure a detailed shipping inventory of household and personal effects (including serial numbers) is in the carry-on luggage and a copy is at home with a designated representative.

15) Obtain extra prescriptions in generic terms and include a sufficient supply of essential medicine with the luggage.

16) Obtain an international driver's license for all family members who drive. Some countries do not recognize an international driver's license but they issue one of their own, provided you have a valid home country license. Bring a supply of photographs as they may be required in the overseas location for driver's licenses and other identification cards.

17) Bring a notarized copy of your marriage certificate.

18) Arrange for someone to have power of attorney in case of an emergency.

19) Close your safety deposit box or leave your key with someone authorized to open it if necessary.

20) Notify Social Security Administration or corporate accounting department (for pensions) where to deposit any U.S. income. Make sure the bank account a d routing numbers are correct.

21) Bring copies of the children's school transcripts. If they are to take correspondence courses, make arrangements prior to departure and hand-carry the course material.

22) At least learn the Language basics prior to going to a foreign country. Trying to integrate with the new culture without the ability to communicate can be frustrating if not impossible.

23) Learn about the country's people and way of life before moving there. Go to your library, call your intended destination's tourism board and read all of the travel publications (magazines and travel guidebooks) you can to educate yourself.

Though this short article only provides a brief overview of the essentials, use it as a guide to prepare yourself for a smooth transition abroad.

Useful Resources:
Transitions Abroad Magazine 800 293-9373
A Guide to Living Abroad 609-924-9302

INDISPENSABLE SOURCES OF INFORMATION ABOUT LIVING IN COSTA RICA

LIVE IN COSTA RICA is a time-proven company offering well-organized introductory trips from the U.S. for those people interested in moving to Costa Rica. For more information contact them toll-free at: 800-365-2342 E-mail: **crbooks@racsa.co.cr** or **liveincostarica@cox.net** or see **www.liveincostarica.com**. All trips are led by Christopher Howard, the author of this best-selling guidebook and renowned expert on living and doing business in Costa Rica. **See Chapter 1 and this chapter for a sample itinerary.**

TICO TRAVEL also offers trips to Costa Rica. Their trips are designed to introduce retirees, investors and entrepreneurs to the exciting opportunities that await them abroad. They remain committed to individual and high-quality service offering un-biased information about Costa Rica. They offer shorter tailor-made tours for individuals, couples and small groups. Their trips are also led by Christopher Howard. Toll Free 800 493-8426 Fax (954) 493-8466 E-Mail: tico@gate.net, http: www.ticotravel.com.

RELOCATION AND RETIREMENT CONSULTANTS have helped newcomers find success and happiness in Costa Rica for over 15 years. They offer an extensive network of contacts and insider information for potential residents and investors. See www.liveincostarica.com or contact them at: Suite 1 SJO 981, P.O. Box 025216, Miami, FL 33102-5126, E-mail: crbooks@racsa.co.cr or costaricaconsultants@hotmail.com.

SEMINARS ON LIVING IN COSTA RICA are given once a month by the Association of Residents of Costa Rica (ARCR). Do not miss the opportunity to get informed about living in Costa Rica. The topics covered are: Costa Rican Laws and Regulations, Health Care System in Costa Rica, Real Estate - buying, selling and renting, Insurance in Costa Rica, Banking in Costa Rica, Moving and Customs, Living and Retiring in Costa Rica. Call 221-2053 or 233-8068 or fax 255-0061 for more information.

EL RESIDENTE is published by the Association of Residents of Costa Rica and not for sale to the general public. If you join the Association, your membership will include a bi-monthly copy of their newsletter.

Discussion Groups

Over the last few years, online Costa Rican discussion groups have begun to flourish. Joining one or more of these forums is an excellent way to see what issues residents of Costa Rica face on a daily basis and keep up with a lot of what is happening in the local expatriate community. Members can express their problems or concerns and receive a lot of constructive feedback. Many residents contribute daily while others add something occasionally or just simply read what their fellow members have to say. Another reason to follow these groups is that many friendships have been made online. Not a week goes by without numerous activities being mentioned for the group's members.

If you are thinking of moving to Costa Rica a lot of value can be derived from the groups below. What follows is a brief description of each of the major discussion groups. Membership in all of these groups is FREE.

Live in Costa Rica's New Forum (www.costaricabooks.com).
To access, click on the menu at the top of the home page where it says "Forum." We have to put our own forum at the head of the list. Although it is new you will benefit immensely by participating. We will try to answer all of your questions We work with the country's most brilliant minds who contribute to our forum in the fields of real estate, medicine, law, learning the Spanish language, the Internet, communications, moving, banking and more.

Association of Residents of Costa Rica Forum (www.arcr.com)
This forum is for general discussion, questions, news and comments pertaining to living in Costa Rica. Posts include discussion of questions on health care, working in Costa Rica, housing, cost of living environment, social commentary, or any other topic that pertains to life in Costa Rica.

Choose Costa Rica Bulletin Board (www.discoverypress.com)
This group was started as an experiment, a copy of the very successful Mexico Connect forum that deals with living and retiring in Mexico. John Howells, the site's founder says, "I am continually amazed at the number of hits our bulletin board receives, and worry that some day it will be too much to handle. My administrator tries to keep things under control by steadfastly refusing to accept commercial advertising and by encouraging forum participants to stay on the topic (living and travel in Costa Rica)

and to observe rules of common courtesy. That doesn't always happen, but we try."

CostaRicaLiving@yahoogroups.com

CostaRicaLiving is an English-language e-mail group dedicated to the exchange of information about living in or visiting Costa Rica. Our approximately 1000 members are welcome to ask questions, share tips and opinions, make recommendations, network and share experiences about retirement, travel, establishing businesses, bring up families, or virtually any other issue related to Costa Rica. Membership to the group is open. The list is unmoderated, non-commercial, non-religious and non-political. Promotion of personal businesses, sales, rentals and recommendations are accepted. CR Living maintains a separate bulletin board for descriptions of areas of Costa Rica, FAQs, ads, legal advice, announcements and photos. ¡Bienvenidos! (Welcome!).

Costa Rica Pages Forum (www.costaricapages.com)

This group was founded by boy wonder Casey Halloran. He is an expert in the field of internet marketing and runs several successful internet-based tour companies in Costa Rica. His site offers a moderated forum on travel, living, retirement, investment and working in Costa Rica. On the site there are educated discussion and debate on the pros and cons of life in Costa Rica, information and tips on how to find a job and live happily from those who have done it. Several renowned local experts participate in the forum and will be happy to answer all of your questions.

GalloPinto@yahoogroups.com

Gallo Pinto translates as speckled or spotted rooster and is flavored and garnished black bean and rice dish normally served at breakfast. Gallo Pinto is a different kind of Internet Discussion Group, one that welcomes stories, discussions and questions on the Costa Rica and is open for discussion of most all other topics, as long as good taste is observed. The founder of the groups states, "The prime focus is Costa Rica - by expatriates living here, those exploring doing so in the future and ticos (Costa Ricans). We try to dig a bit deeper into all facets of Costa Rican life, and to break many off the old Internet rules along the way. We welcome Q & A's, stories and discussions on the history, culture, politics, religion and everything else about Tico Land and discovering "piggybacking" and short "chat room" type messages. Gallo Pinto also fosters a friendly club-like atmosphere, where members can delve into all things interesting to curious, intelligent, self-disciplined people.'

Useful Websites

www.liveincostarica.com - tours for living here
www.retireincostarica.net - tours for living here
www.costaricabooks.com - books about Costa Rica
www.travel.costaricabooks.com - a tour site
www.primecostaricaproperty.com - good retirement homes
www.costaricagolfproperties.com - real estate
www.costaricaspanish.net - learning Spanish
www.drivetocentralamerica.com- making the trip by car
www.investincentralamerica.com - investment information
www.blujeweltravel.com - more information on Costa Rica
www.ticotravel.com - tour information
www.escapeartist.com - Excellent information for expats
www.costaricapages.com - excellent directory
www.arcr.net - Association of Residents
www.interbusonline.com - bus information
www.gallopinto.com - A forum, news group
www. CostaRicaLiving@yahoogroups.com - a forum
www.discoverypress.com - a forum, news group
www.registronacional.go.cr - hall of records
wwww.hospitalsanjose.net - Cima Private Hospital
www.clinicabiblica.com - another private hospital
www.clinicacatolica.com - another good private hospital
www.fishel.co.cr - largest pharmacy chain
www.racsa.co.cr - telecommunications site
www.filetax.com/expat.hmtl - expat tax site
www.orcag.com - Panamanian corporations
www.drivemeloco.com car insurance
www.sanborns.com - car insurance
www.aerocasillas.com - private mail service
www.liveinnicaragua.com - living in Nicaragua
www.primenicaraguaproperty.com. - retirement property
www.liveinpanama.com - living in Panama
www.panamaretirementproperties.com - real estate

ADDITIONAL TOUR ITINERARIES
(Continued from Chapter 1)

7-Day Beach Tour:

Saturday: Arrive in San Jose. We will meet you at the airport and transport you to the Presidente Hotel. There will be a brief orientation on your way to the hotel.

Sunday: Quepos Beach where you will stay at the beautiful Hotel Tres Banderas . On the way you will see a sampling of a couple of new develpoments. You will eat lunch at The Great Escape featuring their great fish tacos and more. In the afternoon you'll view Manuel Antonio National Park - touted to be the best national park on the country. Dinner will be at the hotel.

Monday: The second stop are Dominical Beach and the Ojochal area where you'll be staying at the Posada Playa Tortuga. We'll have lunch at the hotel and then go down the coast to the beautiful village of Ojochal. This area is really interesting. It just recently became accessible when the new costal highway was finished.

Tuesday:
The final stop is Jaco Beach where you'll stay at the beachfront Arenal Pacifico Lodge. You'll tour the five star Marriott Los Sueños resort, marina and golf course. You will also see a sampling of a couple of developments in the area. Finally, you will view one of the most beautiful sunsets in the world from a spectacular hilltop at the Hotel Villas Caletas. The view really has to be seen to believed.

Wednesday: Return to San Jose, free afternoon and evening

Thursday: Informative Seminar with the Association of Residents of Costa Rica (ARCR) lunch at the seminar. Please see chapter I for the schedule of topics and speakers.

Friday: Second day of the seminar. Please see chapter I for the schedule of speakers and topics. Dinner at an exotic restaurant.

Saturday: Transportation to the airport. This tour is for those who are certain they want to only explore the beach as their option. It includes the majority of your meals, and all of your transportation while in Costa Rica. Hotel and continental breakfasts are included.. Airfare is not included.

Combination Tour (beach and 6 –day Central Valley Tour):

Saturday: Arrive in San Jose. We will meet you at the airport and transport you to the Presidente Hotel. There will be a brief orientation on your way to the hotel.

Sunday: Leave for the Beach. First stop at Quepos Manuel Antonio (see the description above).

Monday; Dominical/Ojochal (see the description above).

Tuesday: The final stop is Jacó. (see the description above).

Wednesday: Return to San Jose, free afternoon and evening.

Thursday: Informative Seminar with the Association of Residents of Costa Rica (ARCR) lunch at the seminar. Please see chapter I for the schedule of topics and speakers.

Friday: Second day of the seminar. Please see chapter I for the schedule of speakers and topics. Dinner at an exotic restaurant.

Saturday: Breakfast at the hotel
Tour of the city of San José including: Clínica Bíblica Hospital, markets, San Perdro Mall, University of Costa Rica, Hipermás mega superstore, neighborhoods where Americans live (Los Yoses, Barrio Escalante, Sabana Norte, Sabana Sur, Rohrmoser, and Escazú) Hospital Cima and Multiplaza Mall. Continue tour around the Central Valley to see the other choice areas where foreigners reside: Escazú, Santa Ana, San Antonio de Belén, Ciudad Cariari, Alajuela, Heredia and Moravia.
Lunch at La Cocina de Doña Lela where they serve authentic Costa Rican cuisine.
Free night

Sunday:
Breakfast at the hotel

Tour the areas west of San José including the city of Atenas, Grecia, Alajuela and a view a couple of homes.

Mouth-watering buffet lunch at El Banco de Mariscos.

Final questions, answers and other concerns.

Monday: Transportation back to the airport.

This tour is our most popular. It allows you to see both the beach and the Inland Valley extensively. Airfare is not included

6-Day Guanacaste Beach Tour

Located in the North Pacific region of Costa Rica, Guanacaste is famous for its string of beautiful beaches. Many of the beaches have white sand, excellent surf breaks, world-class sport fishing, skin diving and unparalleled beauty.

Day 1 - Arrival and airport pick-up and on to the Hotel Presidente

Day 2 - Depart for Flamingo Beach after breakfast buffet at the hotel. Lunch in Flamingo. In the afternoon you will se a sampling of local properties. View the sights, recreational activities and property in the area Dinner.

Day 3 - Breakfast in Flamingo. Transportation to Tamarindo Beach. See the sights along the way. Lunch. Sampling of homes in the afternoon. The rest of the afternoon is free. Dinner.

Day 4 - Breakfast and transportation by bus aand ferry to Tambor Hills and the Barceló Resort. Lunch. Tour of the surrounding area. Typical Costa Rican dinner.

Day 5 - Breakfast at the hotel and early departure for the Hotel Torremolinos in San José.

Day 6 - Buffet breakfast at the hotel and departure.

*For more information on pricing and availability of these unique tours Call (U.S. & Canada): 800 365-2342, E-mail us at: crbooks@racsa.co.cr or liveincostarica@cox.net or see www.liveincostarica.com.

SUGGESTED READING

BOOKS

Costa Rica Handbook, by Christopher D. Baker. Moon/Avalon Publications. The longest, most extensive and best guidebook to date—over 750 pages of invaluable information.

The New Key to Costa Rica, by Beatrice Blake. Ulysses Press, Berkeley, CA. An excellent, easy to follow guide . We recommend it highly — a must for anyone visiting Costa Rica. The new edition has been expanded to 380 pages.

Living Abroad in Costa Rica, by Erin Van Rheenen. Another fine publication from Avalon Publications. An excellent compliment to this guidebook.

Choose Costa Rica, by John Howells. Discovery Press. A long-time favorite with people who want to make the move. Mr. Howells has been a part-time Costa Rican resident for many years. Another must read if you plan to move here.

The Costa Rica Traveler, by Ellen Searby. Windham Bay Press, Box 1198, Occidental, CA 95465. This book and *"The New Key to Costa Rica"* are guidebooks for tourists as well as locals.

Escape from America, by Roger Gallo. Available from: http://www.escapeartist.com. This book is a must read for anyone who wants to relocate overseas. It has the answers to all of your questions plus profiles of the best countries in which to live. We recommend this book highly.

The Freedom Handbook, a Guide to Personal Freedom, Wealth and Privacy by Charles Freeman. Freedom Publications, P.O. Box 115, St. Helier, Jersey, Channel Islands, via Great Britain. This guide contains a wealth of useful information for the expatriate.

Amcham's Guide to Investing and Doing Business in Costa Rica, by The American Chamber of Commerce of Costa Rica. AMCHAM, P.O. Box, 4946, San José, Costa Rica. An updated guide containing good information on Costa Rica's business and investment climate.

The Essential Road Guide for Costa Rica, by Bill Baker $19.95. A good guide book if you plan to do a lot of driving in the country.

*The Legal Guide to Costa Rica, by Roger Petersen $29.95. Everything you need to know about Costa Rica's complex legal system. Also available through Costa Rica Books.

Costa Rica - A Travel Survival Kit, by Rob Rackowiecki. Lonely Planet Publications, Inc. Excellent.

Guide to the Perfect Latin American Idiot, by Plinio Apuleyo Mendoza, Carlos Alberto Montaner and Alvaro Vargas Llosa. Madison Books, 4720 Boston Way, Lanham, Maryland 20706. This bestseller must be read by anyone in the United States or Canada who is interested in Latin America.

The World's Retirement Havens, by Margret J. Goldsmith. This guide briefly covers the top retirement havens in the world. Most of the material is still current since it was published in 1999. You may obtain this guide from John Muir Publications, P.O. Box 613, Santa Fe, New Mexico 87504.

The Costa Ricans, by Richard, Karen, and Mavis Biesanz. Waveland Press, Prospect Heights, IL.

*How You Can Avoid Losses Buying Costa Rican Real Estate, by Bill Baker, $29.95. Another excellent publication by Mr. Baker deals with the real estate market in Costa Rica and helps the reader develop a plan for investing. This book may be ordered through Costa Rica Books.

Happy Aging With Costa Rican Women, by James Y. Kennedy. This one-of-a-kind book tells about all the trials and tribulations many *gringos* have with Costa Rican women. It is available through www.amazon.com.

How I Found Freedom in An Unfree World, by Harry Browne, Liam Works — Dept. FB, P.O. Box 2165, Great Falls, MT 59403-2165 or toll- free 1-888-377-0417. This book will revolutionize your life.

*Driving the Pan-American Highway to Mexico and Central America, by Raymond & Audrey Pritchard, $18.95. This is the only book available if you are planning to drive from the U.S. to Costa Rica via the Pan-American Highway. It is available from Costa Rica Books.

Costa Rican Spanish Survival Course and 90 minute cassette, by Christopher Howard. Costa Rica Books. A book of basic survival Spanish with a section on Costa Rican idioms. A 90 minute cassette is included for pronunciation purposes. Available from www.costaricabooks.com or Amazon.com.

Purchasing Real Estate in Costa Rica, by Attorney Alvaro Carballo. Apartado 6997-1000, San José, Costa Rica. FAX: 011-(506) 223-9151.

Insurance in Costa Rica, by David R. Garrett. Garrett and Asociados, SJO 450, P.O. Box 025216, Miami, FL 33102-5216.

A Travelers Guide to Latin America n Customs and Manners, by Elizabeth Devine. Published by St. Martin's Press. Helps the newcomer understand the Latin way of life.

Bell's Walking Tour of Downtown San José, by Vernon Bell. A good guide for exploring the downtown area. P.O Box 185, 1000, San José, Costa Rica. E-mail: home-stay@racsa.co.cr.

PERIODICALS

Costa Rica Today newspaper is a free publication that is published weekly. It is more for tourists and upbeat than the *Tico Times.* See Chapter 5 for details.

The Tico Times newspaper is also published weekly. It is worth subscribing to if you plan to live in Costa Rica. See Chapter 5 for subscription details.

Costa Rica Outdoors, is a magazine that covers almost all of the country's outdoor activities. To subscribe write to: Costa Rica Outdoors, Dept. SJO 2316, P.O. Box 025216, Miami, FL 33102-5216. You can also call or fax 011-(506)-282-6743.

VIDEOS

Costa Rica Unica, is an informative video dealing with history, the people, archeology, ecology and touring. It provides an in-depth view of the country. This fine video may also be ordered from our company. The price is $22.95.

★All of the titles above with an asterisk are available through Costa Rica Books by calling toll-free 800-365-2342. You may also order some of the titles above from Amazon.com or by viewing www.costaricabooks.com.

Frequently Asked Questions

How can I teach school or volunteer in Costa Rica?

There are several U.S.-curriculum and English-medium schools in Costa Rica, and some of them recruit teachers in the U.S. If you are interested in teaching school in Costa Rica or another foreign country, see the Department of State's Overseas Schools page for a list of recruiting organizations and for information on schools that are supported by the U.S. Government overseas.

The Peace Corps has a small number of volunteers in Costa Rica. Other U.S. non-profit programs such as WorldTeach have placed volunteers in Costa Rica in past years. The Embassy has no specific information on volunteer opportunities at this time. The Embassy of Costa Rica in Washington, DC (Tel. 202-234-2945) may have additional information about volunteer programs.

Can I receive my social security checks at the Embassy?

Only military personnel can receive their social security checks at the U.S. Embassy. The recipient should have at least 20 years of service. In order to receive checks at the Embassy, you must fill out a registration form to be submitted to and approved by the Office of the Defense Representative in the Embassy.

At one time all other beneficiaries could receive checks in Costa Rica by registering with the Federal Benefits Unit. You needed to provide the Embassy with your home and mailing addresses, phone number, identification document and social security number. The checks were received through Diplomatic Pouch and are mailed via "Registered Mail" to the address indicated in your registration document. The problem was the checks did not reach your post office box until the middle of the month.

The good news is that a couple of Costa Rica banks now offer direct deposit to your account by the thrid of each month. Please check with the embassy to see whcih banks provide this service and what forms have to be filled out.

What innoculations do I need for Costa Rica? How is medical care in Costa Rica?

There are no required innoculations for Costa Rica, but it is a good idea to check with your physician for recommendations of optional innoculations and health precautions. Costa Rica is suffering an outbreak of dengue fever, although the incidence remains lower than in other Central American countries. Dengue is transmitted by mosquito bite and there is no vaccine. Anyone planning to travel in affected areas should take steps to avoid mosquito bites. These include wearing long sleeves and pants, using insect repellent on exposed skin, and sleeping under mosquito netting.

Medical care in the capital city of San Jose is adequate. However, in areas outside of San Jose medical care is more limited. Doctors and hospitals often expect immediate cash payment for health services. U.S. medical insurance is not always valid outside the United States. Supplemental medical insurance with specific overseas coverage, including provision for medical evacuation, has proven useful in many emergencies.

How can I register with the Embassy?

All travellers should register with the Embassy in case an emergency occurs in Costa Rica or at home.

Come to the Embassy Consular Section, Window C, Monday 8:00 AM-11:30 AM and 1:00 PM-3:00 PM
Tuesday-Friday: 8:00 AM-11:30 AM.

You can also send us your information on-line : include name, passport number, travel plans, local contact in Costa Rica, and next-of-kin contact information in the U.S. Registration on-line will not serve to prove citizenship in case of passport loss, but will provide a basis for which an emergency passport may be issued.

In person registration is necessary to be entered in Embassy records as an American citizen.

Those American citizens who are living in Costa Rica, whether or not they are official residents, should also register.

Do I have access to APO privileges in the U.S. Embassy?

If you are a holder of a U.S. military identification card, you may use the Embassy's Army Post Office privileges.

*Courtesy of the U.S. Embassy

IMPORTANT SPANISH PHRASES AND VOCABULARY

You should know all of the vocabulary below if you plan to live in Costa Rica.

What's your name?	¿ Cómo se llama usted?
Hello!	¡Hola!
Good Morning	Buenos días
Good Afternoon	Buenas tardes
Good night	Buenas noches
How much is it?	¿Cuánto es?
How much is it worth?	¿Cuánto vale?
I like	Me gusta
You like	Le gusta
Where is...?	¿Dónde está...?
Help!	¡Socorro!
What's the rate of exchange	¿Cuál es el tipo de cambio?

I'm sick	Estoy enfermo	day after	
		tomorrow	pasado mañana
where	dónde	week	la semana
what	qué	Sunday	domingo
when	cuándo	Monday	lunes
how much	cuánto	Tuesday	martes
how	cómo	Wednesday	miércoles
which	cuál or cuáles	Thursday	jueves
why	por qué	Friday	vienes
		Saturday	sábado
now	ahora		
later	más tarde	month	mes
tomorrow	mañana	January	enero
tonight	esta noche	February	febrero
yesterday	ayer	March	marzo
day before		April	abril
yesterday	anteayer	May	mayo

June	junio	tall	alto
July	julio	tired	cansado
August	agosto	bored	aburrido
September	septiembre	happy	contento
October	octubre	sad	triste
November	noviembre		
December	diciembre	expensive	caro
		cheap	barato
spring	primavera	more	más
summer	verano	less	menos
fall	otoño	inside	adentro
winter	invierno	outside	afuera
		good	bueno
north	norte	bad	malo
south	sur	slow	lento
east	este	fast	rápido
west	oeste	right	correcto
		wrong	equivocado
left	izquierda	full	lleno
right	derecha	empty	vacío
easy	fácil	early	temprano
difficult	difícil	late	tarde
big	**grande**	best	el mejor
small	pequeño, chiquito	worst	el peor
a lot	mucho	I understand	comprendo
a little	poco	I don't	
there	allí	understand	no comprendo
here	aquí	Do you speak	
nice, pretty	bonito	English?	¿Habla usted inglés?
ugly	feo		
old	viejo	hurry up!	¡apúrese!
young	joven	O.K.	está bien
fat	gordo	excuse me!	¡perdón!
thin	delgado	Watch out!	¡cuidado!

open	abierto	bill	la cuenta
closed	cerrado		
occupied		blue	azul
(in use)	ocupado	green	verde
free (no cost)	gratis	black	negro
against the		white	blanco
rules or law	prohibido	red	rojo
exit	la salida	yellow	amarillo
entrance	la entrada	pink	rosado
stop	alto	orange	anaranjado
		brown	café, castaño
breakfast	el desayuno	purple	morado,
lunch	el almuerzo		púrpura
dinner	la cena		
cabin	la cabina	0	cero
bag	la bolsa	1	uno
sugar	el azúcar	2	dos
water	el agua	3	trés
coffee	el café	4	cuatro
street	la calle	5	cinco
avenue	la avenida	6	seis
beer	la cerveza	7	siete
market	el mercado	8	ocho
ranch	la finca	9	nueve
doctor	el médico	10	diez
egg	el huevo	11	once
bread	el pan	12	doce
meat	el carne	13	trece
milk	la leche	14	catorce
fish	el pescado	15	quince
ice cream	el helado	16	diez y seis
salt	la sal	17	diez y siete
pepper	la pimienta	18	diez y ocho
post office	el correo	19	diez y nueve
passport	pasaporte	20	veinte
waiter	el salonero	30	treinta

40	cuarenta	400	cuatrocientos
50	cincuenta	500	quinientos
60	sesenta	600	seiscientos
70	setenta	700	setecientos
80	ochenta	800	ochocientos
90	noventa	900	novecientos
100	cien	1000	mil
200	doscientos	1,000,000	un millón
300	trescientos		

"If you want to perfect your Spanish, we suggest you purchase our best-selling Spanish book, Christopher Howard's Guide to Costa Rican Spanish. It is a one-of-a-kind pocket-sized course designed for people who want to learn to speak Spanish the Costa Rican way. Please see ad on page 229."

TIQUISMOS

Here are some Costa Rican expressions you should be familiar with if you plan to spend a lot of time in Costa Rica.

Buena Nota!	Fantastic! Great!	**Jale!**	Hurry up!
camaronear	work an extra job	**maje**	pal
chapa	a coin or stupid person	**pachanga**	party
		paja	B.S.
chicha	anger	**panga**	a small boat
chumeco	dark skin	**pulpería**	corner grocery store
chunche	a thing	**queque**	cake
color	shame	**roco**	old person
dar pelota	flirt	**¡Salado!**	Too bad!
fila	line		Tough luck!
gato	blue-eyed person	**soda**	a small cafe
goma	hangover	**Tico**	a Costa Rican
harina	money	**timba**	big stomach
jalar una torta	get in trouble	**tiquicia**	Costa Rica
jamar	to eat	**vos**	you, informal equivalent of tú

IMPORTANT TELEPHONE NUMBERS

GENERAL EMERGENCY 911
BILINGUAL TOURIST INFORMATION 800-343-6332
MUNICIPALITY OF SAN JOSE.....................223-4655, 223-4640
COLLECT CALLS WITHIN COSTA RICA.............................110
TIME OF DAY..112
INFORMATION 113
AT&T (INTERNATIONAL CALLS)......................................114
AT&T 9 COLLECT-CREDIT CARD CALLING.........0-800-011-4114
UNLISTED NUMBERS 115
IMMIGRATION 220-0355
OIJ (Judicial Police) 295-3271
TRANSIT POLICE (ACCIDENTS)..............227-4866 EXT. 205-265
POLICE...117
PARAMEDICS...118
FIRE DEPARTMENT 118
CHAMBER OF COMMERECE 221-0005,221-0389
INTERNATIONAL COLLECT CALLS....................................116
TELEPHONE OUT OF ORDER..119
TELEGRAMS...123
ELECTRIC COMPANY 126
RURAL GUARD 127
AMBULANCE...128
BILINGUAL EMERGENCY SERVICE (Like our 911) 122
MCI 162
ELECOM CANADA...161
U. S. SPRINT (INTERNATIONAL CALLS).............................163
NATIONAL PARKS...192
TOURISM INTITUTE (ICT)......................223-1733, 257-6057
TRAVELER'S INFORMATION 800-0123456
RED CROSS AMBULANCE 221-5818
PUBLIC MEDICAL CENTERS
    HOSPITAL MEXICO 232-6122
    HOSPITAL NACIONAL DE NIÑOS 222-0122
    HOSPITAL SAN JUAN DE DIOS...............................257-6282
    HOSPITAL CALDERON GUARDIA 257-7922
CLINICA BIBLICA (private hospital with 24 hour pharmacy).........257-5252
CLINICA CATOLICA (private hospital) 283-6616
PSIQUIATRICO (Psychiatric Hospital)............................232-2155
AMERICAN EXPRESS assistance 0-800-120-039
DIRECT DIALING TO U.S.A. ....001+area code and number
U.S. EMBASSY (3 a.m.–4:30 p.m., M–F)................................220-3939

U.S. EMBASSY (after hours, weekends) 220-3050
CANADIAN EMBASSY (anytime)..255-3522
AIRPORT INFORMATION (24 hours)..441-0744

PHONE NUMBERS FOR SPECIAL SERVICES

Accountants

MITRY BREEDY...290-4050
HOUSEMAN, DAVID ....223-2787 or 239-2045

Alarms

ADT..257-7373

Automobile Repair

H.M.S. (English spoken, reliable and honest) 223-0348

Banks

BANCO CREDITO AGRICOLA DE CARTAGO 251-3011
BANCO DE COSTA RICA...255-1100
BANCO NACIONAL DE COSTA RICA..223-2166
BANCO BANEX (PRIVATE) 221-6344
BANCO LYON (PRIVATE)..221-2212
SCOTIA BANK (PRIVATE) 287-8747

Bottled Water

ALPINA. 256-2020
CRISTAL..442-5453

Business and Secretarial Services

BILINGUAL SECRETARIAL SERVICES..228-4367
TEMPO 222-7844

Car Rentals

EUROCAR (our first choice) 257-1158
AVIS RENT-A-CAR. 232-9922

BUDGET...223-3284
HERTZ..221-1818

Car Services

EMERGENCY AUTOSERVICES 221-2053
TOWING..381-6534 or 258-4248

Credit Card Companies

AMERICAN EXPRESS...233-0044
DINNERS CLUB..233-0455
VISA...223-2211

Customs Agents

ABC MOVERS 227-2645, 226-9010

Dentists

ACOSTA, ARTURO...228-9904
SANDRA FERNANDEZ...257-3382
HIRSCH, RONALD (CHILDREN'S DENTIST) 222-1081
RAWSON, BERNAL..257-4735

Doctors

AGGERO, ROLANDO...255-4476
ARCE, LUIS R. (EAR, NOSE AND THROAT)..........................235-5653
ARELLANO, ALFONSO (CARDIOLOGIST)............................233-5435
BOLAÑOS, PEDRO (ACUPUNTURE) 231-3165
ESQUIVEL, JULIO (GYNECOLOGY) 220-1010
GABRIEL,PATRICK (CHIROPRACTOR) 296-0020
KOGEL, STEVEN (AMERICAN PSYCHIATRIST). ....253-4502 or 225-7149
LABORATORY LABIN 222-1987
MURRAY, CHARLES (PSYCHOLOGICAL COUNSELING) 260-9902
NUNEZ, RODOLFO (DERMATOLOGY) 222-6265
PARDO, ROGELIO (INTERNAL MEDICINE) 222-1010
RUBINSTEIN, BERNARDO (OPHTHALMOLOGIST) 221-7709

Errands

RAPHA NISSI MULTISERVICES...................................250-5940, 257-0305

Interpreters and Translators

CHRISTOPHER HOWARD ......From U.S.: Suite #1 SJO 981, P.O. Box 025216-5216, Miami FL 33102 or Local address: Apartado Postal 7349-1000, San José, Costa Rica. ....Tel: 261-8968

Laundry

LAVA Y SECA...224-5098
DRY CLEANERS USA (many locations) 220-1570,231-7396

Maids

CINDERELA DOMESTIC SERVICES...TEL/FAX 262-2834, BEEPER 256-7890 CODE 2084

Mailing Services (private)

AEROCASILLAS..255—4567
TRANS-EXPRESS INTERLINK 296-3973/296-3974
STAR BOX...221-9092

Real Estate

PRIME COSTA RICA PROPERITIES 261-8968
(e-mail: buycostarica@hotmail.com)
RELOCATION AND RETIREMENT CONSULTANTS 261-8968

Taxis

AEROPUERTO...241-0333
COOPEIRAZU 254-3211
COOPETAXI...235-9966
COOPETICO 224-7979
TAXI ALFARO..221-8466
TAXI COOPEGUARIA 226-1366
TAXIS DE CARGA Y MUDANZAS (For moving)............................223-0921

Tours and Travel Agencies

TICO TRAVEL 800-493-8426

INDEX

NOTES

Special Services for Newcomers

The time-tested business listed in this special section provide excellent services. We have interviewed hundreds of foreigners who have utilized these services and are very pleased with them.

Thank you

Travel Store, Ltd.

322

Health Visions®

MEDICAL BENEFITS FOR U.S. MILITARY RETIREES AND DISABLED VETERANS

Our Mission is to provide the highest quality health care possible to our Military Retirees, their families, and qualifing Windows and their families. **Health Visions Corporation** recently established in Costa Rica is offering immediate access to you and your family's health care. HVC is structured in such a way that total medical care and medications are provided with no out of pocket cost to you. The following documents are required:

- A current U.S. military retired ID card (20 years active duty)
- 65 years or over must have medicare part B
- Current ID cards for all dependents under 21 years of age, Up to 23 years of age if in college with proof of enrollment
- Copy of DD 214
- DISABLED VETERANS TREATED FOR SERVICE CONNECTED DISABILIES.

Unremarried widows must have the above related documents for their husband.

FOR FURTHER INFORMATION IN COSTA RICA
CALL (506) 260-0535 / 265-6505, 836-2328
EMAIL: retireeva@racsa.co.cr
WEBSITE: www.healthvisionscostarica.com

Centro Lingüístico
CONVERSA
Founded 1975

Spanish
so many schools, so many questions...

WHY Conversa?
30 years of experience in Costa Rica
ALL LEVELS

Tiny groups (maximun of 4 students per class)
Several lodging options
High staff to student ratio
Highly experienced instructors
Saturday morning tutorials
Host family programs

Two locations:

Santa Ana
Children's Program
Meals included
Daily transportation to/from campus
Beautiful 6-acre campus
Swimming pool
Volleyball court
View of Santa Ana valley
On - campus lodges

San José
On - site internet access
One block form the Paseo Colón
Video room
Flexible schedules
Language lab
Cozy environment

1-800-367-7726
www.conversa.net
info@conversa.net

Farmacia
AL VAREZ

Taking care of your health

BEST PRICES IN COSTA RICA

- Free injections
- Free blood - pressure test
- We can help you in English

• **Zocor** • **Glucovance** • **Yasmin** • **Generic Viagra** •
• **Cialis** • **Lipitor** • **Lopresor** •

Attention Americans!!

Did you know Prescriptions are not required
on most products in Costa Rica?

And did you know that you can take a 90-day
supply back to the U.S.A.?

And did you also know you'll save up to
80% compared to most U.S.A. drugstores?

237-5425 or 263-3300

Open Mon-Sat. 9 a.m. - 6 p.m.
Heredia, 150 mts. East
of the Courthouse
(Tribunales de Justicia)

327

Quiropráctica
familiar

Gentle and effective treatment
to relieve pain,
restore health and stay well.

Specializing in headaches, neck pain,
low-back pain, and wellness care.

Serving the Western San Jose Area.

Dr. Jason Ramke, D.C.
Board Certified (USA)
Life University Graduate (Atlanta, GA)

506-220-3041
www.quiropracticafamilar.com

330

Hotel América

40 rooms, each with:

- Bathroom
- Solar-heated water
- Direct-dial Telephone
- Fan
- Cable TV
- Laundry
- Restaurant
- Conference Room
- Media Facilities
- Free Parking Lot

$35 Single
$ 45 Double
$ 55 Triple

Hotel Ceos

$ 18 Single
$ 28 Double
$ 33 Triple

 ## Hotel D'Cristina

$ 15 Single
$ 25 Double
$ 30 Triple

Hotel Heredia

$ 15 Single
$ 25 Double
$ 30 Triple

**We offer you kind attention!
For other services
e-mail: info@hamerica.net
website: www.hamerica.net**

For reservation in Hotel América,
Hotel Ceos, Hotel Heredia and
Hotel D'Cristina call:
Tel: (506) 260-9292 • Fax: (506) 260-9293

10% Discount

Charming Tropical Oasis in San José...
Sleep well • Laugh Often • Live long.

Hotel Dunn Inn

"Your Home Away From Home"
"Sleep well • Laugh Often • Live long"

Whether traveling on business or pleasure it would be an honor to have you as our guest. We strive to provide the best service in San José and every effort is made to ensure an ejoyable and memorable visit. From the moment you arrive you will experience firsthand the warmth of Costa Rican hospitality and enjoy all the benefits of a full service hotel with excellent value.

For more information or reservations please contact:

Ph: (506) 222-3232 • Fax: (506) 221-4596
Ave. 11, Calle 5 - Barrio Amón, San José

www.hoteldunninn.com   dunninn@racsa.co.cr

"Your Home Away From Home"

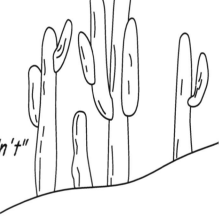

LINCOLN SCHOOL

Excellence since 1945

- Founded in 1945 as a non profit institution, committed to academic excellence and fostering moral and social values, in a bilingual and multicultural environment

- Current 7.9 acre campus in Moravia, with new 17.3 acre property, ten minutes from current location

- Three full diploma options: US High School Diploma, International Baccalaureate Diploma and Costa Rican Ministry of Education Diploma

- Course of studies in English with US textbooks and instructional material

- Early Learning Center at 2.6 years of age, through grade 12

- International Calendar (2004-2005 school year begins August 9)

- Excellent bus transportation system

For additional information please call us at 247-0847, e-mail: develop@lincoln.ed.cr
www.lincoln.ed.cr